Best Antiqu

A Travel Guide to America's Greatest Places to Antique

Wilbert and Deanne Fuller

Deebil Publishing Co.

Wichita, Kansas

Copyright © 2005 by Wilbert and Deanne Fuller.
All rights reserved. No part of this book may be reporoduced by any
means without permission of the publisher. Exceptions are made for brief
excerpts to be used in published reviews. For information address Deebil
Publishing Co.

Deebil Publishing Co.
P.O. Box 783169
Wichita, KS 67278-3169

ISBN: 0-9670517-0-3

Important notice: The information on antique places and activities listed in
this antique travel guide has been validated by phone and/or personal visit
with the operators thereof and is assumed to be accurate. However, the
information is subject to change. Neither the authors, editors, printers or
publisher assume any responsibility for errors, omissions or changes
which may occur.

Best Antiquing USA is available from the publisher.
Price is $19.95 post paid.
For information call toll free 1-888-317-7217
Orders or comments for the editors should be directed to:
Deebil Publishing Co.
P.O. Box 783169
Wichita, KS 67287-3169

Fourth Edition
Printed in U.S.A.

*This book is dedicated to all those antiquers
who love the adventure of antiquing;
who have arrived at an antique show or market
too early or too late, or passed by a great
antique place because they didn't know it was
just around the corner or while traveling,
had an unscheduled evening when they could
have enjoyed an antique auction,
had they only known...*

Take the time to journalize your antiquing travels. You will later treasure the good memories made as you list a new antique mall, outdoor market or recorded the name of an antique dealer you would like to contact again in the future. We have reserved portions of the guide for your "TRAVEL NOTES."

Also, we would appreciate hearing from you on how you were abel to use this guide. Send us your thoughts on any suggestions, or locations you believe we should check out, that should be included in Fuller's Best Antiquing USA.

Happy Antiquing - the Fuller's

TRAVEL NOTES

Contents

Contents cont'd

Great Antiquing Getaways

Using The Guide

The purpose of this book is to make your antiquing more pleasurable and more profitable by organizing for easy reference, the information on major antique markets, shows, malls, auctions and antique districts coast to coast.

We have added "25-Great Antiquing Getaways" to this edition. They are found on the last pages of selected states. We have arranged the Getaways as antiquing trails with occasional suggestions for dining, lodging, leisure points of interest as well as the best time of the year to shop a great market.

We have created for this guide an innovation that you will not find in other antique and collectibles travel guide, i.e. Perpetual Calendars. Many antique/collectible markets and shows are repeated, such as the third Sunday every month or the second weekend of every June. We have taken advantage of this fact in preparing our Perpetual Calendars by listing events by city using the maps and Perpetual Calendars, you will be able to find major antique markets and shows to visit while traveling the route with most places to search for antiques and collectibles. There are references to help you find auctions to include on your trip. The Calendar of Weekly Events lists markets and shows occuring every week. Markets and Shows occuring *irregularly* are listed seperately.

The maps are not intended to be accurate for travel. Their purpose is to show where the most antiques and collectibles are to be found. It is suggested that you travel by a map or atlas like Rand McNally's which numbers the Interstate Highway exits as we have used the exit numbers as main reference points in giving directions. You will need to use the city maps in your atlas to find numbered highway exits in the cities.

Using The Guide, contd

Major Antique Districts and Villages, if any, are then listed. Since the schedule of auctions often change, it is essential that you call for confirmation and directions. Markets are more stable, but State Fairs, etc., can upset a market's schedule, so call to be sure.

Each place is listed only because our visit there or research indicates that is is a place with a sufficient quantity of antiques and collectibles to make it worth shopping. Hours and days open are given so you will not spend time driving to a place that is closed. The information in each listing has been checked with the operators by telephone and/or by a visit and should be correct. However, due to the changeable nature of the business, some errors are inevitable.

In the past dozen years, we have traveled over a half a million miles to all of the 48 states and there are some some generalizations. Even if, as Lowell has said, "Generalizations are apt to be as dangerous as they are tempting." So, to generalize; The Southwest is best for Native American and Western items, the West Coast is best for Orientals, also Native American and Western items. The Midwest and South are best for oak furniture and primitives. The East Coast is best for Early American and European antiques. The south and Battleground areas such as Fredericksburg, VA and Gettysburg, PA are best for Civil War items and militaria. Retirement areas such as Florida, Arizona and California are prime antiquing areas for all kinds of antiques and collectibles, as are all of the large cities. The most intriguing generalization of all, is that a great find can be made *anywhere at anytime.*

Some of our favorite restaurants across the country are listed for your consideration. Mail comments to the publisher at the address on the copyright page.

Weekly and Holiday Events
Subject to change - call to confirm

Weekends	Sundays Only	Holidays
CT- Woodbury-Sat. FL-S Orlando/Mt. Dora ME- Woolwich MO-W Kansas City MS- Jackson NJ- Lanbertville NM- Albuquerque NM- Santa Fe NY- NYC Annex, Sat. NY- NYC, Grnd Bazaar OK- Tulsa, Sat. PA- Kutztown, Sat. PA- Middletown, Sat. RI- Charlestown TX-S Houston/Pearland VT- Wilmington WV- Bluefield, Sat. WV- Harpers Ferry	DC- Washington MA-E Rowley MA-W Grafton MA-W Hadley MA-W Hubbardston MD- Columbia NH- Nashua NY- Bouckville NY- Buffalo/Clarence PA- Adamstown WI- Shawano Holiday Abbreviations: LD = Labor Day J4 = July 4th MD= Memorial Day CD = Columbus Day WE = Weekend S&S= Sat and Sun	CA-N Oakhurst- MD S&S, LD WE. CT- Hartford - S&S bef LD WE. IA- Solon - J4 MI- Howard City - MD, J4, LD WE. MN- Minneapolis/ Elko- F,S&S of MD,J4,LD NY- Rhinebeck - MD & Columbus WE VA- Hillsville - LD & preceding F, S&S WI- Cedarburg - Labor Day WV- Harpers Ferry - MD, J4, LD S,S&M

Non-Scheduled Markets and Shows
Call for Dates

CA-N	San Francisco Cow Palace, 1 WE in Feb, May, Aug & Nov
CA-S	Costa Mesa Antique Show, 1 WE in Mar & Oct
CA-S	Del Mar - Del Mar Antique Show, 1 WE in Jan, Apr, Jul & Nov
CA-S	Pasadena - Bustamante Antique Show, 1 WE in Mar, Jun, Aug & Dec.
CO-	Denver - World Wide Show, 1 WE in Mar, Jul, Oct
CO-	Denver - Buchanan Flea Mkt, 1 WE per month
CT-	Wilton, Mar, Sept & Dec
IA-	Des Moines, 1 WE per month, May, Jun, Sep & Oct.
IA-	Dubuque, 1 Sun in Feb, Apr & Oct
FL-S	Deland, 1 WE in Dec, Jan, Feb, Mar & Sep.
FL-S	Ft. Lauderdale, 3 Shows in winter season
IL-	Chicago O'Hare, 1 WE in Apr, Aug & Nov.
IL-	Sandwich, 1 Sun monthly, May thru Oct.
IN-	Evansville - Collectors Carnival, 1 WE in Apr, Aug & Oct.
KS-	Wichita, 1 WE per month except Jul & Aug.
Ky-	Louisville, 1 Fri, S&S, every month
MD-	Baltimore, Saturday before Easter
MN-	Minneapolis show, 1 WE in Feb, Jul & Nov.
MO-W	Kansas City - The Monthly Flea Market, 1 Sat per month.
OH-	Akron, 1 WE mid Jul & late Oct.
OR-	Salem, 1 Sun per month, Sept thru Jun.
TX-S	Round Top in Mar or Apr and Oct or Sep.
WI-	Elkhorn, 1 Sun in May, Jun, Jul,Aug & Sep.

January - Perpetual Calendar
Monthly/Yearly/Markets/Shows

1st Sun Weekend

AL-	Birmingham
CA-N	Alameda
CA-S	Glendale
FL-S	West Palm Beach
IL-	Chicago/St. Charles
KS-	Hutchinson
NC-W	Charlotte
OH-	Urbana
SD-	Sioux Falls
TX-N	Canton
WA	Tacoma

2nd Sun Weekend

CA-S	Pasadena
CA-S	Los Angeles
GA	Atlanta
NC-W	Greensboro
NY-	Triple Pier
OK-	Oklahoma City

3rd Sun Weekend

AZ-	Phoenix
CA-N	San Mateo
CA-S	Long Beach
FL-S	Orlando/Mt. Dora
IL-	Chicago Dupage
NC-E	Raleigh
NY-	Triple Pier
OH-	Columbus
OH-	Springfield
SC-	Charleston
TN-	Memphis
TX-N	Dallas

4th Sun Weekend

CA-S	Santa Monica
CA-S	Torrance
FL-S	Miami Beach
FL-S	Miami
GA	Atlanta
KS-	Wichita
NY-	Piers 88 & 90
OH-	Columbus
TN-	Nashville
TX-N	Canton
VA-	Norfolk

Perpetual Calendar - February
Monthly/Yearly/Markets/Shows

1st Sun Weekend	2nd Sun Weekend
AL- Birmingham	CA-S Pasadena
CA-N Alameda	CA-S Los Angeles
CA-S Glendale	GA Atlanta
FL-S Miami	NC-W Greensboro
FL-S West Palm Beach	ND- Minot
IL- Chicago/St. Charles	NYC Triple Pier
KS- Hutchinson	OK- Oklahoma City
NC-W Charlotte	
ND- Mandan	
OH- Medina	
OH- Urbana	
SD- Sioux Falls	
TX-N Canton	

3rd Sun Weekend	4th Sun Weekend
AZ- Phoenix	CA-S Santa Monica
CA-S Long Beach	CA-S Torrance
FL-S Orlando/Mt. Dora	GA Atlanta
IL- Chicago Dupage	KS- Wichita
NYC Triple Pier	OH- Columbus
OH- Columbus	PA- Philadelphia
OH- Springfield	TN- Nashville
SC- Charleston	TX-N Canton
TN- Memphis	VA- Richmond
TX-N Dallas	

12

1st Sun Weekend		2nd Sun Weekend	
AL-	Birmingham	CA-S	Pasadena
CA-N	Alameda	CA-S	Los Angeles
CA-S	Glendale	GA	Atlanta
DC-	Washington	NC-W	Greensboro
FL-S	West Palm Beach	ND-	Minot
IL-	Chicago/St. Charles	NY-	Triple Pier
KS-	Hutchinson	OK-	Oklahoma City
NC-W	Charlotte		
ND-	Mandan		
OH-	Medina		
OH-	Urbana		
OR-	Portland		
SD-	Sioux Falls		
TX-N	Canton		

3rd Sun Weekend		4th Sun Weekend	
AZ-	Phoenix	CA-S	Santa Monica
CA-S	Long Beach	CA-S	Torrance
IL-	Chicago Dupage	GA	Atlanta
NY-	Triple Pier	KS-	Wichita
OH-	Columbus	MD-	Baltimore
OH-	Springfield	NJ-	Atlantic City
SC-	Charleston	OH-	Columbus
TN-	Memphis	TN-	Nashville
TX-N	Dallas	TX-N	Canton

13

1st Sun Weekend	
AL-	Birmingham
CA-N	Alameda
CA-S	Glendale
FL-S	West Palm Beach
IL-	Chicago/St. Charles
KS-	Hutchinson
NC-W	Charlotte- Sepctacular
ND-	Mandan
OH-	Medina
OH-	Urbana
SD-	Sioux Falls
TX-N	Canton
TX-S	Round Top

2nd Sun Weekend	
CA-S	Pasadena
CA-S	Los Angeles
GA	Atlanta
MO-E	St. Louis
NC-W	Greensboro
ND-	Minot
NJ-	Rancocas Woods
OK-	Oklahoma City
LA-	Washington

3rd Sun Weekend	
AZ-	Phoenix
CA-N	Sacto/Folsom
CA-S	Long Beach
IL-	Chicago Dupage
KY-	Burlington
MA-	Hadley
MI-S	Ann Arbor
MN-	St. Paul
OH-	Columbus
OH-	Springfield
OK-	Oklahoma City
SC-	Charleston
TN-	Memphis
TX-N	Dallas

4th Sun Weekend	
CA-N	Petaluma
CA-S	Santa Monica
CA-S	Torrance
GA	Atlanta
KS-	Wichita
MI-S	Allegan
NC-W	Liberty
OH-	Columbus
PA-	Adamstown Ext
PA-	Kultztown Ext
TN-	Nashville
TX-N	Canton

1st Sun Weekend		2nd Sun Weekend	
AL-	Birmingham	CA-S	Pasadena
CA-N	Alameda	CA-S	Los Angeles
CA-N	Lodi	GA	Atlanta
CA-N	San Mateo	MA-W	Brimfield
CA-S	Glendale	NM-	Rochester
FL-S	West Palm Beach	NC-W	Greensboro
IA-	What Cheer	ND-	Minot
IL-	Chicago/St. Charles	NJ-	Stanhope
IN-	Lawrenceburg	OK-	Oklahoma City
KS-	Hutchinson	VA-	Fisherville
KS-	White Cloud		
MI-S	Centreville		
NC-W	Charlotte		
ND-	Mandan		
OH-	Medina		
OH-	Urbana		
OK-	Sparks		
TX-N	Canton		

3rd Sun Weekend		4th Sun Weekend	
AZ-	Phoenix	CA-S	Santa Monica
CA-N	Martinez	CA-S	Torrance
CA-S	Long Beach	GA	Atlanta
IL-	Bloomington	KS-	Wichita
IL-	Chicago Dupage	MD-	Baltimore
KY-	Burlington	NJ-	Atlantic City
MA-	Handley	OH-	Columbus
MI-	Ann Arbor	TN-	Nashville
NJ-	Stanhope	TX-N	Canton
OH-	Columbus		
OH-	Springfield Ext		
SC-	Charleston		
TN-	Memphis		
TX-N	Dallas		

15

1st Sun Weekend	2nd Sun Weekend
AL- Birmingham	CA-N Fremont
CA-N Alameda	CA-S Pasadena
CA-N S.F. Deco	CA-S Los Angeles
CA-S Glendale	CT- Hartford/Farmington
FL-S West Palm Beach	GA- Atlanta
IN- Lawrenceburg	MI-S Centreville
IL- Chicago/St. Charles	MN- St. Paul
KS- Hutchinson	NC-W Greensboro
MI-S Midland	ND- Minot
NC-W Charlotte	NJ- Far Hills
ND Mandan	OK- Oklahoma City
OH- Burton	
OH- Urbana	
TX-N Canton	
WY- Casper	

3rd Sun Weekend	4th Sun Weekend
AZ- Phoenix	CA-S Santa Monica
CA-S Long Beach	CA-S Torrance
IA- Walnut	GA Atlanta
IL- Bloomington	KS- Wichita
IL- Chicago Dupage	MA-E Topsfield
KY- Burlington	MI-S Allegan
MA- Hadley	NY- Bouckville
MI-S Ann Arbor	OH- Columbus
OH- Columbus	PA- Adamstown Ext
OH- Springfield	PA- Kultztown Ext
SC- Charleston	TN- Nashville
TN- Memphis	TX-N Canton
TX-N Dallas	

16

1st Sun Weekend

AL-	Birmingham
CA-N	Alameda
CA-S	Glendale
FL-S	West Palm Beach
IA-	Solon
IN-	Lawerenceburg
IL-	Chicago/St. Charles
NC-W	Charlotte-Spectacular
ND-	Mandan
OH-	Medina
OH-	Urbana
TX-N	Canton

2nd Sun Weekend

CA-S	Pasadena
CA-S	Los Angeles
GA	Atlanta
KS-	Sparks
MA-W	Brimfield
MI-	Centreville
NC-W	Greensboro
ND-	Minot
OH-	Cleveland
OK-	Oklahoma City
WY-	Jackson Hole

3rd Sun Weekend

AZ-	Phoenix
CA-S	Long Beach
IL-	Bloomington
IL-	Sandwich
KY-	Burlington
MA-	Handley
MI-S	Ann Arbor
NC-E	Raleigh
NY-	Syracuse/Liverpool
OH-	Cleveland
OH-	Columbus
OH-	Springfield Extrav
OR-	Portland
SC-	Charleston
TN-	Memphis
TX-N	Dallas

4th Sun Weekend

CA-S	Santa Monica
CA-S	Torrance
CO-	Colorado Springs
MI-S	Allegan
MI-N	Midland
NH-	Wolfeboro
NY-	Rhinebeck
OH-	Columbus
TN-	Nashville
TX-N	Canton
WI-	Cedarburg

1st Sun Weekend		2nd Sun Weekend	
AL-	Birmingham	CA-S	Pasadena
AL-	Gadsen	CA-S	Los Angeles
CA-N	San Juan Bautista	GA-	Atlanta
CA-N	Alameda	KY-	Covington
CA-S	Glendale	ME-	Union
FL-S	West Palm Beach	MI-S	Centreville
IA-	What Cheer	NC-W	Greensboro
IN-	Lawrenceburg	ND-	Minot
IL-	Chicago/St. Charles	OK-	Oklahoma City
MI-N	Howard City	WY-	Jackson Hole
NC-W	Charlotte		
ND	Mandan		
TX-N	Canton		

3rd Sun Weekend		4th Sun Weekend	
AZ-	Phoenix	CA-N	Martinz
CA-S	Long Beach	CA-S	Santa Monica
IL-	Bloomington	CA-S	Torrance
IL-	Chicago Dupage	GA	Atlanta
IL-	Sandwich	MA-E	Topsfield
KY-	Burlington	MI-S	Allegan
MA-	Hadley	OH-	Columbus
MI-S	Ann Arbor	TN-	Nashville
MN-	Oronoco	TX-N	Canton
MN-	Rochester	VA-	Hillsville
NM-	Santa Fe		
NY-	Bouckville		
OH-	Columbus		
OH-	Springfield		
SC-	Charleston		
TN-	Memphis		
TX-N	Dallas		
WY-	Jackson Hole		

18

September - Perpetual Calendar
Monthly/Yearly/Markets/Shows

1st Sun Weekend	
AL-	Birmingham
CA-N	Alameda
CA-S	Glendale
CT-	Farmington
FL-S	West Palm Beach
ID-	Ketchum/Sun Valley
IN-	Lawrenceburg
IL-	Chicago/St. Charles
KS-	White Cloud
NC-W	Charlotte
ND-	Mandan
OH-	Medina
OH-	Urbana
SD-	Sioux Falls
TX-N	Canton
WA-	Tacoma
WI-	Cedarburg

2nd Sun Weekend	
CA-S	Pasadena
CA-S	Los Angeles
GA	Atlanta
MA-W	Brimfield
NC-W	Greensboro
ND-	Minot
NJ-	Stanhope
OK-	Oklahoma City

3rd Sun Weekend	
AZ-	Phoenix
CA-N	Sacto/Folsom
CA-S	Long Beach
IL-	Bloomington
IL-	Chicago Dupage
IL-	Sandwich
KY-	Burlington
MA-	Handley
MI-S	Ann Arbor
NJ-	Stanhope
OH-	Burton
OH-	Columbus
OH-	Springfield Extrav
SC-	Charleston
TX-N	Dallas

4th Sun Weekend	
CA-N	Petaluma
CA-N	Santa Monica
CA-S	Torrance
GA-	Atlanta
KS-	Wichita
MI-N	Allegan
MI-S	Midland
MN-	Rochester
NC-W	Liberty
OH-	Columbus
PA-	Adamstown Extrav
PA-	Kutztown Extrav
TN-	Nashville
TX-N	Canton

1st Sun Weekend	
AL-	Birmingham
CA-N	Alameda
CA-N	Lodi
CA-S	Glendale
FL-S	West Palm Beach
IA-	What Cheer
IL-	Chicago/St. Charles
IN-	Lawrenceburg
KS-	Hutchinson
MI-N	Howard City
NC-W	Charlotte
ND-	Mandan
OH-	Medina
OH-	Urbana
SD-	Sioux Falls
TX-N	Canton
TX-S	Round Top
VA-	Richmond
WI-	Cedarburg
WY-	Casper

2nd Sun Weekend	
CA-S	Pasadena
CA-S	Los Angeles
GA-	Atlanta
MI-S	Centerville
LA	Washington
MN-	St. Paul
MO-E	St. Louis
NC-W	Greensboro
ND-	Minot
NJ-	Rancocas Woods
NY-	Rhinebeck
OH-	Cleveland
OK-	Oklahoma City
VA-	Fisherville
VT-	Quechee

3rd Sun Weekend	
CA-N	San Jose
CA-S	Long Beach
IL-	Bloomington
IL-	Chicago Dupage
IL-	Sandwich
KY-	Burlington
KY-	Mt. Sterling
MA-	Hadley
MI-S	Ann Arbor
NJ-	Atlantic City
OH-	Columbus
OH-	Springfield
OK-	Oklahoma City
SC-	Charleston
TN-	Memphis
TX-N	Dallas

4th Sun Weekend	
CA-S	Santa Monica
CA-S	Torrance
GA	Atlanta
KS-	Wichita
MD-	Baltimore
OH-	Columbus
OR-	Portland
TN-	Nashville
TX-N	Canton

20

November - Perpetual Calendar
Monthly/Yearly/Markets/Shows

1st Sun Weekend

AL-	Birmingham
CA-N	Alameda
CA-S	Glendale
FL-S	West Palm Beach
IL-	Chicago/St. Charles
KS-	Hutchinson
MI-S	Ann Arbor
NC-W	Charlotte, Spectacular
ND-	Mandan
OH-	Medina
OH-	Urbana
SD-	Sioux Falls
TX-N	Canton

2nd Sun Weekend

CA-S	Pasadena
CA-S	Los Angeles
GA	Atlanta
NC-W	Greensboro
ND-	Minot
OK-	Oklahoma City
SC-	Charleston

3rd Sun Weekend

AZ-	Phoenix
CA-S	Long Beach
CA-S	San Mateo
FL-S	Ft. Lauderdale
FL-S	Orlando/Mt. Dora
IL-	Chicago Dupage
OH-	Columbus
OH-	Springfield
TN-	Memphis
TX-N	Dallas

4th Sun Weekend

CA-S	Santa Monica
CA-S	Torrance
GA-	Atlanta
KS-	Wichita
NC-	Winston-Salem
OH-	Columbus
TN-	Nashville
TX-N	Canton

Perpetual Calendar - December
Monthly/Yearly/Markets/Shows

1st Sun Weekend

AL-	Birmingham
CA-	S.F. Deco
CA-N	Alameda
CA-S	Glendale
DC-	Washington
FL-S	West Palm Beach
IL-	Chicago/St. Charles
KS-	Hutchinson
NC-W	Charlotte
ND-	Mandan
OH-	Medina
OH-	Urbana
OK-	Tulsa
SD-	Sioux Falls
TX-N	Canton

2nd Sun Weekend

AL-	Birmingham
CA-S	Pasadena
CA-S	Los Angeles
GA-	Atlanta
MO-E	St. Louis
NC-W	Greensboro
ND-	Minot
OK-	Oklahoma City
SC-	Charleston

3rd Sun Weekend

AZ-	Phoenix
CA-S	Long Beach
IL-	Chicago Dupage
OH-	Columbus
OH-	Springfield
OR-	Portland
TN-	Knoxville Extrav
TN-	Memphis
TX-N	Dallas

4th Sun Weekend

CA-S	Santa Monica
CA-S	Torrance
GA	Atlanta
KS-	Wichita
MD-	Baltimore
OH-	Columbus
TN-	Portland
TX-N	Nashville

__TRAVEL NOTES__

ALABAMA

72

72

Huntsville

31

59

Guiwin

Gadsden

78

65

A Pell City

20

Birmingham

Chelsea

Tuscaloosa

59

65

20

Montgomery

Millbrook

85

80

Selma

65

231

A
Flomaton

Mobile

Daphne
Foley

LEGEND
2 Ⓐ = 2 Auction Companies
● = Cities w/ Antique Malls listed in guide

ALABAMA

WEEKEND ANTIQUE EVENTS   (See city listing for details)
Birmingham Fairgrounds Flea Market **1st weekends Fri, Sat & Sun**
ANTIQUE DISTRICTS/VILLAGES
Foley, AL

AUCTION / ESTATE SALE CO.'S
Gu-Win, AL 35563
B & B Antiques and Auctions
Antique auctions
P.O. Box 430
Monthly auctions, call for dates
205-468-2213
3 mi E of Guin on 43S

Pell City, AL 35054
Pell City Auction Co.
Antique Auctions
Hwy 231 S, P.O. Box 74
Every Friday night at 7 P.M.
205-525-4100
I-20 Exit 158 S, 10 mi.

Pensacola/
Flomaton, AL 36441
Flomaton Auction
Antique auctions only
320 Palafox Street
Call for next auction date
251-296-3059

ANTIQUE MALLS, MARKETS & SHOWS
BIRMINGHAM, AL 35208
Fairgrounds Flea Market
500 dealers, 30 % antiques & collectibles
Fairgrounds
Fri 3-7; Sat 9-5, Sun 9-5 free
800-362-7538
I-20 Exit 120 and follow signs
1st weekend of every month except Dec which is 1st 2 weekends
Fairgrounds Flea Market
130 Wildwood Parkway #108
Birmingham, AL 35209

BIRMINGHAM, AL 35020
Hanna Antique Mall
100 dealers
2424 7th Avenue South
Mon-Sat 10-5:30; Sun 1-5:30
205-323-6036
I-65 Exit 8th Ave W to 24th St,
L to 7th Ave, then turn R

BIRMINGHAM, AL 35233
Peck & Hills Antique Mall
55 dealers
2400 7th Avenue South
Open Mon-Sat 10-5
205-252-3179
I-65 Exit 8th Ave W to 24th St,
L to 7th Ave, then turn R

ALABAMA

BIRMINGHAM/
HOOVER, AL 35216
Antiques Supermall
140 dealers
3454 Lorna Rd.
Open Mon-Sat 10-6; Sun 1-6
205-823-6433
I-459 S exit 13 1st R, intersection of
Lorna Rd & 459

BIRMINGHAM, AL 35733
5th Ave Antiques
45 dealers, 25,000 sq. ft.
2410 5th Ave.
Mon-Sat 10-5, Clsd Sun
3blks to 5th Ave turn R

CHELSEA, AL 35043
Chelsea Antique mall
85 dealers
14569 Hwy 280 East
Mon-Fri 10-5:30; Sat 10-6; Sun 1-5
205-678-2151
15 mi S of Birmingham on US Hwy 280

DAPHNE, AL 36526
Daphne Antique Galleria
27,000 sq ft, 75 dealers
1699 Hwy 98 E
Open winter Mon-Sat 10-5:30; Sun 1-
5:30,after April 1,half hour later
251-625-2200
5 mi S of I-10 Exit 35

FOLEY, AL 36535
Gas Works Antique Mall
70 dealers
813 N. McKenzie
Open Mon-Sat 10-5; Sun 1-5
251-943-5555
Hwy 59

FOLEY, AL 36535
Old Armory Mall
30 dealers
712 N. McKenzie
Open Mon-Sat 10-5; Sun 1-5
251-943-7300
Hwy 59

FOLEY, AL 36535
Hollis Ole Crush Antique Mall
75 dealers
200 S. McKenzie
Open Mon-Sat 10-5; Sun 1-5
251-943-8154
Hwy 59

GADSDEN, AL
World's Longest Outdoor Sale-So. End
3000 vendors, en route
US Hwy 127
Hours vary place to place, runs 9 days
800-327-3945 for info & confirmation
Extends 450 mi N along
US Hwy 127 to Covington, KY
Starts Sat, 1st weekend in Aug
www.127 sale.com

ALABAMA

GARDENDALE, AL 35071
Gardendale Antique Center
300 dealers
2405 Decatur Hwy.
Open 7 days 10-6
205-631-7451
**I-65 Exit 272.Mt.Olive Rd to 2nd light
to Decateur Hwy about 1 1/2 mi
N on Hwy 31, 1/4 mi**

HOMEWOOD, AL 35209
See Birmingham/Homewood
HOOVER, AL 35216
See Birmingham/Hoover

HUNTSVILLE, AL 35801
Railroad Station Antique Mall
50 dealers, 3 stories
315 Jefferson Street
Open Tue-Sat 10-6; Sun 1-6
256-533-6550
At Jefferson Street Exit off I-565.

HUNTSVILLE, AL 35803
Red Rooster Antique Mall
32 dealers
12519 S. Memorial Parkway
Mon-Fri 10-6; Sat 10-5; Sun 1-5
256-881-6530
**US Hwy 231same as Memorial Park-
way S of Huntsville.**

HUNTSVILLE, AL 35803
Packards Antique Mall
80 dealers
8503 Whitesburg
Open Mon-Sat 10-5; Sun 1-5
256-881-1678
US Hwy 231.

HUNTSVILLE, AL 35803
Desotos Antique Mall
50 dealers, +20 new booths
8402 Whitesburg
Open Mon-Sat 10-5; Sun 1-5
256-883-0181
US Hwy 231.

MADISON, AL 35758
Hartlex Antique Mall
150 dealers
181 Hughes Rd.
Open Mon-Sat 10-7; Sun 1-5
256-464-3940
**Across from City Hall off Hwy 72 on
Hughes Rd.**

MOBILE, AL 36606
Cotton City Antique Mall
90 dealer booths
2012 Airport Blvd.
Open Mon-Sat 10-5:30;Sun 1-5:30
251-479-9747
**2.2 mi E of I-65 on Airport Blvd E,
in town take Gov't St W.**

MONTGOMERY, AL 36117
Montgomery Antique Galleries
50 dealers
1955 Eastern Blvd
Open Mon-Sat 10-6; Sun 1-6
334-277-2490
I-85 Exit 6 S 1 mi.

ALABAMA

Southeast Antiques & Collectibles
18,000 sq.ft.
2530 East South Blvd.
Mon-Sat 9:30-5:30; Sun 1-5:30
July & Aug closed Sundays
334-284-5711
email-seac@knology.net
I-65 Exit 168 E on South Blvd
Dealers, Decorators, & Antique
Collectors.
Wholesale and retail. No Middleman.
Alabama's largest importer of Euro-
pean Antiques.

SELMA, AL 36701
Selma Antique Mall
60 dealer spaces
1400 Water Avenue
Open Mon-Sat 10-6, Sun 1-5
334-872-1663
From town going W on US Hwy 80
turn R on first St after crossing bridge

TUSCALOOSA, AL 35401
Southern Home Antiques & Collectibles
40 dealers
620 Greensboro Ave.
Open Mon-Sat 10-5:30; Sun closed
205-391-9320
Downtown historic area, I-20/59 Exit
359 to 7th St, turn R, at end of block.
Mall on left.

TUSCALOOSA, AL 35405
Hobby Horse Antique Mall
30 dealers
5500 Montgomery Hwy
Open 7 days Mon- Sat 10-5, Sun 1-5
205-752-1630
Just off I-20/59 Exit 73
S to Montgomery Hwy (US 82)

TRAVEL NOTES

TRAVEL NOTES

ARKANSAS

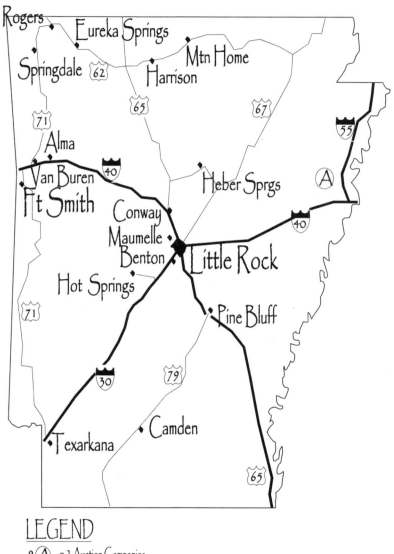

Rogers

Eureka Springs

Mtn Home

Springdale [62]

Harrison

[71]

[65]

[67]

[55]

Alma

[40]

Van Buren

Ft Smith

Heber Sprgs

(A)

[40]

Conway

Maumelle

Benton

Little Rock

Hot Springs

[71]

Pine Bluff

[30]

[79]

Camden

Texarkana

[65]

LEGEND

2 (A) = 2 Auction Companies

● = Cities w/Antique Malls listed in guide

ARIZONA

MAJOR ANTIQUE EVENTS

Phoenix Fairgrounds Antique Market, 500 dealers in Winter, 100-150 in summer,
3rd weekend of every month, none in Oct.

ANTIQUE DISTRICTS/ VILLAGES

Phoenix/ Glendale and Phoenix Scottsdale Rd.

ANTIQUE AUCTIONS

Phoenix/ Mesa
Allard Auctions
All Native American and western Items
Holiday Inn Resort US 60 & Country
Club Blvd.
2nd weekend in Mar & Nov
1-888-314-0343
Doug & Steve Allard
P.O. Box 1030
St. Ignatius, MT 59865

ANTIQUE MARKETS, MALLS & SHOWS

PHOENIX, AZ 85082-1172
Phoenix Antique Market
500 dealers in winter, 100-150 in summer.
State Fairgrounds
 1826 W. McDowell Rd.
Sat 9-5; Sun 10-4; adm $2; park $5
602-943-1766 or 800-678-9987
N. of downtown
At 19th Ave & McDowell Rd.
with exits off I-10 & I-17.
3rd weekend, none in Oct.
Jack Black Enterprises
P. O. Box 61172
Phoenix, AZ 85082-1172
phxantique@jackblack.com

PHOENIX, AZ 85007
The Antique Market
65 dealers
1601 N. 7th Ave
M-Sat 10-6, Sun 11-5
602-255-0212
I-10 Exit 7th Ave, 2 blks N on 7th
In Willow Historic District next to
Willow Bakery.

PHOENIX, AZ 85003
Historic District Antiques
40 dealers
539 W. McDowell Road
Mon-Sat 10-6; Sun 11-6
602-253-3778
I-17 Exit 200 E

PHOENIX, AZ 85018
Antique Gatherings
70 dealers
3601 E. Indian School
Mon-Sat 10-6; Sun 11-5
602-956-8203
I-17 Exit 202 E

ARIZONA

PHOENIX, AZ 85029
Brass Armadillo Antique Mall
600 dealers
12419 N. 28th Dr.
Open 7 days 9-9
602-942-0030
**I-17 and Cactus Rd, 1 bk west
& 28th Dr**

PHOENIX, AZ 85012
Central Antiques and Interiors
35 dealers
36 E Camelback
Open Mon-Sat 10-6; Sun 12-5
602-241-1636
**At Central and Camelback, in
shopping center.** *Two beautiful shops
in one central Phoenix location. We
are overflowing with fine quality art,
furniture, porcelain, pottery, glass,
silver, vintage lighting, Native
American arts and more. Represent-
ing some of the best antique dealers
in the Southwest.*
RICHARD@ANTIQUEGALLERYAZ.COM

PHOENIX, AZ 85012
Antique Gallery
75 dealers
5037 N. Central Avenue
Mon-Sat 10-5:30 Sun 12-5;
602-241-1174
**At Central and Camelback, in
shopping center.
RICHARD@ANTIQUEGALLERYAZ.COM**

PHOENIX /
APACHE JCT., AZ 85220
Superstition Grand Antique Mall
80 dealers
201 W. Apache Trail
Open 7 days 10-5:30, winter 9-6
480-982-1004
25 mi E on US 60

PHOENIX /
GLENDALE, AZ 85301
Apple Tree Antique Mall
6000 Sq. ft
5811 W. Glendale Ave.
Open daily 10-5
623-435-8486
**I-17 Exit 205 W 4 mi; or I-10 Exit 138 N
on 59th Dr, 5 mi to Glendale Ave E
30 shops at Glendale, 58th & 57th.**

PHOENIX /
GLENDALE, AZ 85301
A Mad Hatters Antique Mall
100 booths 240 showcases
5734 W. Glendale Ave.
Mon-Sat 10-6, Sun 11-5
623-931-1991
I-17 Exit 205, W 4 mi on Glendale Ave.

PHOENIX /
SCOTTSDALE, AZ 85257
Antique Trove
150 dealers, 25,000 sq. ft.
2020 N. Scottsdale Rd.
Open 7 days 10-6
480-947-6074
**202 East, Scottsdale Exit/Rural
3 mi. N.**

PHOENIX /
SCOTTSDALE, AZ 85257
Antique Center
185 dealers
2012 N. Scottsdale Rd.
7 days 10-6
480-675-9500
**US 60 Hwy Exit 3 (Rural rd) N or
Loop 202 Exit Scottsdale Rd N.**

**In Phoenix there is a *La Madeline*
French Bakery and Cafe in Fashion
Square Mall in Scottsdale, and one at
Camelback & 32nd. A favorite eatery
of ours.**

**If driving between Phoenix and
Flagstaff and you can spare one-half
hour take Hwy 179/89A through
Sedona and Oak Creek Canyon for
some of the most beautiful scenery
this country has to offer.**

**We enjoyed lunch at *L'Auberge de
Sedona*, a French restaurant on the
river in downtown Sedona at 301
L'Auberge Lane. A lovely restaurant
in a scenic setting.
928-282-1661**

**In Tucson we head for the *Arizona
Inn Restaurant*, 2200 East Elm St., a
Tucson favorite for years, 520-881-
5830**

TUCSON, AZ 85716
The American Antique Mall
100 dealers
3130 E. Grant at Country Club
Open Mon-Sat 10-5:30; Sun 11-4:30
602-326-3070
I-10 Exit 256 E

TUCSON, AZ 85710
Firehouse Antique Center
40 dealers
6522 E 22nd St.
Mon-Sat 10-5, Sun 12-4
520-571-1775
I-10 Exit 259 E

**In Yuma, AZ we found a delightful
Oasis for food and lodging, the *Shilo
Motor Hotel and Restaurant* at 1530
Castle Dome Rd, just off the I-8 Exit at
the east end of town; 520-782-9518.
Julieanna's Patio Cafe in the Picacho
Medical Center, near corner of 25th &
19th Ave. at 1951 W. 25th St, would be
another. 520-317-1961**

GREAT GETAWAY TO ANTIQUE PHOENIX & SCOTTSDALE

WHEN: Nov. thru April, 3rd
Sat & Sun.

WHERE: Phoenix Antique Market at the State Fairgrounds, 9-5, w/500 dealers, adm $2.00, park $5.00 at 19th Ave and McDowell Rd with exits off I-10 and I-17.

ANTIQUING: After the Fairgrounds Market go N on I-17 to Exit 205., Glendale Ave.

1. Go W on Glendale Ave to *Mad Hatters Antique Mall*. 100 booths & 200 showcases and *Apple Tree Antique Mall* at 5734 and 5811 W. Glendale Ave. Many antique shops in the area.

2. After Glendale, a 600 dealer mall to see in the evening or Sunday morning would be the *Brass Armadillo*, as they are open 7 days a week from 9AM to 9 PM, and located at I-17 Exit 210, Cactus Rd.

3. After the *Brass Armadillo*, take I-17 So. to Exit 203, Camelback Rd., East to Central and the two antique malls there in the shopping center, *Central Antiques & Interiors,* and *Antique Gallery* at Central and Camelback.

4. From here go W on Camelback to 7th Ave So. to 1601 N. 7th Ave, *The Antique Market* with 75 dealers.
5. Then continue S. on 7th Ave to McDowell Rd. E to 539 W McDowell for *Historic District Antiques*, with 55 dealers.

6. Now go E on Mc Dowell Rd to Hwy 51 N to Indian School Rd E to 3602, *Antique Gatherings* with 70 dealers.
Restaurant: La Madeline French Bakery & Cafe at 32nd & Camel back, our favorite. There is also a *La Madeline* in Fashion Square Mall at Camelack & Scottsdale Rd.

7. *Antique Trove & Antique Center*, 300 dealers plus in quality antiques, 2012 & 2020 N. Scottsdale Rd.
Leisure: Heard Museum, 2301 N. Central. Famous for Native American Artifacts. Adm $7.00 Also Pueblo Grand Museum, a prehistoric Hohokam Village Ruin with platform mound, irrigation canals & replicas of pit houses at 4619 E. Washington. Expwy 202 E to 32nd St S to Washington E. Adm $2.00, Sun free.

If you are heading N out of Phoenix your Getaway can be greatly enhanced by leaving I-17 at Exit 298 and taking Hwy 179 into Sedona.for some of the most incredible scenery in America.

Restaurant:: Enjoy a meal at *L'Auberge de Sedona* lovely French restaurant, in a gorgeous setting overlooking Oak Creek at 301 L'Auberge Lane, downtown Sedona. 928-282-1661. Moderately expensive.
(Continue N up Oak Creek Canyon for more spectacular scenery.)

TRAVEL NOTES

ARKANSAS

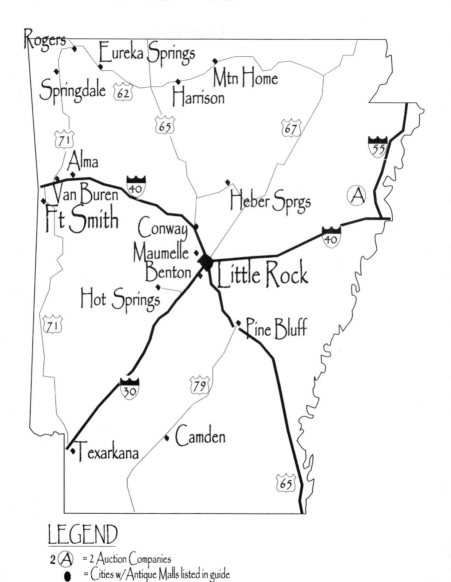

Rogers
Eureka Springs
Mtn Home
Springdale 62 Harrison
71
65 67
55
Alma
40 Van Buren
Ft Smith Heber Sprgs A
Conway 40
Maumelle
Benton Little Rock
Hot Springs
71
Pine Bluff
30
79
Camden
Texarkana
65

LEGEND

2 (A) = 2 Auction Companies
● = Cities w/ Antique Malls listed in guide

ARKANSAS

ANTIQUE DISTRICTS/ VILLAGES
Van Buren Historic District, Hot Springs Central Ave., N. Little Rock at Crystal Hill Rd and Eureka Springs

ANTIQUE MALLS, MARKETS/ SHOWS

ALMA, AR 72921
Sister's Antique Mall & Flea Market
100 dealers, 12,000 sq. ft.
Hwy 71 N
Mon-Sat 9-5, Sun 1-5
501-632-0829
I-40 Exit 13 N, turn N on Hwy 71, 1 1/2 blks on right

BENTON AR 72015
Benton Antique Mall
52 dealers
18325 I-30.
Mon-Sat 10-5; Sun 12-5
501-778-9532
I-30 Exit 118, 15 mi S of Little Rock

CAMDEN, AR 71701
Downtown Antique Mall
60 dealer spaces
131 S. Adams SE
Mon-Sat 10-5; Sun 1-5
870-836-4244
Camden is 50 mi E of I-30 Exit 44, mall in the middle of downtown

EUREKA SPRINGS, AR 72632
Yesteryear Too Antique & Collectible Mall
125 dealer spaces, 17,500 sq. ft.
Hwy 62 E
Open year round 10-6, winter 10-5
479-253-2002
In NW AR 39 mi E of Rogers
15 antique shops here
on Hwy 62, Spring & Main Sts
there is another Yesteryears Mall with 160 dealers about 2 blocks W of here on Hwy 62E

HOT SPRINGS, ARK 71913
Old South Antique Mall
35 dealers
5444 Central Ave.
Open 9-5 except Sun
South edge of town on Hwy 7 across the lakes
There are 30 antique shops in Hot Springs, 15 on Central St.

LITTLE ROCK/BRYANT AR 72022
Paarlain's Antique Mall
10 dealer
25014 Hwy I-30
Open 5 days 9:30-5 closed Tue & Wed
Sun 1-5
501-847-4978
Between Exits 126 & 128 off I-30

ARKANSAS

LITTLE ROCK/ KEO, AR 72083
Morris Antiques
8 bldgs of furniture
Open Tue-Sat 9-5;Closed Sun & Mon
501-842-3531
I-440 Exit 7 E, 8 mi on
US Hwy 165

N. LITTLE ROCK, AR 72114
Argenta Antique Mall
20 dealers
201 E. Broadway
Mon-Sat 10-5; Sun 1-5
501-372-7750
Downtown; I-30 Exit 141-B(Broadway)

N. LITTLE ROCK, AR 72118
Crystal Hill Antique Mall
60 dealers
5813 Crystal Hill Road
Open 7 days 9-5
501-753-3777
I-40 Exit 148 to Crystal Hill Rd,
turn R

N. LITTLE ROCK, AR 72118
Twin City Antique Mall
50 dealers
5812 Crystal Hill Rd.
Open 7 days 9-5:30
501-812-0400
At I-40, Exit 148

MAUMELLE, AR 72113
I-40 Antique Mall
41 booths
13021 Long Fisher Road
Mon-Sat 10-5; Sun 1-5
501-851-0039
I-40 Exit 142
West of North Little Rock on frontage
road at deadend.

MOUNTAIN HOME, AR
On US Hwy 62
There are 8 single and multi-dealer
shops on US Hwy 62 through
Mt. Home, AR

OZARK, MO
Yesteryears Antique Mall
162 dealer booths
105 N. 20th St.
Open daily 9-6
winter 9-5
417-485-2646
Jct 65 Hwy 14

ROGERS, AR 72756
Yesteryears Antique Mall
100 booths
3704 W. Walnut
Open Mon-Sat 10-6, Sun 12-6
winter close -5 PM
501-636-9273
1 mi E of US 71 Bypass on
Business 71

ROGERS, AR 72756
Homestead Antique Mall
100 dealers
3223 Hudson Rd.
Open Mon-Sat 10-6, Sun 12-6
501-631-9003
I-540 Exit 86 E 1/2 mile

HARRISON, AR
**We found Neighbor's Mill Bakery &
Cafe at 1012 Hwy 62/65 in Harrison to
be serving what mught be called
"Ozark Gourmet " food. 870-741-6455**

SPRINGDALE/
TONTITOWN, AR 72770
Tontitown Flea Mkt & Antique Mall
120 booths
Hwy 412 W
Mon-Sat until 5; Sun 12-5
501-361-9902
1 block W of Hwy 112

SPRINGDALE/
TONTITOWN, AR 72770
Yesteryears Antique Mall
300 booths
Hwy 412 W
Mon-Thur 10-6, Fri & Sat 10-8, Sun 12-6
winter close 5 PM
501-361-5747
**W of US 71 on Hwy 412
Several other shops nearby**

**In Springdale our favorite place
to eat is the *Market Place* at Jct
of Hwy 71 and US Hwy 412 by
the Holiday Inn. Varied menu and
delicious food. 501-750-5200.**

SPRINGDALE, AR 72764
Famous Hardware. Antique Mall
14,700 sq. ft.
113 W. Emma
Mon-Sat. 10-5, Sun 1-5
479-756-6650
Downtown

**In Texarkana, if you like "home
cooked" type meals, you will like the
"Dixie Diner". Chicken & dumplings
like"Mother used to make", great
deserts like fresh strawberry pie &
blackberry cobbler. 3200 State Line off
Hwy 30 down by the bowling alley.**

VAN BUREN, AR 72956
**I-40 Exit 7, then I-540 Exit 1 to
downtown Historic District, walk to 12
shops & malls.**

CALIFORNIA
North

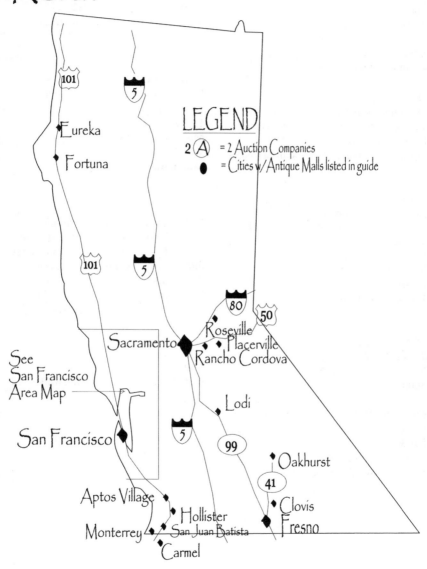

LEGEND

2 (A) = 2 Auction Companies

● = Cities w/ Antique Malls listed in guide

101

5

Eureka

Fortuna

101

5

80

50

Roseville

Sacramento

Placerville

Rancho Cordova

See
San Francisco
Area Map

Lodi

San Francisco

5

99

Oakhurst

41

Aptos Village

Clovis

Hollister

Fresno

Monterrey

San Juan Batista

Carmel

CALIFORNIA - NORTH

WEEKEND ANTIQUE EVENTS
Alameda Point Antiques Faire, **1st Sundays** (Call to confirm)
San Francisco Art Deco Society Show, **1st weekend in Jun & Dec**
San Francisco Cow Palace, 600 booths, **1- Wk end in Feb, May, Aug, Nov**
Petaluma Outdoor Antique Fair, **last Sunday in Apr & Sep.**
Lodi Street Faire, **1st Sun of every May & Oct**
Fremont/Niles, Niles Antique Fair, 500 dealers **Last Sun in Aug**,
Oakhurst Mountain Peddler's Show, **Memorial & Labor Day weekends**
Sacramento/Folsom; 300 dealers, **3rd Sun in Apr and Sep**
San Juan Bautista Annual Flea Market, 150 dealers, **1st Sun in Aug**

ANTIQUE DISTRICTS/VILLAGES
Martinez, Petaluma, Placerville, Roseville, Sacramento, Folsom, Fremont/ Niles, San
Anselmo, Sebastapol

AUCTION/ESTATE SALE CO'S

San Francisco, CA 04103
Butterfield and Butterfield
Antique furniture and collectors sale
220 San Bruno Ave
Monthly
415-861-7500 Call for details

San Leandro,CA 94177
Albino Auction
Antique,estate, general auctions
720 Williams St.
Every other Mon & Tue at 7PM
510-483-2672 Call for details

ANTIQUE MALLS, MARKETS & SHOWS
ALAMEDA, CA
Alameda Point Antiques Faire,
1st SUN
200 booths indoors, 750 outdoors
At the former Alameda Naval Air Station
Open 6AM-$15,7:30-$10, 9AM-$5
510-869-5428, or 510-522-7500
Antiques by the Bay
1000 Central Ave.
Alameda, CA 94501
**From I-880 Southbound take the
Broadway Alameda Exit, turn R at 5th
St to Bdwy, enter Webster Tube, Turn R
at Atlantic.**

CALIFORNIA - NORTH

APTOS VILLAGE, CA 95003
Village Fair Antiques
25 shops
417 Trout Gulch Road
Thur-Sun 10-5
831-688-9883
**Between Santa Cruz and Watsonville
Downtown in the Village of Aptos,
which is on Hwy 1.**

CARMEL, CA
**There are about 10 antique shops in
downtown Carmel off 6th & 7th Sts.
on Delores, Ocean & Lincoln.**

EUREKA/
FORTUNA, CA 95540
Fernbridge Antique Mall
30 dealers
597 Fernbridge Dr.
Open 7 days 10-5
707-725-8820
**US 101 Exit Fernbridge Dr.
about 15 mi S of Eureka**

FREMONT/
NILES, CA
Back On Track Antique Show
200-300 booths of juried antiques
Outdoors on Niles Blvd, Adm free
510-792-8023
**2nd Sunday in June (12th)
From Frwy 880 Exit Niles Blvd E**
Niles Mwerchant Assoc
P.O. Box 2672
Niles District, Fremont, CA 94536

FREMONT/
NILES, CA
Niles Antique Faire
500 dealers, antiques, collectibles, crafts
Outdoors On Niles Blvd & side streets
5 A.M. to 4 P.M; adm free; park $3
510-742-9868
**Last Sunday in Aug
From Fwy 880 Exit Niles Blvd E
16 antique shops on Niles Blvd**
Niles Merchant Assoc
P.O. Box 2672
Niles District, Fremont, CA 94536

FRESNO, CA 93710
Chesterfield's Antiques & Collectible
40 dealers
5092 N. Blackstone
6 days 11-5; Sat 10-6; Sun 12-5, clsd Tue
559-225-4736
**Frwy 41 Exit Shaw W to
Blackstone N.**

FRESNO, CA 93728
Fulton's Folly Antique Mall
60 dealers
920 E. Olive Ave.
Open 7 days 10:30-5:30
559-268-3856
Hwy 99 Exit Olive Ave E 4 1/2 mi

FRESNO /
CLOVIS, CA 93612
Clovis Antique Mall
35 dealers
532 Fifth Street
Mon-Sat-10-5:30; Sun 11-5
559-298-1090
**Off Hwy 41 take Bullord Ave
Exit E to Clovis;
Street fair here March & Oct.**

FRESNO/ CLOVIS, CA 93612
Fourth Street Antique Mall
45 dealers
402 Pollasky, Corner 4th & Pollasky
Open daily 10-5:30
559-323-1636
In Oldtown Clovis with a dozen other antique shops

HEALDSBURG, CA 95448
Mill Street Antiques
35 dealers;100 dealers in Healdsburg
44 Mill Street
Open 7 days 10-5
707-433-8409
16 mi N of Santa Rosa on US 101 take Central Healdsburg Exit, left at 2nd light.

LODI, CA
Street Faire
450-700 dealers; 50% antiques & collectibles, some art & crafts
Downtown
Open 8-4; free adm & parking
209-367-7840
30 mi S of Sacramento on Hwy 99 First Sunday every May and Oct
Lodi Chamber of Commerce
35 So. School St.
Lodi, CA 95242

MARTINEZ, CA 94553
Olde Towne Antiques
30 plus dealers
516 Ferry Street
Open Mon-Sat 10:30-5:30; Sun 11-5:30
925-370-8345
I-680 Marina Vista Exit to downtown

MARTINEZ, CA 94553
Ferry Street Antiques
20 dealers
716 Main St.
Open 10:30-5,Tue-Sat; Sun 12-5 clsd Mon
925-370-9091
Downtown, there are 20 antique stores in Martinez, most within walking distance. AlsoMartinez Peddlers Faire in downtown Martinez 295 booths. Usually in May and in August; call for dates, 510-370-8480

MONTEREY, CA 93940
Cannery Row Antique Mall
135 dealers
471 Wave St
Open Mon-Fr -10-5:30, Sat 10-6; Sun 10-5 in winter, summer hours vary.
831-655-0264
21,000 sq. ft. Located in the Historic *Cannery Row district. Browse two floors of unique antiques and collectibles. Complimentary coffee. FREE PARKING. Voted "Antique Mall of the Year"- Professional Antique Mall Magazine..*

CALIFORNIA - NORTH

NAPPA, CA 94559
Silverado Antique Center
45 plus dealers
835 Lincoln Ave.
Open daily 10-5:30, Sun 12-5:30
707-253-1966
**Located in the historic former Feed
Mill at the Wine Train Tracks off Hwy
29 Lincoln Ave Exit**

OAKHURST, CA
Oakhurst Mountain Peddler's Fair
300 dealers, antiques, collectibles, crafts
Rd 426 & Sierra Way
Open Sat 10-6, Sun 8-4; adm free;
outdoors rain or shine
559-683-7766
**36 mi N of Fresno
Sat/Sun of Memorial Day
and Labor Day weekends**
Chamber of Commerce
49074 Civic Circle
Oakhurst, CA 93644

PETALUMA, CA 94952
Petaluma Collective
20 dealers
300 Petaluma Blvd N
7 days 10-5:30
707-765-2920
**45 mi N of San Francisco, on US 101
downtown**

PETALUMA, CA 94952
Chelsea Antiques
35 dealers
148 Petaluma Blvd N
Open 7 days 10-5:30
707-763-7686
**Downtown, among 30 antique shops
Street Fair last Sunday in Apr & Sep
is held in downtown Petaluma.**

PLACERVILLE, CA 95667
Placerville Antiques & Collectibles
22 dealer
448 Main St
Open 7 days 10-6
530-626-3425
**US Hwy 50, 43 miles E of Sacramento,
Placerville Exit to downtown. 8 antique
shops on Main**

SACRAMENTO, CA
See page 49 for area malls with map.

**San Anselmo, known as Northern
Calfornia's Antique Capital. Aprox. 20
mi N of San Francisco, just off US 101.
There are 35 antique stores, many of
them collectives, most on or just off Sir
Francis Drake or San anselmo Ave.
Exit at San Alselmo off US 101 at San
Rafael.**
SAN ANSELMO, CA 94960
Legacy Antiques
35 shops
204 Sir Francis Drake Blvd.
Mon-Sat 10-5:30; Sun 11-5:50
415-457-7166
Antique district

SAN ANSELMO, CA 94960
Pavilion Antiques
40 dealers
610 Sir Francis Drake Blvd.
Mon-Sat 10:30-5:30; Sun 12-5
415-459-2002
Antique district

SAN CARLOS, CA 94070
Antique Trove
150 dealers
1119 Industrial Way
Mon-Sun 11-6
650-593-1300
Off Interstate 101, San Carlos Exit W to
1st light which is Industrial St, turn S.

SAN FRANCISCO, CA 94111
Thomas Livingston Antiques
8 antique shops in 400 block Jackson St.
414 Jackson
Shops closed on Sundays
415-621-3800
Take the cable car to Powell & Jackson
and walk east on Jackson.

SAN FRANCISCO, CA
Antiques & Collectible Show, Cow Palace
350 booths
Cow Palace
Adm $5; parking $5, Fri $20 adm.
503-282-0877 (call for exact dates)
Hwy 101 Exit Cow Palace,
or Hwy 280, follow signs
One weekend in Feb, May, Aug & Nov
Palmer Wirfs & Assoc.
4001 NE Halsey
Portland, OR 97232

SAN FRANCISCO, CA
Art Deco - 60s Sale
200 dealers, Deco including 40s- 60s
Concourse Exhibit Ctr 8th & Brannan
Sat 10-6; Sun 11-5; adm $8; indoors
650-599-3326 or 415-383-3008
Bay Bridge 9th St Exit to 8th St, 2nd
light; Hwy 101 N 7th St Exit to 6th St., R
on Brannon; 1st Wkend,
Jun & Dec.
Peter & Deborah Keresztury
1217 Waterview Dr.
Mill Valley, CA 94941
www.artdecosale.com

SAN JUAN BAUTISTA, CA
San Juan Bautista Annual Flea Market
150 dealers, all antiques
On main streets of town
Open 8-5; adm & some park free;
outdoors
831-623-2454
30 mi S of San Jose on US 101
First Sunday in August
Every year
Chamber of Commerce
P.O. Box 1037
San Juan Bautista, CA 95045-1037

SAN JOSE, CA 95128
Antique Colony
55 dealers, 15,000 sq. ft.
1915 W. San Carlos St
Open Mon-Sat 10-6; Sun 11-5
408-293-9844
I-880 Exit San Carlos St. W
7 antique shops on San Carlos

CALIFORNIA - NORTH

SAN MATEO, CA 94402
Collective Antiques
40 dealers
55 E. 3rd Ave
Mon-Sat 10-5; Sun 12-5
650-347-2171
From US 101 Exit 3rd Ave W.

SAN MATEO, CA 94402
Hillsborough Antique Show & Sale
175,00 sq. ft, 550 dealers
San Mateo County Expo Center
Thur-Sat 11-8, Sun 11-5; Adm $6, Pk $5
208-939-7460 or 650-574-3247
**Next to Bay Meadows at Delaware
&25th, Hwy 92 W off US 101, Dela-
ware St**
3rd Wk in Jan, 1st in May, 3rd in Nov
Hillsborough Antique Show
P.O. Box 1216
Merdian, Idaho
www.hillsboroughantiqueshow.com

SEBASTOPOL, CA 45472
Antique Society
120 dealers
2661 Gravenstein Hwy
Open 7 days 10-5
707-829-1733
5 mi W of Santa Rosa on Hwy 116

SEBASTOPOL, CA 45472
Sebastopol Antique Mall
65 dealers
755 Petaluma Ave.
Open daily 10-5
707-823-1936
**Exit US 101 at Santa Rosa Hwy 116 W
8 shops on 116 at Sebastopol.**

TRAVEL NOTES

46

GREAT ANTIQUE GETAWAY TO THE CALIFORNIA WINE COUNTRY

WHEN: Anytime, but if it is a 1st Sunday of the month, you could visit **Alameda Point Antiques Faire**, with 950 exhibitors. Go either before or after antiquing the wine country. See text under Alameda for details.

WHERE: Napa and Sonoma Counties wine country.

LODGING: Our choice would be the Doubletree Hotel in Rohnert Park near Santa Rosa. Charming California architecture with 2 tennis courts and whirlpool. Ask for promotions or package deals, 707-584-5466. Courtyard, Holiday Inn Express, Days Inn, other motels/hotels and Bed & Breakfasts in area.

LEISURE: Consider a leisure 3 hr. Wine Train ride with wine tasting, gourmet brunch, lunch or dinner in a 1917 dining car during a 36 mi tour of the wine country. www.winetrain.com or 1-800-427-4124.

ANTIQUING:

1ST Day, starting at Santa Rosa N on US 101, 16 mi to Central Hearldsburg Exit, then left at 2nd light to antique shops with 100 dealers.

2. Return to US101N 7 mi to Jct Hwy 128 So. to lunch in wine country at a restaurant such as *TraVigne Italian Restaurant*, 1/2 mi So of St. Helena on Hwy29, 707-963-4444.

3.Then the *Antique Shoppe* at 1551 Soscal Ave, downtown Napa. 2 blocks N of 1st St.

4. Next *Silverado Antique Center* at 835 Lincoln Ave. at the Wine Train tracks, Napa. If time permits, Hwy 29 S to I-780 into Martinez with 20 antique shops on Ferry St.

2ND DAY: From Rohnert Park, take Hwy 116 W to *Sebastopol's Antique Society*, 2661 Hwy 116.

Next *Sebastopol Antique Mall* at 755 Petaluma Ave (Hwy 116). 15 shops on Hwy 116 here. Return on Hwy 116 to US 101 So. to 30 antique shops in beautifully restored Victorian era downtown Petaluma. Most shops on Petaluma and Kentucky Streets.

After Petaluma go So. on US 101 to San Anselmo Exit for 35 antique shops, mostly on Sir Francis Drake and San Anselmo Blvd.

There is more great antiquing in the Sacramento and Bay area that can be found in our book on the way home.

CALIFORNIA
~ San Francisco

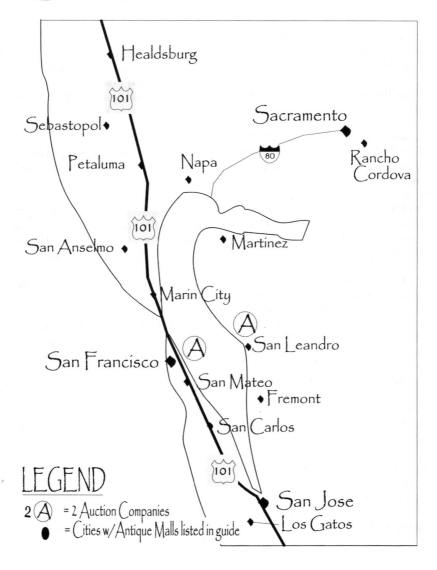

Healdsburg

101

Sebastopol

Sacramento

Petaluma

Napa

80

Rancho Cordova

San Anselmo

101

Martinez

Marin City

A

San Francisco

A

San Leandro

San Mateo

Fremont

San Carlos

LEGEND

2 (A) = 2 Auction Companies
● = Cities w/ Antique Malls listed in guide

101

San Jose

Los Gatos

SACRAMENTO/
ROSEVILLE, CA 95678
Antique Trove
250 dealers,40,00 sq. ft.
236 Harding Blvd
Open 10-6 Mon-Thur, Fri & Sat 10-8,
Sun 10-6
916-786-2777
**Off I-80 Douglas West Exit, go W to 1st
R Harding Blvd.**
*Voted best Antique Store in Sacra-
mento area! Over 3000 antique price
guides and references books for sale.*

SACRAMENTO, CA 95819
Lecoop Antique & Garden Architectual
Antique row of 3 shops
866 57th Street
Wed-Sat 11-5, Sun 12-5 10:30-4:30
916-457-9183
Between H & J Streets

SACRAMENTO /
FOLSOM, CA
Peddler's Faire & Antique Market
300 dealers
On Sutter Street, Old Town Folsom
Open 8:00-to 4:00; adm free
916-985-7452
**U.S. 50 Hwy Exit Folsom Blvd;
N 3 mi 3rd Sun in Apr & Sep,**
Sutter Street Merchants Assoc.
P.O. Box 515
Folsom, CA 95763

SACRAMENTO/
FOLSOM, CA 95630
Folsom Mercantile Exchange
40 dealers
724 Sutter St.
7 days 11-5
916-985-2169
**US Hwy 50 E Exit Folsom Blvd
N 3 mi to Sutter St. L**

**Walk to 8 shops in Folsom
In a historic gold rush, railroad town,
minutes from Sacramento with many
shops, restaurants and historical
attractions.**

SACRAMENTO/
RANCHO CORDOVA, CA 95742
Antique Plaza Mall
250 dealers
11395 Folsom Blvd
Open 7 days 10-6
916-852-8517
**10 mi E of Sacramento off U.S. 50 Hwy
between Sunrise & Hazel**

SACRAMENTO/ ROCKLIN, CA 95677
Antique Plaza Rocklin
100 dealers, 35,000 sq.ft.
4401 Granite Dr.
Open 7 days 10-6
916-315-1990
**I-80, 15 miles E of Sacto Exit, Rocklin
Rd , N. to Granite Dr., then R.**

CALIFORNIA-South

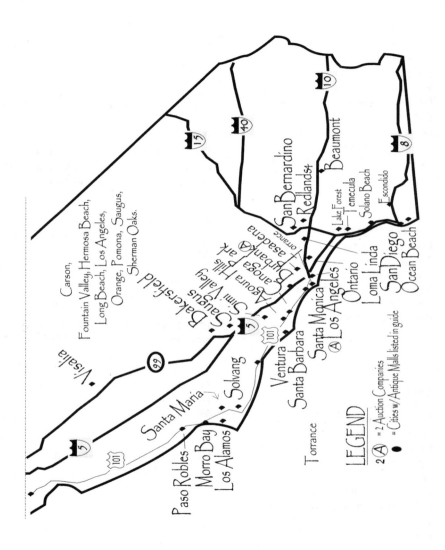

CALIFORNIA - SOUTH

WEEKEND ANTIQUE EVENTS
Costa Mesa Antique Show, **one weekend in Mar & Oct**
Del Mar Antique Show, **one weekend in Jan., Apr.,Nov.**
Glendale Show, **1st Sundays.**
Long Beach Veterans Stadium Market, **3rd Sundays**
Pasadena Rose Bowl Flea Market, **2nd Sundays**.
Pasadena-Bustamante Antique Show, **Mar, Jun, Aug & Dec**.
Santa Monica Airport Antique & Collectibles Mkt.,**4th Sundays**
Torrance Antique Street Faire, **4th Sundays**

ANTIQUE DISTRICTS/VILLAGES
L.A- La Cienga & Melrose, Orange, Pasadena, Pomona, San Diego's
Newport Ave, Summerland, Temecula & Ventura.

Mimi's cafe **in Orange County at**
Beach Blvd. and Garden Grove Blvd. is
a favorite of ours. There are 17 other
Mimi's Cafes **in other cities, mostly in**
Orange County near freeway exits. Ask
most anyone where the nearest *Mimi's*
is located.

AUCTION/ESTATE SALE CO'S
(Call to confirm)

Burbank/Sun Valley, 91352
Oscars Antique Auction
Fine antique auctions
7624 San Fernando Rd
Last Sunday of each month at 9AM
818-767-6176
NW of Burbank-Glendale Airport
Off I-5 N of Hollywood Way & S of
Sunland Blvd

Los Angeles, CA 90018
Orril's Auction Studio, Inc.
Antiques and collectibles auctions
1910 W. Adams Blvd.
Each Tue at 9:30 AM
310-277-7373 or 818-366-7859
2 blks E. of Western St., 2 blks S of I-
10

ANTIQUE MARKETS, MALLS/ SHOWS

AGOURA HILLS, CA 91301
Agoura Antique Mart
50 dealers
28863 Agoura Rd.
Open Mon-Sat 10-6; Sun 11-5
818-706-8366
From US 101 Exit Kanan Rd
S to Agoura Rd , Left

CALIFORNIA - SOUTH

BAKERSFIELD, CA 93301
Central Park Antique Mall
85 dealers
701 19th Street
Open 7 days 10-5
661-633-1143
**Hwy 99 Exit Rosedale Hwy E
to "Q" St, S to 19th St Right**

BAKERSFIELD, CA 93301
Five and Dime Antiques
110 dealers
1400 19th St.
Open Mon-Sat 10-5; Sun 12-5
661-323-8048
**Hwy 99 Exit Rosedale Hwy E
to"Q" St, S to 19th St Right
10 shops on 19th St & 8 more on
"H"St.**

BEAUMONT, CA 92223
Levis Red Barn
60 dealers
504 W. 6th Street
7 days
951-845-8608
At Freeway 60 & I-10 Junction

BEAUMONT, CA 92223
Beaumont Antique Mall
60 dealers
450 E. 6th St.
Open 7 days 10-5
951-845-1397
**E on 6th St from 60 & I-10 Junction
Malls and shops nearby**

CANOGA PARK, CA 91303
Collectible Glitz Miss La de da-s
One of 8 shops in Antique Row
21435 Sherman Way
Mon & Tue 10-5; W-Sat 1-6, Sun 12-5
818-347-9343
**US 101 N to Woodland Hills Exit
Canoga Ave. E on Sherman Way**

CARSON, CA 90745
Memory Lanes Antique Mall
275 dealers
20740 S. Figueroa
7 days 10-6
310-538-4130
**I-110 Exit Torrence Blvd.,
E to Figueroa Left**

COSTA MESA, CA
Costa Mesa Antique show & Sale
200 dealers
Orange County Fairgrounds
Fri & Sat 11-8, Sun 11-5, Adm $8, park free
800-943-7501
**Fwy 55 E, and Exit Fair Dr. or 405 Fwy Exit
Fairview Rd. One weekend in Mar & Oct**
Calendar Antique Shows
P. O. Box 939
Indian Rocks Beach, FL 33785

CULVER CITY, CA 90230
Culver City Antique Center
75 shops, 30,000 sq ft
5431 S. Sepulveda
Open Mon-Sat 11-6:30; Sun 12-5
310-391-1996
2 mi N of LA Int'l Airport

DEL MAR, CA
Del Mar Antique Show & Sale
275 dealers
San Diego County Fairgrounds
Fri-Sat 11-8, Sun 11-5 Adm $8, Park $6
Call for dates
1-800-943-7501
www.calendarshows.com
Calendar Antique Shows
P.O. Box 939
Indian Rocks Beach, FL 33785
**I-5 Exit Via de la Valle W to 1st stop
light, L on J Durante. One weekend in
Jan, Apr, and Nov**

**In Del Mar our favorite restaurant is
Pasta Pronto. Homestyle cooking with
a gourmet slant at 2673 De La Valle.
858-481-6017**

ESCONDIDO, CA 92025
Hidden Valley Antique Emporium
70 shops
333 E. Grand Ave.
Daily 10-5, Sun 11-5
760-737-0333
**I-15, Hwy 78 Exit E to Broadway,
R to Grand, L on Grand.**

ESCONDIDO, CA 92025
Escondido Antique Mall
60 shops
135 W. Grand Avenue
Open daily 10-5:30
760-743-3210
**I-15 Valley Pkwy Exit E to Maple,
left on Maple, R on Grand**

FOUNTAIN VALLEY, CA 97208
Old Chicago Antiques Mall
110 shops
18319 Euclid
Daily 10-6, Fri 10-8, Sun 11-6
714-434-6487
**I-405 and Euclid Ave between
Hwy 55 & I-605**

GLENDALE, CA
The Glendale Show
60 dealers; antiques & collectibles
Glendale Civic Auditorium
Open 9:30-3:00PM
209-358-3134
**Exit Mountain St off Fwy 2
1401 N. Verdugo Rd.
1st Sun every month**
Bustamante Co
P.O. Box 637
Atwater, CA 95301

HERMOSA BEACH, CA 90254
Stars Antique Market
72 dealers
526 Pier Avenue
Open Mon-Sat 11-6; Sun 11-5
310-318-2800
**Downtown
From I-405 take Artesia Blvd W
to Pacific Coast Hwy N**

53

CALIFORNIA - SOUTH

LAKE FOREST, CA 92636
El Torro Antique Mall
70 dealers
23710 El Torro Rd
Mon-Sat 10-6, Sun 11-6
949-588-8979
In the Saddleback Valley Plaza at El Torro Rd & Rockfield

LAKE FOREST, CA 92630
Lake Forest Antique Mall
170 dealers
23222 Lake Center Drive
Open daily 10-6, Sun 11-5
949-597-1189
Exit I-5, Lake Forest E, to Rockfield then R

LAKE FOREST, CA 92630
Cranberry Manor
30 dealers
23720 El Toro Rd. #E
Open M-Sat 10-6, Sun 11-5
949-586-1329
In Saddleback Valley Plaza at El Toro Rd. in shopping center.

LOMA LINDA, CA 92354
Loma Linda Antique Mall
60 shops
24997 Redland Blvd.
Open 7 days 10-:30-5:30
909-797-4776
I-10 Tippecanoe Ave off-ramp

LONG BEACH, CA 90808
The Village Vault
60 spaces
5423 Village Rd
Open Mon-Fri 10-6; Sat 10-6, Sun 11-5
562-425-7455
From I-405 Exit Bellflower Blvd. N. to Carson St., then 1 block past Carson to Viking Way, left 1 block.

LONG BEACH, CA
Outdoor Antique & Collectibles Market
800 dealers, all antiques & collectibles
Veterans Stadium
Open 7-2; adm $5.00; free parking
323-655-5703
I-405 Exit Lakewood Blvd, N 1 1/2 mi R on Conant to stadium
3rd Sunday every month, some 5th Sun
Americana Enterprises
PO Box 69219
Los Angeles, CA 90069

LONG BEACH, CA 90804
Long Beach Antique Mall
50 dealers
3100 E. Pacific Coast Hwy (Hwy 1)
Open Mon-Fri 10-5:30; Sat 11-5:30; Sun 11-5
562-494-2526
I-405 Exit Cherry Av S to Hwy 1 Left.

LOS ALAMOS, CA 93440
 Depot Mall
50 dealers
PO Box 805
Open Mon-Sat 10-5; Sun 12-5
805-344-3315
One-half block W of Los Alamos Exit of 101, 50 mi N of Santa Barbara
In the Pacific Coast RR Station

LOS ANGELES/ WEST HOLLYWOOD
CA 90048
Evans & Gerst
Group of shops in area
520 N. San Vicente
Most shops closed on Sun
Hours vary shop to shop
310-657-0112
Near Pacific Design Center
N of Wilshire on La Cienaga
where there are 20 shops, crossing
La Cienaga is Melrose and Melrose
Place with 40 Antique Shops.

MISSION VIEJO, CA
Landmark Antique Mall
100 spaces, 18,000 sq. ft.
28331 Marguerite Pkwy
Open M-Fri 10-6, Sat & Sun 10-5
949-364-1444
I-5 Exit Avery Pkwy E to Marguerita
Pkwy
L 2 blks in shopping center

MORRO BAY /
CAYUCOS, CA 93430
Rich Man-Poor Man Antique Mall
70 dealers
146 N. Ocean Ave.
Open 10-5, 7 days
805-995-3631
4 mi N of Morro Bay
Downtown Cayucos
4 other shops nearby

MORRO BAY, CA
3 or 4 antique shops on Morro Bay
Blvd. Most shops closed Tue, otherwise
11-4. Hwy 1 Exit Morro Bay Blvd into
town.

ONTARIO, CA 91762
Ontario Antique Center
72 dealers
203 W. B Street
Open Mon-Sat 10-5; Sun 11-5
909-391-1200
Downtown, Euclid Av Exit from I-10
or Hwy 60 to B Street, 1 block W

ONTARIO, CA 91762
Treasures 'n' Junk Antique Mall
70 dealers
215 S. San Antonio
Mon-Sat 10-5; Sun 11-5
909-983-3300
Downtown Ontario, 2 blks W of Euclid

ORANGE, CA 92866
Country Roads Antiques
100 dealers
204 W. Chapman
Open Fr- &-Sat 10-6; Sun-Thur 10-5
714-532-3041
Newport Fwy (55) Chapman Exit W

ORANGE, CA 92866
Orange Circle Antique Mall
125 dealers
118 S. Glassell
Mon 10-5; Tue-Thru Sat 10-6; Sun 11-6
714-538-8160
Garden Grove Freeway (22)
Exit Glassell Ave N
30 shops at Glassell & Chapman

CALIFORNIA - SOUTH

PASADENA, CA
Pasadena Rose Bowl Flea Market
2100 dealers
Rose Bowl
Adm 6 A.M. $10; 9 A.M. $7; park free
323-560-show or 323-588-4411
**Between Linda Vista Ave. exit N off
134, and Lincoln Ave. exit N from I-210
2nd Sunday of every month**
R.G. Canning Attractions
P.O. Box 400
Maywood, CA 90270-0400

PASADENA, CA 91101
Novetry's Antique Gallery
60 dealers
60 N Lake Av
Open Tue-Sun 11:00-5:30
626-577-9660
Lake Exit off I-210 S

PASADENA, CA 91105
Pasadena Antique Center & Annex
130 dealers
480 S. Fair Oaks Ave.
Open daily 10-6
626-449-7706
**Downtown S of Colorado Blvd. Antiques
also at 444 and 446 S. Fair Oaks. I-210
Exit Fair Oaks Ave S.**

PASADENA, CA 91105
Antiques on Fair Oaks
22,000 Sq. Ft.
330 S. Fair Oaks
Mon-Sat 10-6, Sun 11-6
626-449-9590
I-210 Exit Fair Oaks South to #330

PASADENA, CA 91105
Pasadena Antique Mall
50 dealers
35 S. Raymond #130
Mon 10-5, Tue-Sun 10-9
626-304-9886
**I-210 Exit Fair Oaks S, L on Green,
one block, then L on Raymond.**

PASADENA, CA
Bustamante Antique Show
235 dealers, all antiques & collectibles
Pasadena Center, 300 E. Green St.
Fri-Sat 11-7; Sun 11-5; adm $7, seniors
$4
209-358-3134
**At Euclid & Green, 1 block S of Colo.
Av 3 days in 1st half of Mar, June,
Aug & Dec. Call for exact dates.**
Bustamante Enterprises, Inc.
P.O. Box 637
Atwater, CA 95301-0637
www.bustamante-shows.com

**About 25 miles S of Paso Robles on
US 101 at San Louis Obispo is the
Madonna Inn devoted primarily to
newlyweds with heart -shaped beds,
and unbelievable decor. Very interesting for lunch or coffee break.**

PASO ROBLES, CA 93446
Great American Antique Mall
40 dealers
1305 Spring St.
Open 7 days
805-239-1203
US 101 Spring St. Exit to 1305 Spring

POMONA, CA 91766
Robbins Antique Mall
140 dealers
200 E. 2nd Street
Open 7 days 11-5
909-623-9835
I-10 Garey Ave. Exit S

POMONA, CA 91766
Pomona Antique Center
75 dealers
162 E. 2nd St.
Open Mon-Fri-10-4, Sat & Sun 10-5
909-620-7406
I-10 Exit Garey Ave S

POMONA, CA 91766
Olde Towne Pomona Antique Mall
8000 sq ft, 65 dealers
260 E. 2nd St.
Open Mon-Fri 11-5; Sat 10-5, Sun 12-5
909-622-1011
I-10 Exit Garey Ave S
About 25 antique malls & shops on 2nd
St. Street Fair last Sat Jan, Mar, Sep
& Nov.

REDLANDS, CA 92373
Precious Times Antique Mall
125 shops
1740 W. Redlands Blvd.
Open Daily 10-4:45
909-792-7768
I-10 Exit Alabama St.
S to Redlands Blvd. R

REDLANDS, CA 92373
Antique Exchange Mall
50 dealers
31251 Outer Hwy 10
Open Thur-Tue 10:30-5, closed Wed
909-794-9190
At Yucaipa Blvd. Off ramp
There are 11 other antique shops
on Outer Hwy 10 within a mile

RIVERSIDE, CA 92501
Mission Galleria Mall
100 dealers, 35,000 sq. ft.
3700 Main St.
Mon-Sat 10-5:30, Sun 11-5:30
909-276-8000
Downtown

Our very favorite Mexican restaurant
is _Casa de Pico's_ in Old Town San
Diego. Take the Old Town Exit off I-5
just S of I I-8. It's worth the wait to eat
on the patio. You have to drive several
blocks into Old Town to get to _Pico's_ on
Juan St in the Bazaar del Mundo.

CALIFORNIA-SOUTH

A great place for cocktails is the lobby or terrace of La Valencia Hotel in La Jolla with its panoramic view. It is also a great place to eat. For a quick informal meal we like the *Gerard Gourmet* at 7837 Girard Ave in downtown La Jolla.

SAN DIEGO. CA
Adams Antique Row
Many blocks of Adams Ave have shops selling used furniture, used books, some antiques, junk, etc.
I-805 Exit E on Adams St just So. of I-8

SAN DIEGO/ OCEAN BEACH, CA 92107
Newport Avenue Antiques
40 booths
4836 Newport Avenue
Daily 7 days 10-6
619-224-1994
I-8 W to end, Exit Sunset Cliffs Blvd. W to Newport Ave R

SAN DIEGO/ OCEAN BEACH CA 92107
Ocean Beach Antique Mall
40 dealers
4847 Newport Ave.
Mon-Sat 10-6, Sun 12-6
619-223-6170
I-8 W to end. Exit Sunset Cliffs Blvd. W to Newport Ave R

SAN DIEGO/ OCEAN BEACH, CA 92107
Newport Ave. Antique Center
150 dealers, 18,000 sq. ft.
4864 Newport Ave
Open 7 days 10-6
619-222-8686
I-8 W to end, Exit Sunset Cliffs Blvd W to Newport Ave R
6 Malls within one block

SAN DIEGO, CA 92101
Olde Cracker Factory Antiques
100 dealers
448 W. Market
Open 7 days 11-5
619-233-1669
Downtown;10th Av Exit off I-5, S 10 blocks to Market, W about 1 mi

SAN DIEGO/ LA MESA, CA 92042
La Mesa Antique Mall
40 shops
4710 Palm Ave.
Open 7 days 10-6
619-462-2211
Fwy 94, Exit Spring St. N to Palm Dr. 8 Antique shops 8200-8300 La Mesa Blvd
N on Palm Ave to La Mesa Blvd. R

SAN DIEGO /
SAN MARCOS, CA 92078
San Marcos Antique Village
65 shops
983 Grand Avenue
Open 7 days 10-5:30
760-744-8718
**Frwy 78 to San Marcos Blvd.,
W to Grand, R to shops**

SAN DIEGO /
SOLANA BEACH, CA 92075
Antique Warehouse
101 shops
212 S. Cedros Ave.
Closed Tue; otherwise open 10-5
858-755-5156
I-5 Exit Solana Beach W to Cedros S

Great restaurant here called *Pasta
Pronto.* **at 117 W. Plaza St. at US 101. A
couple of blocks north of the Antique
Warehouse 858-481-0634.**

SANTA BARBARA /
SUMMERLAND, CA 93067
Summerland Antique Collective
25 dealers
2194 Ortega Hill Rd
Open 7 days10-5
805-565-3189
**At Summerland Exit of Hwy 101
There are 10 shops you can walk to
all on this frontage Rd to US 101.**

SANTA MARIA /
NIPOMO, CA 93444
 Antique Plus
35 dealers
104 Cuyama Lane
Open 7 days 10-5
805-922-2205
**From US 101 take Hwy 166 E
(Bakersfield Exit) West 1 block.**

SANTA MONICA, CA
Santa Monica Outdoor Antique Mkt
250 dealers, all antiques & collectibles
South side of the Santa Monica Airport
Adm $5.00 at 8 A.M.; 6-8 A.M. $7
323-933-2511
**Airport Ave off Bundy, near intersec-
tion of I-10 & I-405**
4th Sunday every month
Marketplace Productions
P.O. Box 36436
Los Angeles, CA 90036

SANTA MONICA, CA 90404
Wertz Brothers Antique Mall
194 booths & showcases
1607 Lincoln Blvd.
Mon-Sat 10-6, Sun 12-6
310-452-1800
I-10 Exit Lincoln Blvd. W

CALIFORNIA-SOUTH

SAUGUS, CA 91322
Country Antique Fair Mall
100 shops
21546 Golden Triangle
Open daily 10-6
661-254-1474
I-5 Exit Valentia Blvd E.

SHERMAN OAKS, CA 91423
Sherman Oaks Antique Mall
100 dealers
14034 Ventura Blvd.
Open Mon-Sat 11-6; Sun 12-5
818-906-0338
I-405 Exit Van Nuys Blvd S to Ventura Blvd. then L

SIMI VALLEY, CA 93063
Penny Pinchers Antique Mall
72 booths
4265 Valley Fair St
Open Mon-Sat 10-5; Sun 11-5
805-527-0056
**Fwy 118 Tapo Canyon Exit, S to Cochran St,
E to Tapo St, S to Valley Fair Antique Row.**

SOLVANG, CA 93463
Solvang Antique Center
85 dealers
486 First St.
Open 7 days 10-6
805-688-6222
Buellton/Solvang Exit off US 101 about 30 mi N of Santa Barbara

TEMECULA, CA 92592
Chaparral Antique Mall
50 dealers
28465 Front St. (Hwy 79)
Open Mon-Sat 10-5, Sun 115
951-676-0070
I-15 Exit Hwy 79 which turns into Front St. 8 shops on Main St and 8 on Front St

TORRANCE, CA 90501
Torance Antique Street Faire
150 Vendors
1313 Satori Ave.
Open 8-4; park free
310-328-6107
I-405 Fwy Exit Crenshaw Blvd S. to Torrance Blvd. L to Sartori, 4th Sunday of every month.

VENTURA, CA 93001
Nicholby Antiques Mall
50 dealers
404 E Main
Open Mon-Sat 10:30-5:30; Sun 12-5
805-653-1195
US 101 Ventura Exit to Main St from the North . From So. Exit California St. to Main

VENTURA, CA 93001
Times Remembered
30 dealers
467 E. Main St.
Daily 10:30-5:30; Fri & Sat til 9
805-643-3137
**US 101 Ventura Exit to Main St.
25 antique shops & malls on Main St.**

GREAT ANTIQUE GETAWAY TO LOS ANGELES

WHEN: Last weekend of the month for Santa Monica Market which is the last Sun of each month.

WHERE: Santa Monica Market, South side of the Santa Monica Airport. Adm. $4.00, 250 dealers gather there. Airport Ave. off Bundy near Jct I-10 & I-405. Open 8:30 AM

LAST SUN OF MONTH: After the antique market, if you wish to attend an auction, go to Burbank/Sun Valley reference in this guide under auctions for details. It starts at 9AM.

WHEN: Antiquing for getaway will start early Sat or Mon: Go N of Wilshire Blvd. on La Cienega area of about 60 Antique shops on La Cienega Melrose, Melrose Place and some adjacent streets. These shops are closed on Sunday.

LODGING: We would stay in West L.A., perhaps the Courtyard at 10320 W. Olympic Blvd.1-800-228-9290

LUNCH: Go back down La Cienega to 3rd St. East 1 mile to Fairfax Ave, where you will find the famous Farmer's Market. Here you can pick and choose your meal from a varity of vendors selling gourmet foods. After lunch you can continue antiquing Melrose & Melrose Place Next go S on La Cienega to I-10W to Lincoln Blvd Exit W to 1607 Lincoln, *Wertz Bro. Antique Mall*, with 194 booths & showcases.

LEISURE: One of the many interesting things to do in L.A. is Olvera St., downtown, "Mexican Old Town". Go N on Main St. past Union Station to the Plaza and Olvera St.

From the Santa Monica Market go to Pasadena for more great antiquing. 1.Take I-10 E to I-110N to I-210E and exit Fair Oak Ave. S. to antique malls at 330 Fair Oaks, as well as 444 & 446 Fair Oaks. Several hundred quality dealers here.

2. Next take Fair Oaks N to Green, R one block then L to 35 S Raymond, *Pasadena Mall.*

3. Go East on Green to Lake Ave N. to *Novetry's Antique Gallery* at 60 N. Lake Ave.

4.After Pasadena go east on I-210 to I-10 E to Euclid Ave. .Exit So. into Ontario to "B" St. W one block to 203 W "B", *Ontario Antique Center.*

5.Next *Treasures and Junk* at 215 San Antonio, 2 blocks W of Euclid.

6.After Ontario go N on Euclid to I-10W to Garey Ave, Exit in Pomana So.to 2nd St. and 3 malls and 20 shops in the 100-200 blocks on 2nd Street.

GREAT ANTIQUE GETAWAY TO ORANGE COUNTY, CA

WHEN: 3rd Sunday of any month, 7AM to 2PM.

WHERE: *Long Beach Antique and Collectibles Market*, with 800 dealers at Veterans Stadium, Adm $5. I-405- Exit Lakewood Blvd N 1 1/2 mi, R on Conant St to Stadium.

ANTIQUING:

1. After the market go S on Lakewood Blvd to I-405N to Carson St Exit W to Figueroa St N to 20740 S. Figueroa St.to *Memory Lane Antique Mall* with 275 dealers.

2. Next, I-405 S to Cherry St Exit S to US Hwy 1,l eft to 3100 E. Pacific Coast Hwy. *Long Beach Antique Mall,* with 50 d ealers.

3. Now continue on US1 to Lakewood Blvd. N to Carson St.E to Bellflower N 1 block to *VillageVault*, 5423 Village Rd, with 60 spaces.

LODGING: Accomodations in the Disneyland area seem to be the most reasonable. Lodging on the Coast , like Laguna Beach, might be more enjoy-able, if you are not going to Disneyland.

RESTAURANTS: In Laguna Beach, Las Brisas at the Top Of The Hill, 361 Cliff Dr., good Mexican food and view of the coastline.

SATURDAY: In Orange, there are 2 antique malls and 30 shops at Glassell & Chapman Ave.Take Frwy 55 N to Chapman W to Glassell or take Garden Grove Frwy E to Glassell N to Chapman since we don't know where you are coming from these are from 2 different directions.

RESTAURANTS:

There are several *MiMi's Cafes* in Orange County mostly at Frwy exits. Their French decor provides charm for eating good American food that is in very large portions - 2 could split .

There is a MiMi's on your way to the next mall, Frwy 55S 2 miles to 17th St Exit, E side of Frwy for Mi Mi's. From Orange take Frwy 55 S. to I-405, N to Euclid Exit S. to 18319 Euclid, *Old Chicago Antique mall* with it's 110 dealers has lots of good stuff.

Next , I-405 S turns into I-5 to Lake Forest Dr. Exit E to Rockfield then R to170 dealer mall , *Lake Forest Antique Mall* at 23222 Lake Center Drive. Continue S on Rockfield to Saddleback Valley Plaza, with 100 dealers in 2 malls.

Now , return to I-5 on El Torro Rd. and continue S on. I-5 and exit Avery Park E to Marguerita Pkwy, L 2 bl ocks in shopping Center, *Landmark Antique Mall,* 28331 Marguerita Pkwy with 100 spaces. To continue antiquing into the San Diego Getaway simply continue South on I-5.

GREAT GETAWAY TO ANTIQUE SAN DIEGO

WHEN: Anytime

LODGING: We like to stay in suburban La Jolla at the La Jolla Inn, 858-454-0133, a small hotel next to the renowned La Valencia Hotel, 858-454-0771. Ocean views, within walking to the beach, coves, shops and restaurants.

RESTAURANTS: In La Jolla, La Valencia Hotel, Girard Gourmet,, 7837 Girard St. for a quick informal meal. The Marine room, 2000 Spindrift Dr..for breathtaking views of the surf & coast, especially at sunset. Go prospect St. N to Torry Pines N 1/2 mi to Spindrift Dr. to the beach.

ANTIQUING:

1ST DAY: I-5 So. to I- 8W to Exit for Sunset Cliffs Blvd. W to Newport Ave. R to 3 malls and several shops on Newport Ave.

Restaurant: Casa de Picos, our favorite Mexican restaurant with a colorful patio is way back in Old Town on Juan St. in Bazaar del Mundo. If it is a nice day to eat on a patio, exit I-5 just So. of I-8, Old Town Exit, and enjoy Casa de Pico.

NEXT: I-5 So. to 10th ave exit So. to Market St. W about 1 mi to *Olde Cracker Factory Antiques,* 60 dealers at 448 W. Market.
Go E on Market St. to19th St N to Fwy 94E to Spring St. Exit N to Palm Dr., *La Mesa Antique Mall,* 4710 Palm Ave with 40 shops.

4th stop after that, Palm Ave N to La Mesa Blvd turn right. There are 8 antique shops 8200-8300 La Mesa .

5th stop, go W on La Mesa Blvd to Spring St N. to I-8W to I-15 S about1 mi to Adams St. Exit E or W on Adams St for shops selling used furniture, old books some antiques & "junk".

2ND DAY:{ Depending on how fast you shop) Not on a Tue, they are closed then, *Antique Warehouse* has 101 booths at 212 S. Cedros. I-5 N to Solono Beach Exit W to Cedros So to the mall.

Lunch: Pasta Pronto, restaurant 2 blocks N of *Antique Warehouse* on Plaza St. W to #117. serves some great lasanga, etc.

From Solona Beach go So. on I-5 to Frwy 56E to I-15 N to Escondido Exit Valley Pkwy E to Maple L on Maple, R on Grand. Two antique malls: 135 W. Grand *Escondido Antique Mall & Hidden Valley Antique Emporium* at 333 E. Grand.

COLORADO

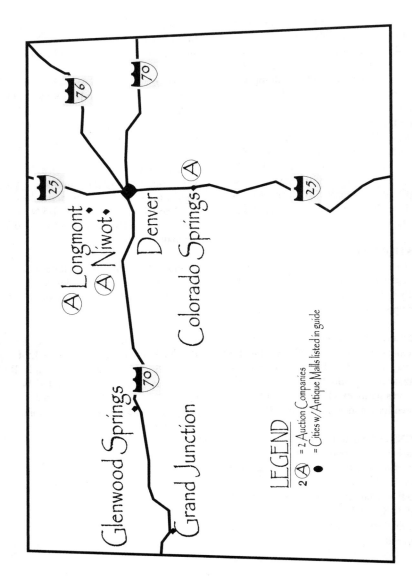

LEGEND

2 (A) = 2 Auction Companies

● = Cities w/ Antique Malls listed in guide

COLORADO

WEEKEND ANTIQUE EVENTS

Buchanan's Monthly Antiques & Flea Market, at Fairgrounds in Brighton/Denver
Once a month Apr. thru Dec., see listing and call for dates.
Denver World Wide Antique Show, 200 dealers, **Mar, Jul,Oct & Nov-dates vary.**
Colorado Springs, Pikes Peak Western Collectibles Show,
    last weekend in July every year.

ANTIQUE DISTRICTS/VILLAGES
South Broadway in Denver, Colorado
Ave in Colorado Springs

AUCTION / ESTATE SALE CO'S
Longmont, CO 80503
Niwot Auction Co.
Antique auction **at Boulder County**
Fairgrounds in Longmont
9595 Nelson Rd
4th Sun at noon
303-652-2030

ANTIQUE MALLS, MARKETS & MALLS

COLORADO SPRINGS, CO 80903
Antiques Gallery Inc.
45 dealers
21 N. Nevada
6 days from 10 -5 PM
719-633-6070
I-25 Exit 142 E to Nevada Ave
Downtown

COLORADO SPRINGS, CO 80903
The Antique Mall of Colorado Springs
80 dealers, & 80 showcases
118 W. Colorado Ave
Mon-Sat 9-6, Sun 12-6
719-520-1415
www.antique-mall-colorado-springs.com
Right behind Antlers Hotel downtown

COLORADO SPRINGS, CO 80903
Downtown shops
20 dealers
405 S. Nevada
Mon-Fri 9:30-5:30; Sat 10-5; Sun 12-4
719-473-3351
I-25 Exit 142 E to Nevada Av. Downtown
8 shops on Colo. Av., I-25 Exit 141 W

COLORADO SPRINGS, CO 80904
Adobe Walls Antique Mall
60 dealers
2808 W. Colorado Ave.
Mon-Sat 10-5, Sun 11-5
719-635-3394
I-25 Exit 141 W

COLORADO SPRINGS, CO
Pikes Peak Western Collectible Show
140 booths of western collectibles
City Auditorium
Fri 12-5 adm $5; Sat 9-5, Sun 9-3 $5
719-635-0588
I-25 Exit 142 E to City Auditorium 1/2 mi
E. at Kiowa & Weber Streets; downtown
Last weekend in July every year
Ruxton's Trading Post.
22 Ruxton Ave
Manitou Springs, CO 80829

COLORADO

DENVER,CO
Buchanan's Monthly Antiques & Flea Market
200 dealers
Fairgrounds in Brighton
Sat 9-5; Sun 11-5; adm $3
One weekend per month
405-478-4050 call for dates
1 mi west of US Hwy 85 on 124th
Brighton Blvd,
Buchanan Productions
PO Box 6534
Edmond, Okla 73083-6534

DENVER, CO 80231
Hampden Street Antique Market (Mall)
100 dealers
8964 E. Hampden
Mon-Thur 10-6,Fri & Sat 10-7, Sun 12-5
303-721-7992
I-25 Exit 201, E 1 mi

DENVER, CO 80014
Classic Treasures Antiques & Collectibles
70 dealers in shopping center
2393 S. Havana St. Unit E-1
M,W,Th, Sat 10-6;T & F10-8; Sun 12-5:30
303-306-9820
I-225 Exit 5 W to Havana and Iliff
in shopping center; or E on Hampden
to Havana N

DENVER, CO 80210
Antique Guild & Antique Market
60 dealers
1298 S. Broadway
Open Mon-Sat 10-5:30; Sun 12-5
303-722-3359 or 744-0281
I-25 Exit Broadway, go S. 2 blks

There is an Antique Row of 25 shops
nearby.

DENVER, CO
World Wide Antique Show
185 dealers
Denver Merchandise Mart
Th-Sat 11-8; Sun 12-5; Adm $7
303-292-6278 ext 5212
1-800-289-6278
I-25 Exit 215 (58th Avenue E).
Call for Mar, Jul,Oct show dates
Worldwide Antique Shows
451 E 58th Ave #4270
Denver, CO 80216
Antiqueshows@denvermart.com
One of the best shows in the US with dealers from 38 States, WWAS offers free appraisals, educational seminars and the finest in antiques. A fully carpeted, climate controlled building features free parking and food on premises.

In Denver our favorite place for lunch is *Andre's Restaurant & Confiserie,* **370 S. Garfield, at Dakota & Garfield, off Cherry Creek North Dr. For Mexican food we prefer** *Senior Ric's,* **13200 E. Mississippi in Aurora.**

DENVER/GOLDEN. CO 80401
Rocking Horse Antique Mall
45 dealers
1106 Washington Ave
Open Mon-Fri 9-6, Sat 9-5 Sun 11-4
Downtown come from I-70 W or 6th AveW
11th or 12th crossstreet in downtown
Golden

LAKEWOOD, CO 80215
Antique Mall of Lakewood
125 dealers
9635 W. Colfax Avenue
Mon-Sat 10-6; Sun 11-6
303-238-6940
I-70 Exit 262 E just past Kipling St
1 blk east of Kipling on Colfax

DENVER/
LAKEWOOD, CO 80226
Main Street Mercantile
70 dealers
1000 S. Wadsworth A
M-Thur 10-6, Fri 10-9, Sun 12-5
303-935-9315
**In shopping center, corner of Mississippi
& Wadsworth. Wadsworth exit
I-70, go South.**

DENVER/
WHEATRIDGE, CO 80033
Brass Armadillo Antique Mall
240 booths & 600 showcases
11301 W. I-70, Frontage Rd. N
Open 9-9 everyday
303-403-1677 or 877-403-1677
**I-70 Exit Kipling Blvd and go W on
North Frontage Rd.**

DENVER/
LITTLETON, CO 80121
Colorado Antique Gallery
250 dealers
5501 S. Broadway
Open Mon-Sat 10-6; Sun 12-6
303-794-8100
4 mi S of US 285 (Hampden Ave)
*Something for everyone! Extensive
selection of fine antiques & collectibles including quality jewelry &
Continental furniture, Western items,
chintz pottery, glassware & books.
Serving antique enthusiasts since
1992, all in a friendly upscale atmosphere.*

GLENWOOD SPRINGS, CO 81601
Little Bear's Antique Mall
40 dealers, 17,000 sq. ft.
2802 S Grand Ave
Mon-Sat 10:00-5:30 everyday
970-945-4505
I-70 Exit 116 S on Grand Ave

GRAND JUNCTION, CO 81501
Haggle of Vendors Emporium
5 dealers
510 Main
Mon-Fri 10-5;summer Thur-8, Sat 10-5; cl
Sun
970-245-1404
**Downtown with some other antique
shops.**

GRAND JUNCTION, CO 81501
Cobweb's Antiques & Stuff
12 dealers
558 Main St.
Open mon- Sat 10-5
970-245-0109
Downtown

NIWOT, CO 80544
Niwot Antiques
40 dealers
180 2nd Ave
Open Mon - Sat 10-5, Sun 12-5
303-625-2587
**Downtown
7 mi NE of Boulder on 119
Other shops in that area**

DENVER/ LAKEWOOD, CO 80215
Stage Stop Antique Mall
140 booths
7340 W. 44th
Mon-Sat 10-6; Sun 11-6
303-423-3630
**I-70 Exit 269, Wadsworth Blvd S to 44th E
1 block**

GREAT GETAWAY TO ANTIQUE COLORADO

WHEN: Specific dates in March, July & Oct. for 200 dealer antique show in Denver, otherwise...anytime.

WHERE: World Wide Antique Show at Denver's Merchandise Mart, I-25 Exit 215 (58th Ave) E. Call 1-800-289-6278 for exact dates. This has some of the best antique dealers from Chicago to Los Angeles.

AUCTION: *Niwot Auction Co.* 4th Sun at noon, Boulder County fairgrounds in Loveland. 303-652-2030.

LODGING: If you like downtown hotels, you will love the 100 year old Brown Palace Hotel for luxury and food is great too at the Brown Palace. 303-297-3111. Motel chains abound in Colorado. Call your favorite. **Casinos** in Blackhawk US Hwy 6 W out of Denver to Hwy 119. 303-271-2500 or 303-777-1111.

ANTIQUING: We start with the "Antique Row" on Broadway, Denver.
1. I-25 Exit Broadway Ave So. to *Antique Guild & Antique Market*, 125 dealers at 1298 S. Broadway and 1212 S. Broadway, plus all the nearby shops.

RESTAURANT: By the time Broadway has been shopped, lunch might be in order at our favorite lunch place, "Andre's Swiss Confiserie" in Cherry Creek North. (Clsd Sun & Mon) They serve until 2:30 PM. Go S on Broadway to Evans Ave E to Colorado Blvd N. then Left at Cherry Creek **North** Dr. Then one block to Dakota St. turn R. Andre's restaurant is in front of you.

2. Next go S on Colorado Blvd to Hampton Blvd E just past Yosemite St., turn R into Shopping Center and *Hampton Antique Mall,* 100 dealers, 8964 Hampton.
3. Go west on Hampton 4 mi to (Littleton), Broadway So to *Colorado Antique Gallery,* set back in shopping center, 200 dealers, 5501 S. Broadway, closes at 6 PM.

4. If it is a Sunday morning, or any evening you can antique from 9AM to 9PM at the *Brass Armadillo*, 240 booths and 600 showcases. I-70 Exit 267 Kipling Exit, W on North frontage road 1 mile. Facing the mountains, it will be on your right.

5. Going E on I-70 to Wadsworth Blvd., So to 44th St. E 1/2 block to *Stage Stop Antique Mall,* 120 booths.

6. Then S on Wadsworth Blvd to Colfax Ave W to 9635 W. Colfax, *Antique Mall of Lakewood,* 125 dealers.

7. Go E on Colfax to Wadsworth Blvd S to *Main Street Mercantile,* 70 dealers, 1000 S. Wadsworth, in shopping center.

If you would like to antique in the mountains, there is an antique store in Morrison on Hwy, and one in Evergreen. To get there from Denver take Morrison Road W off Kipling. Kipling is I-70 Exit 267 South.

In Colorado Springs take I-25 Exit 142 E to Nevada Ave with Antique Malls at 21 N Nevada Ave and 405 S. Nevada. Next go S on Nevada to Colorado Ave (Hwy 24) W to *Adobe Wells Antique Mall*, 60 dealers at 2808 W Colorado Ave.Several antique shops along Colorado Ave.

Antique Show: Pikes Peak Western Collectibles Show, always last weekend in July see text.
Leisure: U S Air Force Acadamy, Garden of the Gods, Broadmoor Hotel

TRAVEL NOTES

69

CONNECTICUT

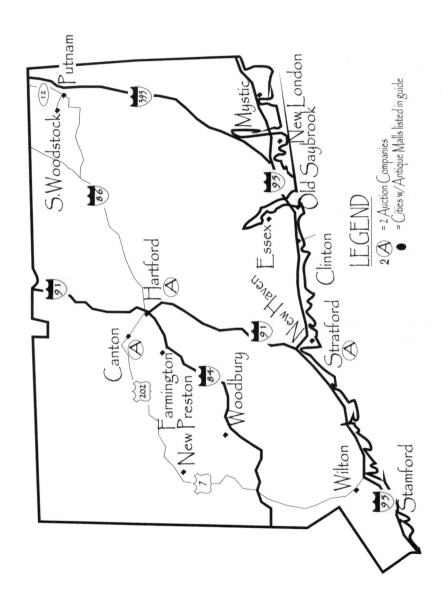

LEGEND

2(A) = 2 Auction Companies

● = Cities w/ Antique Malls listed in guide

Putnam

S. Woodstock

Mystic

New London

Old Saybrook

Essex

Clinton

Hartford

New Haven

Stratford

Canton

Farmington

New Preston

Woodbury

Wilton

Stamford

CONNECTICUT

WEEKEND ANTIQUE EVENTS
Hartford/Farmington Antique Weekend, **2nd weekend in Jun;**
    Sat. and Sun before Labor Day
Wilton Antiques Show , usually 3rd weekend in Jun.
Woodbury, Antiques & Flea Market, Sat. Market, 100 dealers.

ANTIQUE DISTRICTS/VILLAGES
Clinton, New Preston, Putnam, Ridgefield, Stonington & Woodbury

AUCTION/ESTATE SALE CO'S

Wethersfield, CT 06109
Clearing House Auction Galleries
Antiques & collectibles, household
auction
207 Church St.
Every Wed at 7 PM
860-529-3344
I-91 Exit 24

Canton, CT 06019
Canton Barn
Antiques auction
75 Old Canton Rd.
Saturday nights at 7:30
860-693-0601
**12 mi W of Hartford on US 44, in town
turn left off US 44**

Stratford, CT 06615
Lloyd Ralston Gallery
Toy Auction and Train Auction
350 Long Beach Blvd
About every month
203-386-9399
Fax 203-386-9519

ANTIQUE MALLS, MARKETS & SHOWS
CANTON, CT 06019
Balcony Antique Shops
50 dealers
166 Albany Turnpike, Rte. 44
Mon-Sat 10-5; Sun 12-5
860-693-4478
**14 mi W of Hartford on Route 44
Four other shops on Rte 44 in Canton**

CANTON, CT 06022
Collinsville Antique Co.
100 dealers, 20,000 sq. ft.
Rte 179 in Collinsville
Open 7 days 10-5
860-693-1011
**I-84 Exit 39, Rte 4 W to Rte 179, R
into Collinsville, then 1st R after
bridge**

CLINTON, CT 06413
Clinton Antique Center
95 dealers
78 Main St.
Open 7 days 10-5, Clsd Wed Oct-Apr
860-669-3839
I-95 Exit 63 to US Hwy 1

CONNECTICUT

Also nearby 7 antique shops on Main
The Clinton Village Flea Market on
the week-end, May-Oct.

HARTFORD/
FARMINGTON, CT
Farmington Antique Weekend
400-600 dealers, all antiques
Polo Grounds, outdoor & under tents
Adm $10 Sat at 8.AM-5PM,
Sun 10-5 Adm $7.
317-598-0019
**I-84 Exit 39, W 2.5 mi, R 1 mi on Town
Farm Rd. Free parking
2nd S/S in Jun; Labor Day S/S**
Farmington Antique Weekend, Inc.
P.O. Box 580
Fishers, IN 46038

MYSTIC, CT 06355
Mystic River Antiques
40 dealers
232 Greenmanville Ave.
Open 10-5 daily
**Exit 90 off I-95 towards Seaport , 1st
major intersection on the left .**

**In Mystic we highly recommend the
Bravo Bravo Cafe downtown.**

**We found the 150 year old "Old Lyme
Inn" near Old Saybrook to be very
enjoyable. Southbound I-95 take exit
70. and turn R. Northbound take exit
70 turn L off ramp to 1st intersection,
then R on US 1 to 2nd light. Inn on left.
Lunch & dinner 7 days.
1-800-434-5352, also lodging.**

NEW LONDON, CT 06320
New London Antique Center
200 dealer spaces
123-131 Bank St.
Open Mon-Sat 9-6, Sun 10-5
860-444-7598
**I-95S Exit 84 S thru 2 lights, 1 stop
sign, 1 more light, take next L onto
mall parking lot. Center of downtown.**

OLD SAYBROOK, CT 06475
Old Saybrook Antique Center
125 dealers
756-Middlesex Tpk. (Rte 154)
Open daily 11-5
860-388-1600
I-95N Exit 67, N on Rte 154

OLD SAYBROOK, CT 06475
Essex-Saybrook Antique Village
130 dealers
345 Middlesex Turnpike Route 154
Daily 11-5; closed Mon Jan-May
860-388-0689
I-95N Exit 67, N on Rte 154 or
I-95S Exit 68, N on Rte 154

OLD SAYBROOK, CT 06475
The Antiques Depot
95 dealers
455 Boston Post Rd.
Wed-Sun 10-5
860-395-0595
**At train station
on Rte 1, I-95 Exit 67.
450 dealers within 2 mi.**

PUTNAM, CT 06260
The Antiques Marketplace
260 dealers
109 Main Street & Rte 44
7 days 10-5
860-928-0442
I-395 Exit 96 or 97 to downtown
Connecticut's largest and finest
group shop with over 260 rented
booths and showcases.   Visit our
website:
www.antiquesmarketplace.com
There are a dozen antique shops at
Main & Front St. in Putnam.

STAMFORD, CT 06902
Antique and Artisan Center
130 dealers
69 Jefferson St.
Open Mon-Sat 10:30-5:30; Sun 12-5
203-327-6022
I-95N Exit 8, R 2nd light on Canal St
1st left onto Jefferson, or I-95S
Exit 7, L ramp end, L 2nd light

STRATFORD, CT 06497
Stratford Antique Center
200 dealers
400 Honeyspot Road
Open 7 days 10-5
203-378-7754
I-95N Exit 31, R to blue bldg
I-95S Exit 31, straight, 2nd stop
sign L to blue bldg

WOODBURY, CT 06798
Village of 40 Antique Shops, Antique
Capital of Connecticut
I-84 Exit 15 N 6 mi US Hwy 6 to
Woodbury.

S. WOODSTOCK, CT 06267
Scranton's Shops
70 dealers
300 Rte 169
Open daily 11-5
860-928-3738
I-395 Exit 96 W to US 44,
W 4 mi to Rte 169, N 3 mi.

WILTON, CT
Wilton Outdoor Antiques Show
160 dealers, all antiques
On US 7 N of Wilton High School
S/S 10-5, adm $10, Sat 8-10, adm $20
203-762-3525-or call 762-7257
Usually 3rd or 4th weekend in June
I-95 Exit 15 N 5 mi
On US 7 to Wilton
Indoor Shows in Mar, Sept, & Dec
call for dates
MCG Antiques Promotions
10 Chicken St.
Wilton, CT 06897

WOODBURY, CT 06798
Antiques & Flea Market
130 vendors; 70% antiques &
collectibles
Main Street, Rte 6
7-1 P.M.; adm free; park free
203-263-2841
I-84 Exit 15
Rte 6 into Woodbury
Open every Sat, weather permitting
Don Heavens
Box 325
Woodbury, CT 06798

GREAT ANTIQUING GETAWAY TO COLORFUL CONNECTICUT

WHEN: 2nd Sat & Sun in June and Sat & Sun before Labor Day, otherwise, anytime.

WHERE: Farmington Antique Weekend Market, 600 dealers with antiques, outdoors, under tents. Sat 8-5, $10 adm, Sun 10-5 $7

LODGING: Most hotel/motel chains located in the Farmington/ Hartford area. The Marriot, the Hilton Garden and Courtyard advertise discounted rates on weekends. At least one night's stay should be in the Saybrook to Mystic area, as there is a full days antiquing in that area.

LEISURE: Foxwoods Casino is located in the Mystic area, I-95 Exit 92 W 7 mi on Rte 2.

RESTAURANTS: We had a delicious Italian meal at the *Bravo-Bravo Cafe* at 20 E. Main. 860-536-3228, in the historic Whalers' Inn, in Mystic. 860-536-1506. Mystic is a charming old seaport where one can view old wooden ships from the 1800s. In Old Lyme, near Saybrook, we found the 150 yr old Old Lyme Inn to be a great place to eat. 800-434-5352. Northbound on I-95 Exit 70, L to 1st intersection, then R on US 1 to 2nd light. Southbound I-95 Exit 70. turn R. Old Lyme Inn also has lodging.

1. *Stamford Antique Center,* 130 dealers, 69 Jefferson St., I-95 Northbound Exit 8, R 2nd light on Canal St. 1st L into Jefferson. Southbound I-95 Exit 7, L ramp end, L 2nd light.

2.*Stratford Antique Center*, 200 dealers, 400 Honeyspot Rd. I-95 N, Exit 31, R to blue bldg. I-95S Exit 31, straight 2nd stop sign L to blue bldg.

3. Next Woodbury, I-95 S to Expwy 8 N to Exit 22 Rte 67 NW to US 6 into Woodbury and around 40 antique shops in this "Antique Capital" of CT. Plus a Saturday Antique & Flea Market.

RESTAURANT: In Woodbury, a good place to eat is the "Good News Cafe". 694 Main St.

If not attending the Farmington Antique Market, 2 nd Sat & Sun in June or before Labor Day, skip to #6. Expwy 9 South.

4. Farmington Antique Market 2nd weekend in June or Labor Day weekend, I-84 Exit W 2.5 mi, R 1.5 mi on Town Farm Rd. Park free.

5. After market take Rte 10 N 5 mi to US 44/202 W to 2 malls and antique auction Sat at 7:30PM in Canton. 860-693-0601.

GREAT ANTIQUING GETAWAY TO COLORFUL CONNECTICUT

See text for mall & auction details. *Balcony Antique Shops*, 50 dealers, 166 Albany Tpke, (Rte 44). Auction left off US 44 in town at 75 Old Canton Rd., *Collinsville Antique Co.,* 100 dealers, Rte 179 in Collinsville.

6. Get on Expwy 9 South to Rte 81 S. to *Clinton Antique Center* in Clinton, 95 dealers at 78 E. Main. Also nearby shops and Sat Flea Market every week. The Center is closed Wed, Oct-April.

7. Go E on Us 1 to the *Antique Depot*, at 455 Boston Post Rd. (US1) at the train station in Old Saybrook.

8. From Old Saybrook take Rte 154 (Middlesex Tpke) N to *Essex-Saybrook Antique Village*, 130 dealers, at 345 Rte154 and *Old Saybrook Antique Center*, 130 dealers at 756 Rte 154.

9. Next comes the *New London Antique Center*, 200 dealer spaces, I-95 N Exit 84 to stop sign, then 3 more lights to L on Main to Eugene O'Neill Dr. to 125 Bank St. 860-444-7598.

10. N on I-95 to Exit 90 toward Mystic Seaport, 1st major intersection on L is *Mystic River Antiques*, 40 dealers at 232 Greenville Ave.

11. After Mystic go S on US 1 to I-95 Exit 84 N past the US Coast Guard Academy to I-395 N to Putnam and the *Antique Marketplace Mall* with 250 dealers at corner of Main St & Rte 44. There are a dozen nearby shops here.

There are also a dozen nearby antique shops & 70 dealers in *Scranton Shops* in South Woodstock. US 44 W 4 mi to Rte 169 N 3 mi.

This ends the Connecticut Getaway but there is more great antiquing ahead. If you have time, from S. Woodstock continue N on Rte 169 about 20 miles to Sturbridge, MA with 2 very fine malls on Main St. (Rte 20) and at 520 Main St. is a great restaurant "The Whistling Swan." From Sturbridge you could just continue W on I-90 and do the Brimfield/Berkshires Antique Getaway. (see text for details)

TRAVEL NOTES

DELAWARE

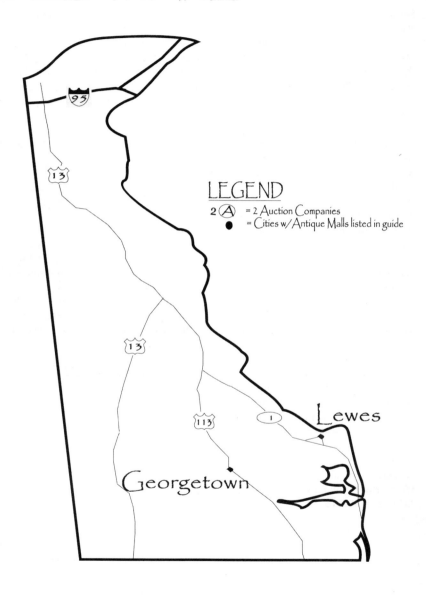

LEGEND

2 (A) = 2 Auction Companies

● = Cities w/ Antique Malls listed in guide

Lewes

Georgetown

DELAWARE

ANTIQUE DISTRICTS/VILLAGES
Georgetown, Newcastle and Lewes

ANTIQUE MALLS, MARKETS & SHOWS

GEORGETOWN
There are half a dozen antique shops in
Georgetown

NEW CASTLE, DE
There are 6 antique shops on Delaware St. downtown #116 to 406 in New Castle.
There are antique shops scattered along US Hwy 13 in Delaware, particularly in
Smyrna and Dover

LEWES, DE 19958
Antiques Village Mall
60 dealers, 3 bldgs.
221 Hwy One
M-Sat.10-5, Sun 11-5, winter cl Wed,
starting Memorial Day open Wed
302-644-0842, 302-645-1940
15 mi E of Georgetown
6 shops in downtown Lewes,
the oldest settlement in Delaware

FLORIDA - North

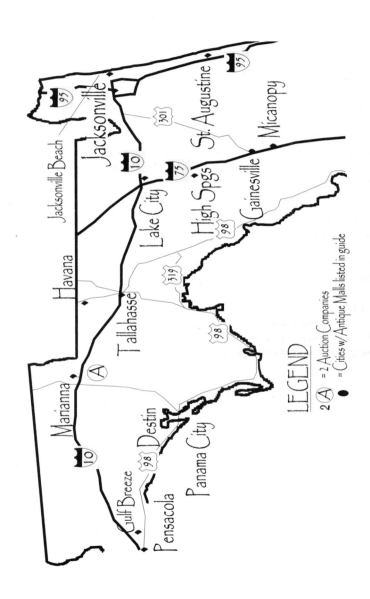

FLORIDA - NORTH

ANTIQUE DISTRICTS/ VILLAGES

High Springs, Micanopy & St. Augustine

AUCTION/ESTATE SALE CO'S

Hillard, FL 32046
Frank's Antique Auctions
10% Buyer premium
551625 US Hwy 1.
1st Sun at 1 PM
904-845-2870
25 mi N of Jax on US 1

ANTIQUE MALLS, MARKETS & SHOWS

DESTIN, FL 32541
Smiths Antique Mall
90 dealers
12500 Emerald Coast Pkwy
Mon-Sat 10-6, Sun 12-5
850-654-1484
4 mi E of Destin on US 98 Hwy
Turn R on Holiday Drive into lot

GULF BREEZE, FL 32561
Annai's Antique Mall
100 dealers, 12,000 sq. ft.
4531 Gulf Breeze Pkwy
Open 7 days, 10-5
850-916-1122
South side of US 98 Hwy

HAVANA, FL
I-10 Exit 29 N on US 27
There are about 20 antique/collectible,
single and multi-dealer shops in
downtown Havana. We enjoyed lunch
on the patio of the *Twin Willow Cafe*
at 211 1st St. The Kentucky Derby
pie is out of this world.

HIGH SPRINGS, FL 32655
Main Street Mall
50 Booths
10 So. Main St.
Mon-Sat 10-5, Sun 12:30-5
386-454-2700
I-75 Exit (Old number) 79, W. 4 mi.

There are a dozen shops downtown
Maps are available from the shops

HIGH SPRINGS, FL 32655
High Springs Antique Center
10 dealers
145 N. Main St
Mon-Sat 10:30-5:50, Sun 12-5:30
386-454-4770
I-75 Old Exit number 79 (High
Springs)
W 4 mi. There are a dozen antique
shops
downtown.

JACKSONVILLE, FL 32246
Avonlea Antique Mall
200 dealers
11260 Beach Blvd.
Mon-Sat 10-6, Sun 12-6, Thur & Fri till 8
904-645-0806
I-95 Exit 106, E on Beach Blvd(US 90)

FLORIDA - NORTH

JACKSONVILLE, FL 32216
Carriage House Antique Mall
75 dealers
8955 Beach Blvd
Mon-Sat 10-6, Sun 12-6
904-641-5500
I-95 Exit 106, E on Beach Blvd(US 90)

JACKSONVILLE, FL 32217
San Jose Antique Mall
85 dealers
2916 University Blvd W
Mon-Sat 10-6, Sun 12-5
904-730-8083
I-95 Exit 346B, W on University
1 mi S on San Jose Blvd, L on Univer-
sity 1 mi E.

LAKE CITY, FL 32005
Webb's Antique Mall
400 dealers
245 S. W. Webbs Glen
Open 7 days 9-6
386-758-5564
I-75 Exit 414 West side of I-75

I-75 Exit 374, Historic Micanopy
13 Antique shops downtown

MICANOPY, FL 32667
Smiley's Antique Mall
200 plus dealers
17020 S. E. County Rd. #234
P.O. Box 218
Open 7 days 10-6
352-466-0707
10 mi. S of Gainesville at the
NE corner of I-75 Exit 374
Florida's largest and finest Antique
Mall !

ST. AUGUSTINE, FL 32084
Uptown Antiques Mall
38 dealers
63 San Marco Ave
Open 7 days 10-5:30
904-824-9156
1 block E of US 1 downtown

ST. AUGUSTINE, FL 32086
St. Augustine Antique Emporium
33 dealers
62 San Marcos Ave
Mon-Sat 10-5:30, Sun 11-5:30
904-829-0544
1 block E of US 1 downtown
There are 25 shops in St. Augustine

We were pleased fo find a Columbia
restuarant, a branch of the well
known *Tampa Columbia.* **This**
restaurant is located in the Old
Quarter at 98 St. George Street in St.
Augustine . It features Cuban and
Spanish dishes. The Cuban bread is
especially great.
Ph. 904-824-3341

80

FLORIDA - NORTH

TRAVEL NOTES

FLORIDA - South

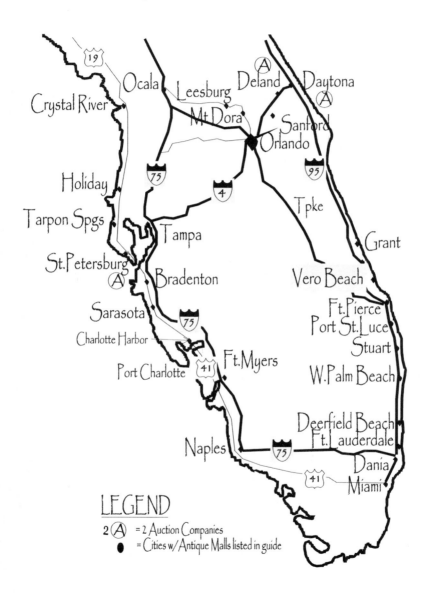

FLORIDA - SOUTH

WEEKEND ANTIQUE EVENTS
Deland-Central Florida Antique Market, 100 dealers,
4 shows during the season plus one in Nov-Jan
Ft. Lauderdale Winter and Fall Antique Show, 300 dealers.
3 shows in winter season
Original Miami Beach Antique Show- **Last week in Jan**
Miami National Antique Show, 350 dealers, Raddison Center,
Fri, Sat & Sun, 4th weekend in Jan
Orlando/Mount Dora, Renningers Antique Fair,
every S&Sun plus 3 extravaganzas 3rd Wk ends in Nov, Jan & Feb
West Palm Beach Fairgrounds Antiques & Collectors Fiar,
usually 1st Sun and preceding Fri & Sat monthly

ANTIQUE DISTRICTS/ VILLAGES
Dania, St. Petersburg, Bellaire Bluffs, Tarpon Springs, & West Palm Beach

AUCTION/ESTATE SALE CO'S

Daytona Beach, FL 32114
Let's Talk Antiques
Antique auction
140 N Beach St.
Call for next auction
386-258-5225 or 800-749-0688

St. Petersburg, FL 33708
Park St. Antique Center
Antique auction
9401 Bay Pines Blvd.
1st and 3rd Fridays at 7PM
727-398-3886

ANTIQUE MALLS, MARKETS & SHOWS

BRADENTON/
ELLENTON, FL 34222
Feed Store Antique Mall
60 dealers
4407 Hwy 301
Open Mon-Sat 10-5, 12-5 Sun
941-729-1379
1 mi W of I-75 Exit 224

CHARLOTTE HARBOR, FL 33980
Harbor Antique Mall & Motel
50 dealers
5000 Tamjami Trail (US 41)
Open Mon-Sat 10-5, Sun 12-4
941-625-6126
Antique Fair 2nd Sat every Month
I-75 Exit Kings Hwy W to US 41 So.

FLORIDA - SOUTH

CRYSTAL RIVER, FL 34429
Heritage Antique Mall
20 dealers
103 NW Hwy 19
Open daily 10-5
352-563-5597
Downtown

DANIA see Ft. Lauderdale
DELAND, FL
Central Florida Antique Market
100 dealers; all antiques & collectibles
Volusia County Fairgrounds
Fri 1-5, $5; Sat 9-5 & Sun 10-4, $3.50
941-697-7272, call for exact dates
I-4 Exit 118, SR 44 1/4 mi E
4 shows, 1 in Nov. Dec, Feb & Jan
Puchstein Promotions
P.O Box 27272
El Jobean, FL 33927
puchs2@yahoo.com

DELAND, FL 32720
Rivertown Antique Mall
35 dealers
114 S. Woodland Blvd (US 17/92)
Open Mon-Sat 10-5
386-738-5111
I-4 Exit Hwy 44W 5 mi to 17/92 Hwy
There are 8 other shops nearby

DEERFIELD BEACH, FL 33441
Hillsboro Antiques Mall & Cafe
250 dealers plus
1025 E. Hillsboro Blvd.
Open Mon-Sat 10-6,Thur 10-9, Sun 12-5
954-571-9988
I-95 Exit 37, E 2 mi on Hillsboro Blvd
E. of US-1

FT. LAUDERDALE/
DANIA, FL 33004-0845
Dania Historic Antique District Assoc.
100 shops on US 1
P.O. Box 845
Most shops open 10-5; Sun 12-5 if
open
1-800-903-2642
Dania is on US 1 just S
of Ft. Lauderdale Int'l Airport

FT. LAUDERDALE, FL
Winter Antiques Show & Sales
250 dealers
Convention Center or War Memorial
Fri 12-9; Sat 12-8; Sun 12-6; adm $8
954-563-6747; call for exact dates
17th Causeway at Eisenhower Blvd;
I-95 Exit 27, E to US 1, N to 17th St E
Three shows in winter season
Dolphin Management
P.O. Box 7326
Ft. Lauderdale, FL 33338

FT. MYERS, FL 33919
12 antique shops on McGregor
Most shops open 7 days 10-5
I-75 Exit 22 W on Hwy 884 to
McGregor

FT. PIERCE, FL 34946
Red Rooster Attic Mall
175 dealers
3128 N US 1
Open daily 10-5; closed Wed, May-
Nov.
772-466-8344
I-95 Exit 65 or 67 E to US 1

GRANT, FL 32949
Grant Antique Mall
100 dealers in 2 bldgs
5900 US 1
Open 7 days 10-5
321-726-6778 or 984-9346
15 mi S of Melbourne

HOLIDAY, FL 34691
Lyon's Head Antique Center
150 dealers
1824 US 19
Open 7 days 10-6
727-943-0021
20 mi N of Clearwater

LEESBURG, FL 32748
Morning Glori Antique Mall
55 dealers
1111 S. 14th St. (Hwy 27)
Open Mon-Sat 10-6; Sun 12-4
Closed Sun May-Oct.
352-365-9977
On US Hwy 27 S
Also a 15 dealer mall at 403 W. Main

MIAMI, FL
Miami National Antique Show and
Sale
400 dealers
Sheraton Expo Centre (formally
Raddison)
Fri & Sat 12-9; Sun 12-6; adm $10
954-563-6747
Free parking
NW 72 Avenue at 836 Expressway
Last Fri, Sat & Sun in Jan 14-16,
2005. Jan 13, 14 & 15th, 2006
Dolphin Promotions, Inc.
P.O. Box 7320
Ft. Lauderdale, FL 33308

MIAMI BEACH, FLA
Original Miami Beach Antique Show
1200 International Exhibitors
Miami Beach Convention Center
Daily 12-9; Last day 12--6; adm $15
239-732-6642
Downtown Miami Beach
Same weekend every year; starts Wed
before last weekend in each year
Andrea Canady
12330 Tamiann Trail
Naples, FL 34113

MT. DORA See ORLANDO/ MT.
DORA

NAPLES, FL 33940
Treasure Island
30 dealers
950 Central
Open Mon-Sat 10-5, Sun closed
239-434-7684
I-75 Exit 16 W to US 41 S to Central,
L. 20 antique shops in area.

FLORIDA - SOUTH

NAPLES, FL 34109
Naples Street Antique Mall
35 dealers
5430 Yahl Street
Open Mon- Sat 10-5, closed Sun
239–591-8182
Off Pine Ridge Rd., one block W of Home Depot Store

OCALA, FL 34471
Ocala Antique Mall
60 booths
3700 S. Hwy 441, Suite D
Open 7 days 10-5
352-622-4468
I-75 Exit 69 E to US 441 S

ORLANDO/
MAITLAND, FL 32751
Hailey's Antique Mall
60 dealers
473 S. Orlando Ave.
Open Mon-Sat 10:30-5:30; Sun 1-4
407-539-1066
Hwy 17/92 , Located in shops at Maitland S of Horatio

MAITLAND, FL 32751
Orange Tree Antique Mall
60 dealers
150 Lake Ave
Open Mon-Sat 10-6, Sun 12-5
407-622-0060
I-4 Exit 87 N on Orlando Ave to Lake Ave. L

ORLANDO/
MOUNT DORA, FL
Renninger's Antique Fair
200-1200 dealers
On US 441, 20 mi N of Orlando
Open 9-5; adm free; park free,except
Extravaganza
800-522-3555
**400+ dealers every 3rd weekend;
1200, 3rd weekends in Nov, Jan & Feb
Every Sat & Sun, 200+ dealers**
Florida Twin markets
P.O. Box 1699
Mt. Dora, FL 32757-1699

ORLANDO/
WINTER GARDEN, FL 34787
Webb's Antique Mall
50,000 sq. ft.
13373 West Colonial (Rte 50)
Open daily 10-6
407-877-5921
**In shopping center, turnpike exit
267B then 1 mi west**
*3 Huge Malls, 1500 booths and cases,
7 days, 10-6, millions of items,
200,000 sq. ft.,Centerville, IND., Lake
City, FL, & Winter Garden, FL*
WEBBANTIQUES@AOL.COM

ORLANDO/
WINTER PARK, FL
**For a great lunch or dinner in a
charming atmosphere, we like
the *Creperie* off the patio at 348 N.
Park Ave. 407-647-4469**

ORLANDO/ WINTER PARK, FL 32789
Orange Tree Antique Mall
90 dealers
853 S. Orlando Ave. (Hwy 17-92)
Open Mon-Sat 10-6, Sun 12-5
407-644-4547
**I-4 Exit 89, E 1 mi to Hwy 17-92 S.
Just So. of Fairbanks**

ST. PETERSBURG, FL 33701
Patty & Friends Antique Mall
60 dealers
1225 Dr. Martin Luther King St. N
Open 7 days 10-4
727-821-2106 or 367-6550
**I-275 Exit 24 E to M. L. King Street
then S**

**In St. Petersburg we like to eat at
the *Columbia Restaurant* at the
end of the pier. Take the elevator
up and enjoy the view and the food.**

ST PETERSBURG, FL 33713
Antique Exchange
130 dealers
2535 Central Ave.
Open Mon-Sat 10-5, Sun 12-5
727-321-6621
**I-25 Exit 5th Ave N, go straight ahead
to Central, R
Multi-dealer shop next door**

ST. PETERSBURG, FL 33705
Gasplant Antique Arcade
100 dealers, 32,000 sq. ft.
1246 Central Avenue
Open 7 days 10-5
727-895-0368
**Downtown - a half dozen antique
shops in the 600 block of Central Ave.**

ST. PETERSBURG, FL 33707
Alice Hauser Antiques
3 shops in one block
7200 W. Central
OpenTue-Sat 10-5; clsd Sun & Mon
727-345-8800

ST. PETERSBURG, FL 33708
Park Street Antique Center
80 dealers
9401 Bay Pines Blvd.
Open Mon-Fri 10-5; Sat 9-5; Sun 9-4
727-392-2198

ST. PETERSBURG, FL 33781
Vintage Antique Mall
50 dealers, 14,000 sq. ft.
7750 Park Blvd (Hwy 694)
Daily 10-5
727-547-6123
I-275 Exit 15, W on Hwy 694

ST. PETERSBURG/
BELLAIRE BLUFFS, FL 33770
Jean's Locker Collectibles
1 of 14 shops nearby in Antique Alley
596 Indian Rocks Rd N, #19A
Most shops Mon-Sat 10-5; Clsd Sun
No Phone
Alt 19 to Bay Drive at Largo W

ST. PETERSBURG/
BELLAIRE BLUFFS, FL 33770
Jewel Antique Mall
35 dealers
2601 Jewel Rd.
Open Mon-Sat 10-5; Sun 12-5
727-585-5568
**Next to shops in Antique Alley off
Indian Rocks Rd N of West Bay Dr.**

FLORIDA - SOUTH

SANFORD, FL 32773
Somewhere in Time
One of 10 antique shops on 1st St.
222 E. 1st Street
Hours vary store to store
407-323-7311
I-4 Exit 51 or 52 into downtown Sanford

SARASOTA, FL 34236
L..A. Freshwater Antique Emporium
25 dealers and 6 nearby shops
527 S. Pineapple Ave.
Open Mon-Sat 10-5
941-951-0477
I-75 Exit 39 W to US 301
S to Ringling Blvd., R to Pineapple, L

SARASOTA, FL 34231
Coral Cove Antique Gallery
40 dealers
7272 S. Tamiami Trail (US Hwy 41)
Mon-Fri 10-8; Sat 10-5; Sun 12-4
941-927-2205
I-75 Exit Clark Rd W
to US 41, S 9/10 mi on right
30 dealer mall at 4123 Clark Rd

**In Sarasota we like to eat at *The Boat-*
house on the dock behind the Hyatt Hotel, just W. of US 41 Hwy in Sarasota.
941-953-1234**

TARPON SPRINGS, FL 34689
Vintage Department Store
150 dealers in 15 shops
167 E. Tarpon Ave.
Open 7 days 11-5
727-942-4675
US Hwy 19 at Tarpon Ave to
Downtown Historic district,
walk to all shops.

VERO BEACH, FL 32967
Company Store Antique Mall
45 dealers
6605 N US Hwy 1
Open Tue-Sun 10-5
772-569-9884
I-95 Exit Rte 60E to US 1

WEST PALM BEACH, FL
Antiques & Collectors Fair
1000 dealers; 2000 in Feb Extravaganza
Fairgrounds
Fri 12-5; Sat 9-5; Sun 10-4:30
561-640-3433; call for exact dates
I-95 Southern Blvd, W 7 mi
Generally 1st Sun of each month &
preceding Fri & Sat, none in Jul & Oct.
Piccadilly Antiques & Collectors Fair
1555 Palm Beach Lakes Blvd
West Palm Beach, FL 33401

WEST PALM BEACH, FL 33405
Elephants Foot
1 of 40 shops antique row
3800 S. Dixie Hwy
Most open Mon-Sat 10:30-5
561-832-0170
**I-95 Exit 68 E on Southern Blvd
to Dixie Hwy N**

WEST PALM BEACH/
PALM BEACH, FL 33480
Yetta Olkes Antiques
1 of 8 antique shops on County Rd
332 S. County Rd.
Mon-Fri 10-5; Sat/Sun by appt.
561-655-2800
**County Rd is Hwy AIA.
There are 10 antique shops on Worth
Ave.**

**If it is a nice day you can't beat lunch
on *Testa's* tropical patio at 221 Royal
Poinciana Way SRAIA. Open also for
breakfast and dinner. Same family
over 75 years. Ph. 561-832-0992.**

GREAT GETAWAY TO ANTIQUE CENTRAL FLORIDA

WHEN: Third Weekend (Sat & Sun) in Nov, Jan, Feb; 1200 dealers. Other third weekends in season, 400 dealers, other weekends, 200 dealers in season. Adm free

WHERE: Renninger's Antique Fair is one of America's greatest antique markets, 20 miles N of Orlando on US 441. Hundreds of dealers set up under huge live oaks trees, plus 200 dealers indoors.

LODGING: The Hilton in Altamonte Springs at I-4, Exit 92 E, and the Courtyard at I-4, Exit 90B, 1/2 mile W are both convenient to all antiquing.

ANTIQUING:

1. For Renninger's Market take Rte 436 W from I-4, Exit 92 to Rte 441, N.

2. After the Market, return on US441 to Apopka, and take the Turnpike S. to Exit 267B, Rte 50 W 1 mi. to *Webb's Antique Mall,* 50,000 sq.ft. at 13373 W. Colonial (Rte 50 in Winter Garden).

Restaurants: When it's time to eat, we suggest you go E. on East-West Expressway to I-4 N to Exit 89E, then to downtown Winter Park. North on Park Ave to *Maison de Crepes* in the Hidden Garden Shops at 348 N. Park Ave, 407-647-4469 or the Briar Patch at 252 N. Park Ave, 407-645-4566.

Leisure: While on Park Ave you may visit the Morse Museum of Art, 445 Park Ave featuring a chapel designed by Tiffany, as well as stained glass windows and pottery and painting of his contemporaries. Adm $3.00.

3. From Park Ave, go back toward I-4 to US17/96, South to Lake Ave, L to *Orange Tree Antique Mall* at 150 Lake Street - 60 dealers.

4. Then back to US17/96 S to *Hailey's Antique Mall,* 60 dealers at 473 S. Orlando Ave in Shops at Maitland.

5. Continue S on Orlando Ave to 853 S. Orlando to the other *Orange Tree Antique Mall* - 90 dealers.

6. For an extended Getaway, take I-4 South to I-275 for a 2 hour drive to St. Petersburg.
See the Great Antique Getaway to St. Petersburg or use our guide to find the best antiquing on your way home.

GREAT GETAWAY TO ANTIQUE ST. PETERSBURG

WHEN: Anytime
    Auctions - *Park St. Antique Center* (Ref item #6) has an antique auction 1st and 3rd Fridays at 7PM.

WHERE: St. Petersburg general area.

LODGING: We found luxury on the beach at *Don Cesar Beach Resort and Spa*. Expensive, but package deals or off season could help - 727-360-1881. Also, the Hampton Inn at I-25, Exit 24 W on 22nd Ave to US 19 S 1/2 mile has been a convient place to stay while antiquing - 727-322-0770.

ANTIQUING:
1. In St. Petersburg take I-275, Exit 24 E to Martin Luther King St., then S to *Pattie and Friends Antique Mall* at #1225 M.L. King Street. Be sure to see both buldings at *Pattie and Friends* with 60 dealers.

2. Next go South to downtown St. Petersburg, then W on Central Ave where there are several antique shops in the 600 block of Central.

3. Next continue on Central to #1246 where you will find *Gas Plant Antiques Mall* - 100 dealers, 32,000 sq.ft.

4. Continue W on Central to the *Antique Exchange* - 130 dealers at 535 W. Central.

5. Now continue W on Central to 34th Street, go North on 34th St to Park Blvd (Hwy 694), Left to 7750 Park for the *Vintage Antique Mall* - 50 dealers.

6. Head West on Park Blvd to Seminole Blvd, left to Bay Pines and the *Park St. Antique Mall* - 80 dealers, at 9401 Bay Pines.

7. Now go back to Seminole Blvd. North to Bay Drive in Largo, West on Bay Dr. to Indian Rocks Rd. (4 blocks) to Jewel, Left to *Jewel Antique Mall* - 35 dealers.

8. Behind *Jewel Antique Mall* is the *Antique Alley* on Indian Rocks Rd. From the parking lot you can walk from one to the other.

9. If you have more time or are heading north, you may proceed north on US 19 about 20 miles to Tarpon Springs. From US Hwy 19 take Tarpon Ave to the downtown Historic district where you can shop 15 antique shops with over 150 dealers.

Restaurant: At least once during our stay in St. Petersburg, we like to enjoy the Cuban cuisine and the view from the *Columbia Restaurant* at the end of the pier in downtown St. Petersburg. When you have more time try the Great Antique Getaway for Central Florida.

GEORGIA

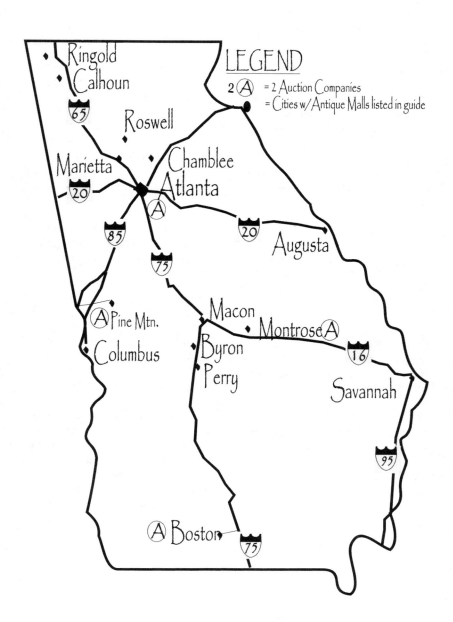

LEGEND

2Ⓐ = 2 Auction Companies
● = Cities w/Antique Malls listed in guide

Ringold
Calhoun
65
Roswell
Marietta
20
Chamblee
Atlanta
Ⓐ
85
20
Augusta
75
Ⓐ Pine Mtn.
Macon
Columbus
Byron
Montrose Ⓐ
16
Perry
Savannah
95
Ⓐ Boston
75

GEORGIA

WEEKEND ANTIQUE EVENTS

Atlanta Scott Antique Market, 1250 dealers,
2nd weekend of every month, Fri, Sat & Sun.
North Atlanta Antique Market., 800 dealers,
4th weekend of every month, Fri, Sat & Sun
Lakewood Antiques Market, 850-1200 dealers,
2nd full weekend of every month,   Fri, Sat & Sun.

ANTIQUE DISTRICTS/ VILLAGES
Atlanta, Chamblee, Marietta, Roswell and Savannah

AUCTION/ESTATE SALE CO'S

Atlanta, GA 30324
Depew Galleries Auction
Prestigious Sales,10% Buyer Premium
1860 Piedmont Rd NE
Collectibles Tue, Antiques Thu; 7 PM
404-874-2286

Montrose, GA 31065
Montrose Auction
Antique Auctions
1702 2nd St., P.O. Box 25
1st Fri at 7 pm
478-376-4559
10% Buyer premium
I-16 Exit 32 or 39, N to US 80
30 mi E of Macon

Pine Mountain, GA 31822
Pine Mountain Auction Center
Antique auctions
202 State Street
1st and 3rd Sun of ea month at 2 PM
(See Pine Mtn. listing)
800-638-9610 or 706-663-8552

We were happy to discover three
La Madeleine **French Bakery and**
Cafes in Atlanta at 35 W. Paces Ferry
Rd, 404-812-9308, 1165 Preimeter
Center West, Dunwoody, 770-392-
0516, & 4101 Roswell Rd, Marietta,
770-579-3040. *La Madeleine's* **is one**
of our favorite eating places in Dallas,
San Antonio & New Orleans.

One of the most beautiful residential
drives in the country, especially in
spring, is by the Governor's Mansion,
in Atlanta. From I-75 Exit 107 W.
Paces Ferry Rd. East to Buckhead.

ANTIQUE MALLS, MARKETS/ SHOWS

ATLANTA, GA
North Atlanta Antique Market
600 booths; all antiques & collectibles
North Atlanta Trade Center
Fri-Sat 9-6; Sun 11-5 adm 4.00
770-279-9853

GEORGIA

North Atlanta Antique Market
I-85 Exit 101 E on Indian Trail Rd, R
on Oakbrook Pkwy, R on Jurgens Ct
4th weekend of every month
North Atlanta Antique Market
1700 Jeurgens
Norcross, GA 30093

ATLANTA, GA
Scott Antique Market
1250 dealers; all antiques & collectibles
Atlanta Expo Center
Fri 9-6; Sat 9-6; Sun 10-4; park free
740-569-4112; adm $ 3.
I-285 Exit 55 (Jonesboro Rd)
2nd weekend every month
Scott Antique Markets
P. O. Box 60
Bremen, OH 43107

ATLANTA, GA
Lakewood Antiques Market/Antique
Show
850 to 1200 vendors
2000 Lakewood Way
Fri & Sat 9-6; Sun 9-5; adm $3; park free
404-622-4488
I-75/85 Exit 243 Hwy 166 (Lakewood
Fwy) E to Fairgrounds
Second full weekend of every month
Lakewood Show
P. O. Box 6826
Atlanta, GA 30315

ATLANTA, GA 30309
The Stalls at Bennett St.
70 dealers
116 Bennett St
Open Mon-Sat 10-5; closed Sun
404-352-4430
I-75 Exit Northside Dr. N to 1st light
R on Collier to Peachtree N 4 lights
to Mick's Restaurant, R into park lot

ATLANTA, GA 30339
Interiors Market (Mall)
45 dealers and 35 dealers at 200
Bennett
55 Bennett St., 2nd location 200
Bennett
Open Mon-Sat 10-5; closed Sun
404-352-0055
There are about a dozen individual
antique shops on Bennett. Enter
through Mick's Restaurant parking
lot.

ATLANTA, GA 30324
There are about 50 antique shops on
Miami Circle
Open Mon-Sat 11-5, clsd Sun
404-237-0599
I-75 Exit E on Paces Ferry Rd
to Piedmont Av. S 2 mi
under RR, L at light.

ATLANTA/
ALPHARETTA, GA 30004
Queen of Hearts Antiques & Interiors
200 dealers
700 N. Main
Open Mon-Sat 10-6; Sun 1-6
678-297-7571
Alpharetta is 12 mi N of I-285 off US
Hwy 9-400

ATLANTA/
CHAMBLEE, GA 30341
Broad Street Antique Mall
100 dealers
3550 Broad St.
Open Mon-Sat 10-5:30; Sun 1-5:30
770-458-6316
1.5 mi S of I-285 off Peachtree
Industrial, turn left at Broad St
www.antiquerow.com/broad

94

ATLANTA/
CHAMBLEE, GA 30341
I-285 Exit , S on Peachtree
Industrial to Broad St L to
Antique Row, 15 bldgs, 100 dealers

ATLANTA/
MARIETTA, GA 30064
Dupre's Antique Market (Mall)
80 dealers
17 Whitlock Ave
Open Mon-Sat 10-5:30; Sun 1-5
770-428-2667
I-75 Exit 112 or 113, W to Downtown
Historic Marietta Square with 20 shops

ATLANTA/
ROSWELL, GA 30076
Historic Roswell Antique Market
100 dealers
1207-C Alpharetta Street
Open Mon-Sat 10-6, Sun 1-5
770-587-5259
8 mi N of I-285 on US 9 Exit 7B; 1 1/2
mi N of Historic area
9 shops on Canton St., 1 block west

ATLANTA/
ROSWELL, GA 30076
Roswell Antique Mall & Flea Market
200 dealers
710 Holcomb Bridge Rd.
Open Mon-Sat 10-6; Sun 12-6
770-642-6964
From US Hwy 19/GA 400
take Exit 7B Roswell 1 mi W
on Holcomb Bridge Rd

AUGUSTA, GA 30907
Antique Marketplace
60 dealers
3179 Washington Rd
Open Mon-Sat 10-6; Sun 12-5
706-860-7909
1 mi N of I-20 Exit 199

CALHOUN, GA 30701
Calhoun Antique Mall
80 dealers
1503 Redbird Rd. NE
Mon-Sat 9-6; Sun 1-5
706-625-2767
Hwy 156 at I-75 Exit 315

COLUMBUS, GA 31904
River Market Antique Mall
75 dealers 20,000 sq. ft.
3226 Hamilton Rd.
Hours:10-6 Mon-Sat,12-6 Sun
706-653-6240
From Atlanta I-85S to I-185 to
Columbus wwwRiver Rd exit, S to
deadend to mall
wwwrivermarketantiques.com

LAKE PARK, GA 31636
Farmhouse Antique Mall
11,000 sq. ft.
1236 Lakes Blvd.
Open 10-6 daily
229-559-0199
Close to Florida border I-75, exit 5

GEORGIA

MACON, GA
Payne Mill Village Antique Mall
150 dealers
364 Rose Ave
Mon-Thur 10-5, Fri-Sun 1-6
478-741-3821
I--75 Exit Bardeman Ave which becomes Vineville (US 41) to Brookdale,
L 1 blk

MACON/
BYRON, GA 31008
Big Peach Antiques & Collectibles Mall
200 dealers
119 Peach Park
Open Mon-Sat 10-7, Sun 10-6
478-956-6256
**I-75 Exit 149, 10 mi S of Macon,
under the Big Peach**

**In Macon we enjoyed the home style
southern cooking at Jeneane's
Restaurant,
4436 Forsyth Rd. I-75 Exit 164 N on
Vineville, which turns into Forsyth Rd.
478-476-4642.**

RINGOLD, GA 30736
Gateway Antiques Center
400 dealers
4103 Cloud Springs Rd
Open 7 days 9-8
706-858-9685
**I-75 Exit 353, W 200 yards,
Suburban Chattanooga, TN**

SAVANNAH, GA 31401
Alexander's Antique Gallery
70 dealers
320 W. Broughton St.
Open Mon-Fri 11-5;Sat 11-6, Sun 12-6
912-232-8205
**Exit Bay St off I-516 E to downtown, R
to Broughton St Maps available here to
32 shops.**

**We certainly enjoyed our luncheon
buffet of Southern cooking at the
Pirates House at 20 E, Broad & Bay
Street. Another well known place for
breakfast or lunch is *Wilkes House* at
107 W. Jones St., famous for it's
family style serving of
Southern cooking.**

TIFTON/CHULA, GA 31793
Sue's Antique Mall
10,000 sq ft
105 Chula-Brookfield Rd.
Open Mon-Sat 10-6; Sun 12-6
229-388-1856
At I-75 Exit 69

VIENNA, GA 31092
Exit 109 Antique Mall
63 dealers
1410 E. Union St.
7 days 8-5
229-268-1442
**At I-75 Exit 109 East side
There are 3 other shops in
the 100 block of Union St., plus 2
nearby shops**

GEORGIA

TRAVEL NOTES

IDAHO

LEGEND

(A) = Auction Companies
● = Cities w/ Antique Malls listed in guide

Coeur d'Alene

Lewiston/Clarkston

(A) Caldwell
Boise

Idaho Falls

Twin Falls

IDAHO

AUCTION/ESTATE SALE CO.'S
Caldwell, ID 83605
Caldwell Auction
Collectors auction
4920 E. Cleveland Blvd.
1st Thu of each month at 6:30 P.M.
208-454-1532

ANTIQUE MALLS, MARKETS & SHOWS
BOISE, ID 83712
The Antique Hub
20 dealers
2244 Warm Springs Ave.
Everyday 11-6
208-336-4748
I-84 Exit 54 N on Broadway to Warm Springs and turn R

BOISE, ID 83705
Antique World Mall
100 plus dealers
4544 Overland Rd.
Open 7 days 10-6, Fri til 9
208-342-5350
I-84 Exit 50 to Overland Rd E to 4544 Overland

COEUR D'ALENE, ID 83814
Coeur d'Alene Antique Mall
90 dealers
N 3650 Government Way
7 days 9:30-5:30
208-667-0246
I-90 Exit 12
2nd Mall at Hwy 95 & 408 Haycroft w/ 35 dealers, Ask for directions to 2 other malls

COEUR D'ALENE, ID 83814
Wiggitt Marketplace
100 dealers, 4 floors
119 N. 4th St
Open 7 days, call for hours open
Phone 208-664-1524
Downtown in 1920's Montgomery Ward Bldg

IDAHO FALLS, ID 83402
Antique Gallery
20 dealers
341 W. Broadway
Mon-Sat 10-6; Sun 12-5:30
208-523-3906
I-15 exit 118, W on Broadway

LEWISTON /
CLARKSTON, WA 99403
The Hangar Antique Emporium
100 dealers
935 Port Way
Tue-Sat 10:30-5:30 PM
509-758-0604
N on 13th to Port Way along the river

TWIN FALLS, ID 83301
Snow's Antiques & Sleigh Works
15 dealers
136 Main Ave.N
Open Tue-Sat 10-5
208-736-7292
I-84 Twin Falls Exit to downtown
4 other shops downtown on Main

TWIN FALLS, ID 83301
Second Time Around
18 dealers
689 Washington St. N
Open Mon-Sat 10-5
208-734-6008
I-84 Exit 174 S to Poleline Rd W to Washington then South

ILLINOIS

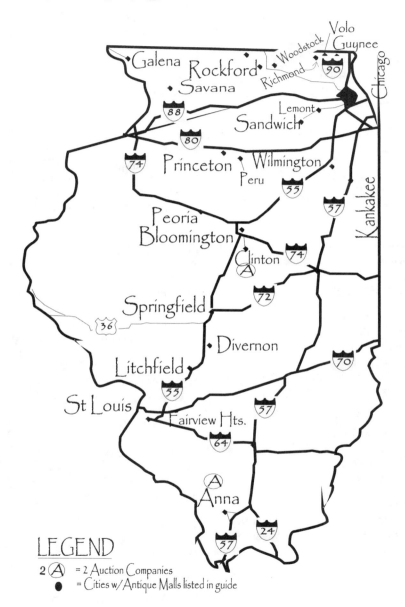

Galena
Rockford
Savana
Woodstock
Volo
Guynee
Richmond
Chicago
88
Lemont
Sandwich
80
74
Princeton
Wilmington
Peru
55
57
Kankakee
Peoria
Bloomington
Clinton
(A)
74
72
Springfield
36
Divernon
70
Litchfield
55
St Louis
Fairview Hts.
57
64
(A)
Anna
57
24

LEGEND
2 (A) = 2 Auction Companies
● = Cities w/ Antique Malls listed in guide

ILLINOIS

WEEKEND ANTIQUE EVENTS
Arlington Heights: Arlington Park Antiques Show- 200 booths
Arlington Racetrack - Apr & Oct
Bloomington; Third Sunday Market, 450 booths, **May thru Oct**
Chicago; Dupage Co. Fairgrounds Flea Mkt., **3rd Sun, no Jul, 2 in Aug**
Chicago; O'Hare Antique Show, 350 dealers, **one Wk-end in Apr, Aug, Nov**
Chicago/St. Charles; Kane Co. Fairgrounds Flea Market
1st Sun & preceeding Sat
Sandwich; Sandwich Antique Markets, 500 dealers, **1 Sun/mo in May-Oct**
ANTIQUE DISTRICTS/ VILLAGES
Chicago Belmont Ave., Galena, Richmond, Volo & Wilmington

AUCTION/ESTATE SALE CO'S

ANNA, IL; 62906
Martin's Antique Auction
PO Box 2
I-57 Exit 30, W.10 mi.
Antique Auctions
last Sat/Sun each mo. at 9:30 AM
618-833-3589 Call to confirm.

CLINTON, IL 61727
Martin Toy Auction
PO Box 333
1st Sun each mo. 11 AM
217-935-8211
Toy auctions
At Bloomington Exit I-55 or I-74 S on Rte 51 to Clinton. Auction is 1.5 mi S of Clinton on Rte 51. Clinton is 20 mi S of Bloomington on US Hwy 51

In Wilmette we like to eat at the Original Pancake House at 153 Green Bay, to enjoy all the Tiffany Glass windows and shades.

ANTIQUE MALLS, MARKETS/ SHOWS

ARLINGTON HEIGHTS, IL
Arlington Park Antiques Show & Sale
200 Exhibitors
Arlington Park Racetrack
Spring & fall, Apr. 2 & 3, Oct. 22 &23,2005
Check local papers for show hours or call 954-563-6747
Dolphin Promotions, Inc
P.O.Box 224
Forest Park, IL 60130

BLOOMINGTON, IL
Third Sunday Market
450 booths, inside and out
Fairgrounds, Rte 9 East
Sun - 8-4, Adm. $5.00
309-452-7926
Early buying Sat. noon $25.
Markets May-Oct, 3rd Sundays
I-55/74 Exit 160-B W on Rte 9, 1 mi
Don & Carol Raycraft
P.O. Box 396
Bloomington, IL. 61702

ILLINOIS

CHICAGO, IL
Dupage County Fairgrounds Flea
Market
Many dealers; antiques & collectibles
2015 Manchester Rd , Wheaton, IL
Open 8-3, indoors, 6AM Adm $20.00,
8AM Adm $5..00
715-526-9769 OR 630-668-6636
**From I-355 Exit Roosevelt Rd. (Rte 38)
thru Wheaton to County Farm Rd N.
3rd Sun, none in July, 2 in Aug.**
Zurko Promotions
211 W. Green Bay
Shawano, WI 54166

CHICAGO./ROSEMONT IL
Chicago O'Hare Summer Antique Show
250 dealers; antiques only
Stephens Convention Center
Adm $10.00; Fri 12-8, Sat 12-7, Sun 12-6
954-563-6747
**Jct I-90 & I-294. By Hyatt on River Rd.
Last wkend -Aug .26-28**
Dolphin Management,
P.O. Box 7320
Ft. Lauderdale, Fl 33338

CHICAGO, IL 60660
Broadway Antique Market
75 dealers, 20,000 sq. ft.
6130 N. Broadway
Open Mon-Sat 11-7, Sun 11-6
773-743-5444
3 Blks South of Lyola University, 3 blks
from lake, E to Broadway, north end of
Lakeshore Dr.

CHICAGO/ BLUE ISLAND, IL 60406
Three Sisters Antique Mall
100 dealers
13042 S. Western Ave.
Mon-Sat 10-6, Sun 11-5
708-597-3331
**294 to Cicero exit 127 th then E to
Western Ave. So I-57- 127th St, Exit to
Western Ave.South 17 mi S. of Chicago**

CHICAGO, IL 60618
Pursuing The Past Antique Mall
25 plus dealers
2229 W. Belmont Ave
Daily 11-6
773-871-3915
**I-90/94 Exit 45-C, Belmont Ave. E.
14 shops on Belmont from 1819-2336**

CHICAGO/
ELK GROVE VILLAGE, IL 60005
Oakton Street Antique Centre
79 dealer spaces
2430 E. Oakton Street
Mon-Sat 10-6; Sun 10-5:30
847-437-2514
I-290 Exit 10, Rte 83 N. to Oakton St. E.

CHICAGO/
ST. CHARLES, IL
Kane County Fairgrounds Antique
Market
100's of dealers, Indoors and Out
Fairgrounds
Open Sat 7-5-, Sun 7-4
Adm $5.00; Park Free
630-377-2252
**On Randall Rd between Hwy 64 & 38
1st Sun & preceding Sat every month**
Kane County Flea Mkt
PO Box 549
St. Charles, IL. 60174

CHICAGO/
ST. CHARLES, IL 60174
Antique Malls - I, II, III
75 dealers
11 N. 3rd St, 301 W. Main & 413 W.
Main
Daily 10-5
630-377-5798 or 630-377-5599 (III)
20 mi W of Chicago on Rte 64
Park and walk to all 3 Malls

CHICAGO/
WHEELING, IL 60090
1 1/2 mi N of Rte 68 (Dundee Rd)
I-94 Exit Rte 22 W to Milwaukee Av. S.
to Wheeling in an Antique village of
11 bldgs. in the 900 block

CHICAGO/
WILMETTE, IL 60091
Heritage Trail Mall
75 dealers
410 Ridge Rd
Mon-Sat 10-5:30, Sun 12-5
847-256-6208
I-94 Exit 34 Lake Ave. E. to Ridge Rd S.

CLINTON, IL 61727
Clinton Antique Mall
100 dealers
Junction Rtes 51 & 54
Mon-Sat 10-5, Sun 11-5
217-935-8846
25 mi S of Bloomington at Jst of Rtes
51 & 54

DIVERNON, IL 62530
Lisa's Antique Malls
150 dealers in 2 buildings
14272 Frazee Rd.#150
Open 7 days 10-6
217-628-1111 or 628-3333
I-55 & Hwy 104 (I-55 Exit 82) Westside
Truckers Homestead Restaurant is a
good stop for good food down from
Lisa's Mall it has a buffet all day.

EL PASO, IL 61738
El Paso Antique Mall
200 dealers
Open 7 days 10-6
309-527-3705
At I-39 Exit 14, Westside of I-39

FAIRVIEW HEIGHTS, IL 62208
St. Clair Antique Mall
200 dealers
315 Salem Place
Open Mon-Sat 10-8; Sun 12-6
618-628-1650
I-64 Exit 12, Hwy 159 N, Rt on Salem
Place at Ramada Inn (15 min E of St.
Louis)

GALENA, IL 61036
Galena Antique Mall
40 dealers
8201 State Route 20
Daily 10-5
815-777-3440
2 mi. SE of town on US Hwy 20
14 mi SE of Dubuque, IA on US Hwy 20
another new mall 1 mi from Galena
Mall, with 4 or 5 shops on Main St.

ILLINOIS

GURNEE, IL. 60031
Gurnee Antique Center
200 dealers, 24,000 sq. ft.
5742 Northridge Dr.
Mon Sat 10-5, Thur till 8, Sun 12-5
847-782-9094
**S of WI border Exit-94 at Hwy 132,
Grand Ave E . Turn S on Dilley's Rd
which becomes Northridge Dr. and
deadends into Antique Center parking.**
*A real antique shop where merchan-
dise is old and of top quality. Featuring furniture, porcelain, pottery, art
glass, jewelry, advertising, art,
primitives and much more.*

KANKAKEE, IL 60901
Kankakee Antique Mall
225 booths
145 S. Schuyler Avenue
Fri,Sat ,Mon -10-5, Sun 12-5, clsd Tue
Wed Thur
815-937-4957
**Downtown, I-57 exit 312 W 1 1/2 mi
to Schuyler Avenue, L then 1st R, park
and enter in back.**

LITCHFIELD, IL 62056
Lisa's Mall III
75 dealers
Route 108
Open 7 days 10-6
217-324-5170
At I-55 Exit 60

PEORIA, IL 61602
Illinois Antique Center
175 dealers
311 SW Water St
Mon-Sat 9-5, Sun 11-5, Thur 9-8
309-673-3354
**Downtown, I-74 Exit 93, S on
Washington St to Liberty, left on
Liberty. Watch for signs on Riverfront.**

PEORIA/
EAST PEORIA, IL 61611
Pleasant Hill Antique Mall
250 dealers
315 S. Pleasant Hill Rd
4 days 7-7, Fri & Sat 7-8, Sun 7-5
309-694-4040
**I-74 Exit 98, S on Pinecrest to 1st stop
light, turn left on Muller, go 1.24 mi,
then left on Pleasant Hill.**

PERU, IL 61354
Peru Antique Mall
250 dealers
2702 May Rd.
Open 7 days 9:30-5:30
815-224-9991
**On I-80 between Exits 73 & 75 on
North side**

PRINCETON, IL 61356
Sherwood Antique Mall
200 dealers
1661 N. Main
Open daily 9-9
815-872-2580
I-80 Exit 56, S 1/2 mi

ILLINOIS

RICHMOND, IL 61356
Emporium 1905
One of 5 shops
10310 N. Main (US Hwy 12)
Daily 11-5, clsd Thur
815-678-4414
**One of 5 single and multi-dealer
shops at Jct of U.S. Hwy 12 and Bdwy**

ROCKFORD, IL 61108
East State Street Mall (1&2))
120 dealers
5301 E. State St & 5411
Daily 10-9
815-226-1566
**I-90 State St Exit, W 2 mi; enter
in back of shopping center
#2 at 5411 E. State St**

SANDWICH, IL 60548
Olde Timers Antique Centre
100 booths, 175 showcases
131 E. Church St. (Rte 34)
Mon-Sat 10-5, Sun 12-5
815-786-6430
In town on Rte 34, 2 blks E of Main St.

SANDWICH, IL 60548
Sandwich Antique Markets
600 dealers, antiques & collectibles
Fairgrounds
**One Sun monthly May-Oct ,
Call for exact dates**
Adm $5.00, park free
773-227-4464 or 773-815-3337
**US 34, 60 mi W of Chicago.
I-88 Sugar Grove Exit, Hwy 47 S to US
34 W**
Robert Lawler Promotions
151 0 N. Hoyne
Chicago, IL 60622-1804

SAVANNA, IL 61074
Pulford Opera House Antique Mall
120 dealers
Rte 84, Great River Road
M-Thur 9:30-5:30, S-S 9:30-8, Sun 11-6
815-273-2661
32 miles S of Galena on Rte 84

SPRINGFIELD, IL 62703
Barrel Antique Mall
120 shops
5850 S 6th St.
Open 7 days 9:30-5:30
217-585-1438
**At I-55 Exit 90, E of Cracker Barrel
Has Aumann Auction House giving
auction once a mo. on premises.**

SPRINGFIELD, IL 62702
Sangamon Antique Mall
90 dealers, 3 floors, 22,000 sq. ft.
3050 Sangamon Ave.
Daily 10-6
217-522-7740
Off I-55 exit 100B

ILLINOIS

VOLO, IL 60073
Volo Antique Mall & Auto Museum
350 dealers, 250 cars
27640 W. Volo Village Rd
Open 7 days 10-5
815-344-6062
20 mi. W of Waukegan, 15 mi W of Six Flags Great America

WILMINGTON, IL 60481
15 mi. S of Joliet on Hwy 53, or I-55 Exit 241 S; I-55 Exit 227 N
12 mi. on Hwy 53. 10 Shops downtown, with flea market.

In Wilmington we enjoyed lunch at an 1871 Victorian B & B which serves a light lunch at 117 S. Kanakee. 1-888-317-8560

WOODSTOCK, IL 60098
Colonial Antique Mall
150 dealers, 35,000 sq. ft.
890 Lake Ave.
Open 7 days 10-5
815-334-8960
Woodstock is 8 mi NW of Crystal Lake near Jct of US 14 & Rte 47

TRAVEL NOTES

INDIANA

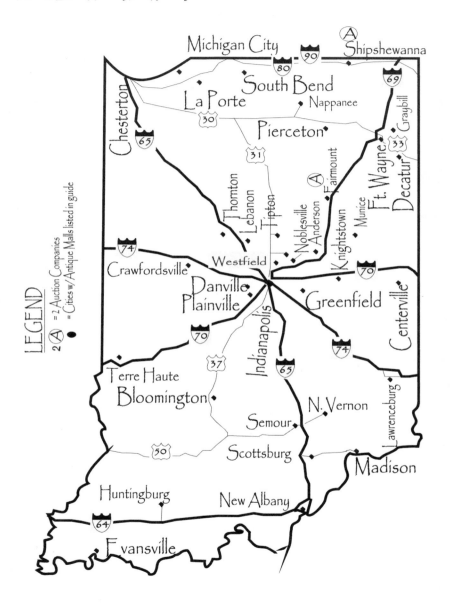

LEGEND

2 (A) = 2 Auction Companies

● = Cities w/ Antique Malls listed in guide

Michigan City

Shipshewanna

South Bend

La Porte

Nappanee

Chesterton

Graybill

Pierceton

Ft. Wayne

Decatur

Thornton

Fairmount

Lebanon

Noblesville

Tipton

Anderson

Munice

Knightstown

Crawfordsville

Westfield

Danville

Plainville

Greenfield

Centerville

Terre Haute

Indianapolis

Bloomington

N. Vernon

Semour

Lawrenceburg

Scottsburg

Madison

Huntingburg

New Albany

Evansville

INDIANA

Lawrenceburg Tri State Antique Market, 250 dealers,
every first Sun May-Oct
Evansville Collectors Carnival Antique & Flea Market, 300 dealers,
Jan, April, & October

ANTIQUE DISTRICTS/VILLAGES
Nappanee, Graybill, Huntingburg

AUCTION/ESTATE SALE CO'S
Indianapolis, IN
Royal Auction
Antique & household auctions
8444 E. Washington
Antique auction, noon, 1st Sundays
317-547-3454 Call to confirm

ANTIQUE MALLS, MARKETS & SHOWS
ANDERSON, IN 46016
Anderson Antique Mall
80 dealers
1407 Main Street
Open Mon-Sat 10-5; Sun 12-5
765-622-9517
I-69 Exit 22, downtown

BLOOMINGTON, IN 47403
Bloomington Antique Mall
120 exhibitors
311 W. 7th Street
Open M-Th 10-5, Fri-Sat 10-6, Sun 12-5
812-332-2290
49 mi S of Indy on Rte 37;
1 block NW of City Square

CENTERVILLE, IN 47330
Webb's Antique Mall
500 dealers
200 W. Union
Open Mon-Sun 8-6
765-855-5551
2 mi S of I-70 Exit 145

CHESTERTON, IN 46304
Yesterday's Treasures Antique Mall
100 dealers
700 W. Broadway
Mon-Sat 10-5, Sun 12-5
219-926-2268
I-94 Exit 26 A, S to downtown,
W on Broadway

CRAWFORDSVILLE, IN 47933
Cabbages & Kings Antique Mall
60 booths, 3 1/2 floors
124 S. Washington Street
Open Mon-Sat 10-5; Sun 12-5
765-362-2577
I-74 Exit 34 (US 231) S to downtown,
Blk South to Courthouse

CRAWFORDSVILLE, IN 47933
Fireside Antique Mall
43 booths
4035 State Road 32 E
Open Mon-Sat 10-5; Sun 1-5
765-362-8711
I-74 Exit 39, 1/2 mi W of SR 32

INDIANA

DECATUR, IN 46733
Yvonne Marie's Antique Mall
75 dealers, 90 % antiques
152 S. 2nd Street
Open Mon-Sat 10-5; Sun 1-5
260-724-2001
**Downtown; 20 mi S of
Ft. Wayne on US 27/33
A 50 dealer mall at 111 Jefferson St.**

EDINBURGH, IN 46124
Exit 76B Antique Mall
550 dealer booths
12595 N Executive Dr.
7 days 12-6
812-526-7676
30 miles S of Indianapolis, on I-55

EVANSVILLE, IN 47712
Franklin Street Antique Mall
75 dealers
2123 W. Franklin
Open Tue-Sat 10-5; Sun 12-4
812-428-0988
**Franklin is north of and parallel to
Lloyd Expressway**

EVANSVILLE, IND
Collectors Carnival Show
300 dealers
**Last weekend in Jan, April, & Oct. at
the 4-H Center, 2nd weekend in Aug**
Set-up Fri shopper 3-8PM, $15
Sat early bird 7-9AM $5 adm, 9AM-4PM
Sat & Sun, $1 adm
1-812-471-9419
Vanderburgh County
Evansville, IN 47714-0537
Hwy 41, 5 mi S of I-64

GRABILL, IN 46741
Country Shops of Grabill
20 dealers, 30,000 sq. ft.
13756 State St
Open Mon-Sat 9-5, Sun 12-5
260-627-6315
**I-69 Exit 116, Rte 1 N to Leo, R at 4 way
stop to Grabill in the heart of Amish
country.**

GREENFIELD, IN 46140
J. W. Riley's Emporium
60 dealers
107 W. Main
Open Mon-Sat 10-5; Sun 12-5
317-462-5268
**I-70 exit 104, S 3 mi.,
4 other antique shops on Main, on Hwy
9 other shops**

HUNTINGBURG , IN 47542
Parker House Antiques
1 of about 8 antique shops on 4th Street
307 E. 4th Street
Open Tue-Sun 12-5; some shops 10-5
812-683-5352
I-64 Exit 57 N 8 mi to downtown

INDIANAPOLIS, IN 46227
Southport Antique Mall
210 dealers, plus 130 showcases
2028 E. Southport Rd.
Mon-Sat 10-8; Sun 12-5
317-786-8246
I-65 Exit 103 (Southport Rd),W 1.7 mi
*36,000 sq. ft. with primitives,
glassware, Flo-blue, furniture, 50's
items, dolls and toys, come see us!
antique@ iquest.net*

INDIANAPOLIS, IN 46203
Indianapolis Downtown Antique Mall
40 shops
1044 Virginia Ave.
Open Mon-Sat 10-5; Sun 12-5
317-635-5336
In Fountain Square
2 block E of I-65 Exit 110

INDIANAPOLIS, IN 46227
Manor House Antique Mall
75 dealers, 20,000 sq. ft.
5454 S. E. St. (US 31)
Open Mon-Sat 10-6; Sun 12-6
317-782-1358
I-74/ 465 Exit 2, S 1/2 mi on US 31,
East St.

INDIANAPOLIS, IN 46220
Allisonville Antique Mall
25,00 sq. ft., 90 Dealers
6230 N. Allisonville Rd.
Mon-Sat. 10-8, Sun 12-6
317-259-7318
I-465 Exit 35, Allisonville Rd South.

INDIANAPOLIS/
ZIONSVILLE, IN 46077
Browns Antiques
3 Bldgs
315 N. 5th (off Main)
Open Mon-Sat 10-5, Sun 10-4
317-873-2284
I-465 Exit 27, N 2 mi on US 421 then L
into downtown Zionsville
6 antique shops on Main St

KNIGHTSTOWN, IN 46148
Knightstown Antique Mall
78 dealers
136 Carey St.
Mon-Sat 10-5; Sun 1-5
765-345-5665
I-70 Exit 115 S

LAPORT, IN 46350
Coachman Antique Mall
100 dealers
500 Lincoln Way, (Hwy 2)
Open Mon-Sat 10-5; Sun 12-5
219-326-5933
I-80/90 Exit 49 S to downtown
3 blocks E of Courthouse

LAWRENCEBURG, IN
Tri-State Antique Market
250 dealers; all antiques & collectibles
At Lawrenceburg, Indiana Fairgrounds
Open 7-3; early birds at 5; adm $3.00
513-738-7256, Call to confirm
1 mi W of Cincinnati Beltway
I-275 Exit 16 W on US 50
May thru Oct, every 1st Sun
Bruce Metzger
P.O. Box 35
Shandon, OH 45063
www.queencityshows.com

MADISON, IN 47250
Lumber Mill Antique Mall
65 dealers
721 W. First
Open Mon-Sat 10-5; Sun 12-5
812-273-3040
Madison is 40 mi NE of Louisville,
KY on the Ohio River.
There are 12 other antique shops in
downtown Madison

111

INDIANA

MADISON, IN 47250
Feed Mill Antique Mall
40 dealers
301 West St.
Open Mon-Sat 10-5, Sun 1-5, Closed Wed
812-265-2534
Downtown

MICHIGAN CITY, IN 46360
The Antique Market of Michigan City
140 dealers
3707 N. Frontage Rd.
Open Mon-Sat 10-5; Sun 12-5
219-879-4084
**I-94 Exit 34, N 1 block on US 42, turn
1st right.**

MUNCIE, IN 47303
Off Broadway Antique Mall
95 dealers
2404 N. Broadway
Open Mon-Sun 10-6
765-747-5000
I-69 Exit 41, 5 mi to Broadway, turn R.

NAPPANEE, IN 46550
Berkholder Dutch Village
45 dealers
71945 CR 101
Tue-Sat 10-5 winter Tue- Sat; 9-5 summer
574-773-2828
**1/4 mi N of US Hwy 6
& 1.5 mi W of SR 19
15 mi S of Elkhart on SR 19 in Nappanee
Walk to other smaller anitque malls.**

NEW ALBANY, IN 47150
Aunt Arties Antique Mall
40 plus dealers
128 W. Main St.
Open Mon-Sat 10-5; Sun 1-5
812-945-9494
Downtown across river from Louisville

NEW ALBANY, IN 47150
Main St. Antique Mall
50 dealers
145 E. Main St.
Open Tue-Sat 10-5, Sun 12-5, clsd Mon
812-948-2222
**Downtown across the river from
Louisville
Take New Albany exit from Hwy 64 over
bridge turn R on State St. straight to
Main, Left and on lefthand side**

NOBLESVILLE, IN 46060
Noblesville Antique Mall
65 dealers
20 N. 9th St.
Open Mon-Sat 10-6; Sun 12-6
317-773-5095
**Nobleville is 12 mi N of Indianapolis
at the Jct of Hwys 32 and 19 on
Courthouse square**

NORTH VERNON, IN 47265
North Vernon Antique Mall
40 dealers
247 E. Walnut St. (US 50 Hwy)
Open Mon-Sat 10-5; closed Sun
812-346-8604
I-65 Exit 49 E 12 mi, downtown

PLAINFIELD, IN 46168
Gilley's Antique Mall & Restaurant
600 booths, 37,000 sq. ft. 7 bldgs
5789 E. US Hwy 40
Open Mon-Sun 10-5
317-839-8779
**US 40 W; 15 mi W of Indianapolis
Off 465 exit 128 Plainfield, go W about
15 miles.**

SCOTTSBURG, IN 47170
Scottsburg Antique Mall
35 dealers
4 S. Main St.
Open Mon-Sat 9-5; Sun 12-5
812-752-4645
I-65 Exit 29 E, downtown, 1 mi from
interstate

SEYMOUR, IN 47274
Crossroads Antique Mall
150 dealers including showcases
311 Holiday Square
Open 7 days 10-5, Sun 12-5
812-522-5675
Jct I-65 & US 50;
behind Holiday Inn at I-65 Exit 50B

SHIPSHEWANNA, IN 46565
Trading Place Antique Gallery
100 dealers, 31,000 sq.ft
P.O Box 185.
May-Oct 9-6, Tue 9-7, Nov-April 9-5
260-768-7090
Downtown Shipshewanna 20 mi E of
Elkhart and 2 mi N on Rte 5. (See
auction section)

In South Bend the 1888 Studebaker
Mansion is now a restaurant,
Tippecanoe Place, **620 W, Washing-**
ton.
The food is very good and the building
and furnishings are most interesting
to an antiquer. 574-234-9077

SOUTH BEND, IN 46637
Unique Antique Mall
107 dealers
50981 US 933 North
Open 7 days 10-5
574-271-1799
On US Hwy 33
Continue N a few mi for more malls
with 300 dealers (see Niles, Michigan)

SOUTHBEND, IN
Antique Avenue Mall
120 booths, 1600 sq. ft.
52345 US 933 (Old 31)
Open 10-6 daily, 12-5 Sun
574-272-2558
2 mi N of Exit 77 on tollroad
See Niles, MI for several more large
antique malls N of South Bend a few
miles on US Hwy 33.

TERRE HAUTE, IN 47807
Nancy's Downtown Mall
100 dealers
9th & Poplar.
Mon,Tue Wed-Sat 10-5;Thur & Fri 10-7,
Sun 12-5
812-238-1129
State Rd 42 (Poplar)

WESTFIELD, IN 46074
Westfield Antique Mall
75 dealers 17,000 sq. ft.
800 E. Main
Mon-Fri 10-6, Sat 10-5, Sun 12-5
317-867-3327
12 mi N of Indianapolis on US 32 and 1
1/2 mi E of Hwy 31.

IOWA

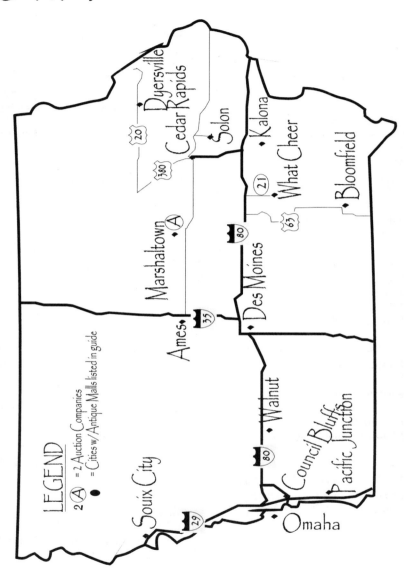

Dyersville

Cedar Rapids

Kalona

Solon

What Cheer

Bloomfield

20

380

21

63

Marshaltown

Ⓐ

80

Des Moines

35

Ames

Walnut

Council Bluff

Pacific Junction

80

LEGEND

2 Ⓐ = 2 Auction Companies

● = Cities w/ Antique Malls listed in guide

Souix City

29

Omaha

114

IOWA

WEEKEND ANTIQUE EVENTS

Des Moines State Fairgrounds, 250 dealers,
**Weekend Market, Sat & Sun, May-Oct, 1 per mo, none
in Jul or Aug.**
Dubuque Flea Mkt/Antique Show, 100 dealers, **One Sun in Feb, Apr & Oct**
Walnut, AMVETS, Market, 500 dealers, **3rd weekend in June**
What Cheer Collector's Paradise Flea Market,
1st Sun and preceeding Sat in April, May, Aug & Oct.

ANTIQUE DISTRICTS/VILLAGES
Kalona, Walnut

AUCTION/ESTATE SALE CO'S
MARSHALLTOWN, IA. 50158
Gene Harris Antique Auction Center
Antique & collectible auctions
203 S. 18th Av.
Most Wed & Sat at 10:00 A.M.
641-752-0600
View Mon-Fri 9-4
email: ghaac@marshallnet.com

ANTIQUE MALLS, MARKETS &
SHOWS
AMES, IA 50010
Antique Ames Mall
75 dealers
203 Main St
Open daily Mon-Sun 10-6
515-233-2519
I-35 Exit 111 W 3 mi to downtown

COUNCIL BLUFFS, IA 51501
Lake Manawa Antique Mall
320 dealers
101 W. So. Omaha Bridge Rd
Open daily 10-7PM
712-366-1562
I-29 Exit 47, W 3 blocks

DES MOINES, IA
The Flea Market
250 dealers; 60% antiques & collectibles
State Fairgrounds
Sat & Sun 9-4; adm free; park free
515-957-3139 Call for dates
2 mi E of I-235 on Hwy 163
one weekend /Mo. except July & Aug.
Elizabeth Rockwell, United Methodist
Church East 26th & Capitol
Des Moines, IA 50317

DES MOINES, IA 50313
Majestic Lion Antique Mall
200 dealers
5048 2nd Ave
Open 7 days 9-7
515-282-LION (5466)
At I-80 Exit 135, north side

115

IOWA

DUBUQUE, IA
Dubuque Flea Market/Antique Show
100 dealers; antiques & collectibles
Dubuque County Fairgrounds
Open 8-4; adm $1; park free
815-747-7745 Call for dates
5 mi W of Dubuque on US 20
Fairgrounds inside & out
One Sun in Feb, Apr & Oct
Jerome F. Koppen
260 Copper Kettle Lane
E. Dubuque, IA 61025

KALONA, IA 52247
Yoder's Antiques
1 of 14 Amish/Mennonite antique shops
435 B Av
Most shops open Mon-Sat 10-5
319-656-3880
Downtown on Ave B, 4th & 5th Streets
Kalona is 15 miles SW of Iowa City
Park and walk to all shops

PACIFIC JUNCTION, IA 51561
Antique Junction Mall
42 dealers
57745 190th St.
Mon-Sat 10-5; Sun 12-5
712-622-3532
I-29 Exit 35, 14 mi S of Council Bluffs

SIOUX CITY, IA 51101
Treasure Trove Antique Mall
100 booths, 200 showcases
925 Dace Ave.
Open 7 days 9-8
712-258-1996
Just off I-29 at Dace Ave between Exits
147A & B

WALNUT, IA 51577
AMVETS Third Weekend Market
300 dealers; all antiques and collectibles
Downtown Walnut
Open dawn to dusk
712-784-2100 Call for dates or 712-784-3710
I-80 Exit 46
All over downtown
3rd weekend in Jun
AMVETS Market
Box 265
Walnut, IA 51577

WALNUT, IA 51577
Walnut Antique Mall
45 dealers
Pearl & Antique City Dr.
Open 7 days Mon- Sat 10-5, Sun 12-5
712-784-3322 winter clsd Sun Dec-Mar
Downtown; I-80 Exit 46
Park and walk to shops & malls
A dozen antique shops and
4 Antique Malls in Walnut.

WALNUT, IA 51577
Granary Antique Mall
100 showcases & 60 booths, 15,000 sq.
ft.
602 Pearl Box 313
Mon-Sat 8-6, Sun 8-6
712-784-3331
Downtown; I-80 Exit 46

WHAT CHEER, IA
Collectors Paradise Flea Market
400 dealers
What Cheer Fairgrounds
Open Sat 7AM, Sun 7AM
641-634-2109 Call for dates
I-80 Exit 201, S 20 mi on Hwy 21
1st Sun & preceding Sat in April, May,
Aug & Oct
Larry Nicholson
PO Box 413
What Cheer, IA 50268

TRAVEL NOTES

KANSAS

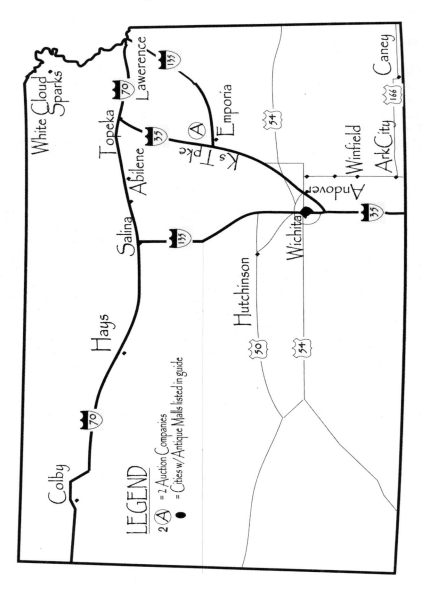

KANSAS

WEEKEND ANTIQUE EVENTS

(For all Kansas City area malls see Kansas City, MO)
Hutchinson Mid America Flea Mkt, 200 dealers,
1st Sun of every month(except none in Sep)
Spark's Flea Market, 400 dealers,
April 28th-1st Sun in May, including preceeding Fri & Sat., and Sept
1-4 Labor Day week-end
White Cloud Flea Mkt, 400 dealers,
1st Sun & preceding Sat in May and Sept
Wichita Coliseum Mid America Flea Mkt., 225 dealers,
See listing for 2005 dates

AUCTIONS

Wichita- Paramount Mall-
Antique auction periodically on Saturdays-call for dates

ANTIQUE DISTRICTS/VILLAGES

Old Town Wichita

ANTIQUE MALLS, MARKETS AND SHOWS

ABILENE, KS 67410
Broadway Antique Mall
20,000 sq. ft
324 N. Broadway
Open 7 days 10-5
785-263-2326
I-70 Exit 275; downtown

ABILENE, KS 67410
Buckeye Antique Mall
25 dealers, 3 floors
310 N. Buckeye
Mon- Sat 10-5:30, Sun 12-5:30
785-263-7696
In downtown historic Abilene

ANDOVER, KS
See Wichita/ Andover

ARKANSAS CITY, KS 67005
Summit Antique Mall
30 dealers
208 S. Summit
Open Mon-Sat 10-5; Sun clsd
620-442-1115
17 mi E of I-35 Exit 4, downtown
Shops on Summit street
at 511 N & 309 S

CANEY, KS 67333
Caney Antique Mall
100 dealers
Open Mon-Sat 9:30-5:30; Sun 1-5
620-879-5478
S Edge of Caney on US 75;
3 mi N of Oklahoma line

KANSAS

EMPORIA, KS 66801
Wild Rose Antique Mall
60 dealers, 75 % collectibles
1505 Road 175
Mon-Sat 10-5; Sun 12-5
620-343-8862
**At I-35 Exit 135 off service road
Ask Tpke toll booth for directions.**

EMPORIA, KS 66801
Poehler Mercantile Antique Mall
40 dealers plus 100 consignments
301 Commercial
Tue-Sat 10-6, Sun 1-5
620-341-9092
Downtown near train tracks

HAYS, KS 67601
Antique Mall of Hays
55 dealers
201 W. 41st St.
Open M-Sat 10-6; Sun 12-6,winter 12-5
Memorial Day thru Labor Day open
8PM except Sun
785-625-6055
**I-70 Exit 159, W 1/4 mi on 41st St
which parallels I-70 on south side**

HOLTON , KS
**An historic town on US 75, 35 mi So of
the Ks-NE line. Three multi-dealer
antique shops around the square. The
Trails Cafe on US 75 at the north edge
of town has been family operated for 13
years. (785-364-2786). We enjoyed
home-style cooking & the bread
pudding.**

HUTCHINSON, KS
Mid America Market
200 dealers
State Fairgrounds; 2100 N. Main
Open 9-4; adm $0.75; park free
620-663-5626
**Usually 1st Sun of every month;except
no Sept.,
Call for exact dates**
Mid-America Markets
P.O. Box 1585
Hutchinson, KS 67504

HUTCHINSON, KS 67501
Yesterday's Treasures Antique Mall
20 dealers, plus 9000 sq ft w/ 200
consignor
20 S. Main
Mon-Sat 10-5;closed Sun
620-662-4439
**Downtown
15 shops on S Main, #112 to #1000,
5 shops are 1 block S of the Mall.**

Kansas City area malls
See Kansas City, MO

LAWRENCE, KS 66044
Antique Mall of Lawrence
70 dealers
830 Massachusetts
Open Mon-Sat 10-6, Sun 1-5
785-842-1328
**Downtown, 20 mi E of Topeka
Exit 204 off Turnpike
Another antique store down the way
from this mall**

SALINA, KS 67401
Auld Lang Syne Mall
60 dealers
101 N. Santa Fe
Mon-Sat 10-5:30; Sun 1-5:30
785-825-0020
I-70 Exit 252, downtown
30 dealer mall across the street

SPARKS, KS
Sparks Flea Market
400 dealers, 85% antiques & collectibles
On Hwy K-7 N & 240th Rd
Open dawn to dusk; adm free; park free
785-985-2411 Confirm dates
23 mi W of St. Joseph, Mo.
April 28- May 1 Sun(3 days before), 3
days before Sept 1-4 Labor Day wk-end
Ray Tackett
P.O. Box 223
Troy, KS, 66087

TOPEKA, KS 66614
Topeka Antique Mall
52 booths
5247 SW 28th Court
Open 7 days 10-5
785-273-2969
Just off Exit 3 of I-470/US 75
(exit for 29th St. & Fairlawn Rd.)
I-470, 1 blk N

TOPEKA, KS 66604
Washburn View Antique Mall
50+ dealers
1507 SW 21st St.
Open Mon-Sat 10-6; Sun 12-5
785-234-0949
From Exit 5 of I-470/US 75 go 2 mi N
on Burlingame/Washburn to 21nd St
Behind Health Mart, on lower level of
Shopping Center

TOPEKA, KS 66611
Wheatland Antique Mall
40 dealers
2121 SW 37th
Open Mon-Fri 10-5:30; Sat & Sun 10-5
785-266-3266
I-470 Exit 5, Burlingame Rd
1 block N in lower level of
Burlingame South Shopping Center.
Other antique malls and shops in the
neighborhood scattered through area.

WHITE CLOUD, KS 66094
White Cloud, KS Flea Market
400 dealers all over town
Hwy 7
Open 8-5, park $2
785-595-3320
W on US 36, 12 mi to Hwy 7,
N 15 mi. 1st Sun, preceding Sat in
May & Sep
White Cloud Tourism
P.O. Box 84
White Cloud, KS 66094

WICHITA, KS
Kansas Coliseum Mid America Mkt.
250 dealers; not all antiques &
collectibles
Kansas Coliseum
Public 9AM, dealers 5:30 AM
620-663-5626
I-135 Exit 17, East 1/4 mi
2005:Jan 9, Jan 23, Feb 13, Mar 13,
Apr 3, Apr 17, Sept. 18, Oct. 2, Oct 23,
Nov 20, Dec 18. No shows Jn, Jl & Aug.
Mid-America Markets
P.O. Box 1585
Hutchinson, KS 67504
Downtown: 2 malls, one being Hewitt
Antique Mall, and A Legacy Antique Mall.

121

KANSAS

WICHITA, KS 67209
Flying Moose Antique Mall
105 spaces
9223 W. US Hwy 54
Open every day but Monday, 10-7,
May-Sept-Sat 10-5 Sun 1-5
316-721-6667

**For a delightful lunch in a
19th century old drug store setting,
we like the *Old Mill Tasty Shop* at
604 E. Douglas in Old Town. Their
steak soup is great, along with a New
York chicken salad sandwich. Another
great restaurant, in E. Wichita, is the
Chelsea Bar & Grill , or more formal
Olive Tree at 2949 N. Rock Rd. 316-
636-1100 . (They are adjacent restaurants)**

WICHITA/
PARK CITY, KS 67219
Annie's Antique Mall
80 dealer spaces
1600 E. 61st St.
Mon-Tue 10-6; Wed-Sat 10-8; Sun 1-6
316-744-1999
I-135 Exit 14 E 1/2 mi
www.anniesantiquemall.com

WICHITA /
ANDOVER, KS 67002
Andover Antique Mall
100 dealers
656 N. Andover Rd
Open Mon-Wed 10-6, Thur til 9 PM,
Fri & Sat 10-6, Sun 12-6
316-733-8999
**I-35 Exit 57 (KS tpke),1/4 mi E
of Hwy 54 on Andover Rd**
*29,000 sq. ft. of quality antiques &
collectibles.Large selection of antique
furniture, primitives , books, china,
pottery, & western artifacts . Open 7
days per week.*

WICHITA,KS 67235
Paramount Antique Mall
175 booths
13200 W. Kellogg (Hwy 54)
Mon-Fri 10-6,Sat 10-6, Sun 12-6
316-722-0500
*Area's largest mall, Showcase Gallery,
ample parking for RVs/ Buses/ Trailers
Voted Best Antique Mall in Discover
Mid-America magazine2004!
Antique Flea Market held every month,
correlated with the Colliseum flea
market weekend.*

TRAVEL NOTES

KENTUCKY

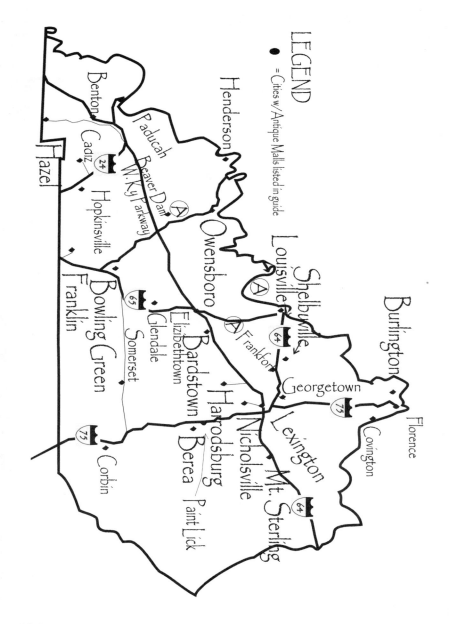

LEGEND

● = Cities w/Antique Malls listed in guide

Benton
Cadiz
Hazel
Paducah
Henderson
Hopkinsville
W.Ky.Parkway
Beaver Dam
Owensboro
Louisville
Shelbyville
Burlington
Franklin
Bowling Green
Somerset
Glendale
Elizabethtown
Bardstown
Harrodsburg
Frankfort
Georgetown
Lexington
Florence
Covington
Corbin
Berea
Paint Lick
Nicholsville
Mt. Sterling

KENTUCKY

WEEKEND ANTIQUE EVENTS

Burlington Antique Show (Market), **3rd Sun Apr-Oct**.
Covington, World's Longest Outdoor Sale, **Starts 1st Sat Weekend Aug**
Louisville KY Flea Market, every month,
   One Fri, Sat & Sun of every month
Mt. Sterling, October Court Days, **3rd Mon in Oct & preceding Wkend**

ANTIQUE DISTRICTS/ VILLAGES
Berea, Cadiz, Harrodsburg, Hazel, Louisville Bardstown Rd.

ANTIQUE MALLS, MARKETS/ SHOWS
BENTON, KY 42025
Antiques Et Cetera Mall
45 dealers
1026 Main St.
Open Mon-Sat 9-5; Sun 1-5
270-527-7922
Purchase Pwky Exit 42 E,
30 mi SE of Paducah

BEREA, KY 40403
Something Old Antique Mall
60 booths
437 Chestnut St.
Open Mon-Sat 10-6; Sun 1-5
859-986-6057
I-75 Exit 76, E (L) 1 mi to
downtown. There are some antique
shops in the 400 block of Chestnut.

BOWLING GREEN, KY 42101
River Bend Antique Mall
42 dealers
315 Beech Bend Rd.
Open Mon-Sat 10-5; Sun 12-5
270-781-5773
From downtown take 31 W Bypass
to Beech Bend Rd.

BURLINGTON, KY
Burlington Antique Show (Market)
350 dealers (early Sun 5-8, adm $5)
Boone County Fairgrounds
Open Sun 8-3; adm $3; park free
513-922-6847
10 mi S of Cincinnati
I-75 Exit 181, W 5 mi, R on KY 338
3rd Sun of each month Apr thru Oct
Burlington Antique Shows
P.O. Box 58367
Cincinnati, OH 45258

CADIZ, KY 42211
Cadiz Antique Mall
60 dealers
34 Main Street
Open 7 days 10-5
270-522-7880
I-24 Exit 65, W 5 mi downtown
There are 7 other Antique Malls &
shops in 2 blocks of Main St downtown

KENTUCKY

COVINGTON, KY
World's Longest Outdoor Sale
3000 vendors en route
US Hwy 127
800-327-3945 for info
**Extends 450 mi S along
US Hwy 127 to Gadsden, AL
Starts Sat of the 1st weekend in Aug
for 9 days**

ELIZABETHTOWN, KY 42701
Heart Land Antique Mall
40 booths
1006 N. Mulberry
Mon-Sat 10-6, closed Sun
270-737-8566
**I-65 Exit 94
7 single and multi-dealer shops
nearby on Dixie and Main St.**

FLORENCE, KY 41042
Florence Antique Mall
40,000 Sq. Ft. , 200 dealers
8145 Mall Rd (Connector Dr)
Open Tu & Sat 10-8, Wed, Thur & Fri
10-6, Sun 12-6, closed Mon
859-371-0600
**I-75N Exit 180 W 1/4 mi to Mall Rd
I-75 S Exit 180A
R 1/2 mi, in shopping center**

FRANKLIN, KY 42134
Heritage Antique Mall
87 dealers
111 W. Washington
Open Mon-Sat 10-5; Sun 1-5
270-586-3880
I-65 Exit 2 or 6 into downtown Franklin

GEORGETOWN, KY 40324
Georgetown Antique Mall
100 dealers in 3 bldg.s
124 W. Main
Mon-Sat 10-5; Sun 1-5
502-863-9033
I-75 Exit 125, I-64 Exit US 62 N

GEORGETOWN, KY 40324
Central Kentucky Antique Mall
40 dealers
114 E. Main
Open Mon-Sat 10-5; Sun clsd
502-863-4018
Downtown, across from courthouse

GLENDALE, KY 42740
Glendale Antique Mall
45 dealers
104 E. Railroad
Open Mon-11-6, Tue-Sat 11-9, Sun 1-6
270-369-7279
I-65 Exit 86 W

GLENDALE, KY 42740
Bennie's Barn
40 dealers, 10,000 sq. ft.
Hwy 252
Open 7 days, Tue-Sat 12-9, M-Sun 1-6
270-369-9677
I-65 Exit 86

GLENDALE, KY 42740
Side Track Shops & Antique Mall
25 shops
212 E. Main Street
Open 11-9; closed Sun & Mon
270-369-8766
**Downtown
7 shops downtown**

HARRODSBURG, KY 40330
Antique Mall of Harrodsburg
130 dealers
540 N. College St.
Open Mon-Sat 10-5; Sun 1-5, clsd Wed
859-734-5191
**On US Hwy 127, 16 mi S
of Blue Grass Pkwy Exit 59.**

HAZEL, KY 42049
Charlies Antique Mall
125 dealers
303 Main St., P.O. Box 196
Mon-Fri 10-4:30; Sat 10:30-5; Sun 1-5
270-492-8175
**Downtown with 11 shops and malls
On US Hwy 641 in KY at TN border.
9 shops & malls on Main in Hazel.**

HENDERSON, KY 42420
Henderson Antique Mall
100 dealer spaces
At Barrett Blvd & Hwy 60
Open Tue-Sat 10-5, Sun 1-5
270-826-3007
**8 mi S of Evansville, IN Exit 81A of
Pennyrile Pkwy. L at light.**

**In Lexington we like to eat the "Hot
Brown" for lunch. It is a Kentucky
regional dish of turkey, bacon, cheese
and eggs at the *Coach House* restaurant, 855 S. Broadway, 859-252-7777.**

LEXINGTON, KY 40508
Lexington Antique Gallery
22 dealers
637 E. Main Street
Open Mon-Sat 10-5
859-231-8197
Business Route 421 or E. Main

LOUISVILLE
Louisville, KY Flea Market
1000 booths
Kentucky Fair & Exposition Center;
indoors
Fri 12-7; Sat 10-7; Sun 11-5; free; park $5
502-456-2244 Call to confirm dates
**I-264 exit 12
One Fri , Sat & Sun every month**
Stewart Promotions
2950 Breckenridge Lane, #4-A
Louisville, KY 40220

LOUISVILLE, KY 40217
Louisville Antique Mall and Cafe
250 dealers
900 Goss Avenue
Mon-Sat 10-6; Sun 12-6
502-635-2852
**I-264 Exit 14, Poplar Level Rd N,
it turns into Goss
11 shops on Bardstown Rd.,**

LOUISVILLE, KY 40229
So.Louisville Antique & Toy Mall
350 showcases & booths
4150 E. Blue Lick Rd.
Open daily 10-6, Sun 12-6
502-955-5303
**I-65 Exit 121 E to Arby's
N 1.5 mi on Blue Lick Rd.
See NEW ALBANY, IN for an 80 dealer
mall and 50 dealer mall across the river**

KENTUCKY

MT. STERLING
October Court Days
1000-2000 dealers
All over downtown, outdoors & in.
Sat 6 AM thru 6 PM. Mon; free
859-498-5343 or 859-498-8732
I-64 Exit 110 to downtown
Third Mon in Oct &
preceding Sat & Sun
Chamber of Commerce
51 N. Maysville
Mt. Sterling, KY 40353

NICHOLASVILLE, KY 40356
Coach Light Antique Mall
80 dealers
213 N. Main Street
Mon-Sat 10-5; Sun 1-5
859-887-4223
10 mi S of Lexington on US 27
Downtown

NICHOLASVILLE, KY 40356
Antiques on Main
30 dealers
221 N. Main Street
Mon-Sat 10-5; Sun 1-5
859-887-2767
Downtown

OWENSBORO, KY 42303
Owensboro Antique Mall
50 dealer booths
500 W 3rd St.
Open Mon-Sat 9:30-5:30; Sun 12-5
270-684-3003
Downtown close to Executive Inn

OWENSBORO, KY 42303
Peachtree Galleries Mall
70 dealers
106 W. 2nd Street
Mon-Sat 10-5, closed Sun
270-683-6937
Downtown
A couple of antique shops nearby.

PADUCAH, KY
I-24 Exit 4, Downtown Paducah Historic
District with 20 antique shops & malls
coming from E. Exit 11

PAINT LICK, KY 40461
Todd's Antique Mall
65 booths
7435 Hwy 21 E
Open 7 days 9-5
859-986-9087
I-75 Exit 76 W 1 mi

SHELBYVILLE, KY 40065
Antiques For You Mall
75 booths
528 Main Street (U.S. 60 Hwy)
Mon-Sat 10-5; Sun 1-5
502-633-7506
I-64 Exit 35

SHELBYVILLE, KY 40065
Shelbyville Antique Mall
50 dealers
524 Main (U.S. 60 Hwy)
Mon-Sat 10-5; Sun 1-5
502-633-0720
I-64 Exit 35

128

SOMERSET, KY 42503
North 27 Antique Mall
150 booths
3000 N. Hwy 27
Open Mon-Sat 10-6; Sun 1-5
606-679-1923
**Cumberland Pwky deadends at
Somerset, L at light 3 mi on Hwy 27**

TRAVEL NOTES

LOUISIANA

Shreveport

W.Monroe

I-20

I-49

Alexandria

Washington

Denham Springs

Baton Rouge

Ponchatoula

(A)

I-10

Lafayette

New Orleans

(A)

US-90

LEGEND

2(A) = 2 Auction Companies

● = Cities w/Antique Malls listed in guide

LOUISIANA

ANTIQUE DISTRICTS/ VILLAGES
Denham Springs, W. Monroe, New Orleans on Royal and Magazine Sts.

AUCTION/ESTATE SALE CO'S
NEW ORLEANS, LA 70115
Neal Auction Co.
Large quality antique auctions
4038 Magazine St.
About every 6 weeks
800-467-5329 or 504-899-5329.

ANTIQUE MALLS/ MARKETS/ SHOWS
**One of our favorites, *La Madeline*
French Bakery and Cafe is located
at 7615 Jefferson Hwy in Baton Rouge.
Take the Jefferson Exit off I-12 N.
If you prefer barbecue with the
"WORLDS LARGEST BAKED POTATO"
loaded, and bread pudding topped with
whiskey sauce, go to *T.J.'s Ribs* at 2324
S. Acadian, at I-10 Exit 157 B. We
enjoyed meals at both places.**

BATON ROUGE, LA 70810
Fireside Antiques
Large importer of European antiques
14007 Perkins Rd
Mon-Sat 10-5, Closed Sundays
225-752-9565
I-10 to Siegen, S to Perkins, L 1 mi

BATON ROUGE/
DENHAM SPGS, LA 70726
Benton Bros. Antique Mall
30 dealers
115 N. Range Ave.
Open Mon-Sat 9-5; Sun 1-5
225-665-5146
I-12 Exit 10 N 2 mi

BATON ROUGE/
DENHAM SPGS, LA 70726
Louisiana Purchase Antique Mall
27 dealers
239 N. Range Ave.
Open Mon-Sat 10-5; Sun 12-5
225-665-2803
I-12 Exit 10 N 2mi
**There are 15 antique shops and malls
on Range Avenue in Denham Springs**

LAFAYETTE, LA 70503
Lafayette Antique Market
40 dealers
3108 Johnston St.
Open Tue-Sat 10-5; Sun 1-5
337-981-9884
I-10 Exit 103. In the center of Lafayette

MONROE/
W. MONROE, LA 71291
I-20 Exit 115; downtown
**15 antique stores on Trenton Street,
and Cotton St.**

NEW ORLEANS, LA 70130
75 antique shops on Magazine St.
Most open Mon-Sat 10-5, closed Sun
**Cross Canal St on Decatur St
then you will be on Magazine St. Drive
19 blocks to antique shops on Magazine
St**

LOUISIANA

In the French Quarter there are many antique shops on Royal Street within walking distance.

For lunch we like *La Madelaine's* French Bakery & Cafe at 547 St. Ann in the French Quarter. We like their Croque Monsieur with French Onion soup and Caesar Salad. For less causal dining we prefer *Bayona Restaurant*, 430 Dauphine St., in the French Quarter. 504-525-4455. (reservations suggested) The Sunday Brunch Buffet on the beautiful patio at the *Court of Two Sisters* is terrific.

WASHINGTON, LA 70589
Washington Old Schoolhouse Mall
100 dealers
123 S. Church St.
Open only Fri, Sat & Sun 9-5
337-826-3580
I-49 Exit 25 W and follow "Antiques " signs. There are 8 shops on Main St. Antique fair on 6 acres with over 200 dealers, 2nd weekend of April & Oct. *Dealers from all over the country come to our fair bringing architecturals, furniture, antique glassware & pottery. Our historic 1930 Deco schoolhouse has everything from French antiques to primitives, and hard to find Louisiana antiques. There is also a 1830 restored mud house on the premises.*

SHREVEPORT, LA 71106
The London Gallery
One of 10 antique shops on & off Line Ave.
5908 Fairfield
Open Tues- Sat 10:30-4:30
318-868-3691
I-20 Exit to I-49S to Piermont Exit, 2 blks to Fairfield, turn S

TRAVEL NOTES

GREAT ANTIQUING GETAWAY TO NEW ORLEANS

WHEN: Anytime

WHERE: New Orleans French Quarter means antiques, street musicians, Mimes and artists at Jackson Square, Historic Buildings with wrought iron balconies, Beignets at *Cafe Du Monde* with a cup of Chickory coffee, and pecan pralines in the French Market, paddlewheels on the river, with great food and history everywhere.

ANTIQUING: Most antique shops are closed on Sunday, so weekdays are for antiquing in New Orleans. Royal Street has high quality antique shops that you can walk to and there are 75 more antique shops on Magazine Street. Drive across Canal St. on Decatur and you will be on Magazine. Drive 19 blocks to the start of 6 miles of scattered antique shops of all types of antiques and collectibles. The National D-Day Museum is at 945 Magazine. The New Orleans Museum of Art in City Park has an extensive collection of Faberge' and paintings by French Impressionists. From the river, take Esplanade about 4 mi to City Park.

LODGING: In the French Quarter, we prefer the Omni Royal Orleans Hotel at 621 St. Louis St. for luxury and they often have great package deals or promotions. 504-529-5333. For more quaint yet nice accomodations, the Place D'Arms Hotel, 625 St. Ann, 800-366-2743 and at Hotel Provincial, 1024 Chartre St.. 504-581-4995. Or check www.NewOrleansPackages.com.

LEISURE: Try a Mississippi river afternoon cruise on the President, a river paddle wheeler in grand style. Also, *Harrah's Casino* is at #4 Canal St. for those who would like to try their luck at gaming.

RESTAURANTS: In a 200 year old Creole cottage with a beautiful patio is our favorite French Quarter restaurant with a great chef and realistic prices, "Bayona" at 430 Dauphine . 504-525-4455, where New Orleans residents dine.

For a quick lunch we enjoy *La Madeline Bakery and Cafe* at 547 St. Ann. A delicious French Quarter Jazz Brunch is served daily on the *Court of Two Sisters* beautiful patio at 613 Royal St. 504-522-7261

MAINE - South

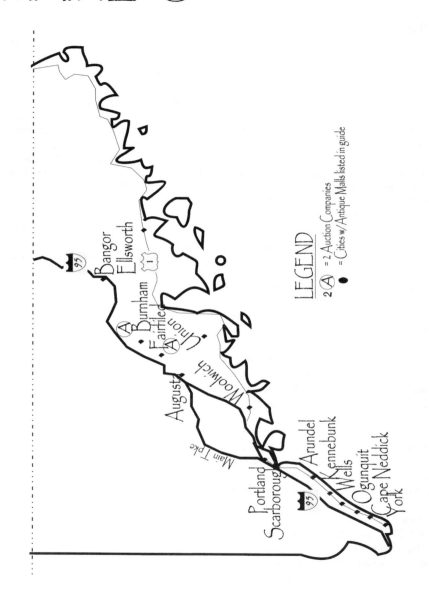

LEGEND

2(A) = 2 Auction Companies
● = Cities w/Antique Malls listed in guide

Bangor
Ellsworth
Burnham
Fairfield
Union
Woolwich
Augusta
Main Tpke
Arundel
Kennebunk
Wells
Ogunquit
Cape Neddick
York
Portland
Scarborough

MAINE - South

WEEKEND ANTIQUE EVENTS

Union Maine Antiques & Festival, **2nd weekend in Aug**
Woolwich, Montsweag Flea Market, outdoor,
    Sat & Sun May thru Oct, also Wed and Fri, Jun thru Aug

ANTIQUE DISTRICTS / VILLAGES
    Wells, US Hwy 1 from York to Kennebunk

AUCTION/ESTATE SALE CO'S

__BURNHAM, ME, 04922__
Houston-Brooks Auctioneers
Antique and household auction
South Horseback Rd.
Every Sunday at 7 A.M. to 3 P.M.
800-254—2214 or 207-948-2214.
I-95 Exit 138 N on Hwy 100,
R in Burnham Village to So Horseback
Rd, right
www.houston-brooks.com

__FAIRFIELD, ME, 04937__
James Julia Auctioner
Antique & collectible sale
P.O. Box 830
About every month, call
207-453-7125 for dates
I-95 Exit 133

ANTIQUE MALLS, MARKETS/ SHOWS

__ARUNDEL, ME 04046-7938__
Arundel Antiques
200+ dealers
1713 Portland Rd. (U.S. 1)
May-Oct10, Mon-Fri 10-5; Sat/Sun 8-6
207-985-7965
I-95 Biddleford Exit then S, on US1
Winter hours Oct 11-Apr daily 10-5

__ELLSWORTH, ME 04605__
Big Chicken Barn Books and Antiques
50 dealers
U.S. Hwy 1
Open daily year around
207-667-7308
S of Bangor between
Bucksport & Ellsworth
www.bigchickenbarn.com

__KENNEBUNK, ME 04043__
Antiques USA
300 dealers
P.O. Box 27 (on US 1)
Open 7 days 10-5
207-985-7766
Heading N I-95 Exit 25, E to US 1

__OGUNQUIT, ME 03907__
The Blacksmith's Mall
65 dealers
166 Main Street, Rte 1, PO Box 795
Open 7 days 9-5, Clsd Wed Nov-Mar
207-646-9643
Between I-95 Exits for York & Wells

In Ogunquit our favorite for a combina-
tion of great seaview and food (and
parking) is " Jackie's Too" at
Perkin's Cove. Lunch & dinner 7 days.
Ph 207-646-4444.

MAINE - South

PORTLAND/
SCARBOROUGH, ME 04074
Centervale Farm Antiques
20,000 sq. ft.
200 US Rte. 1
Open all yr 10-5, Clsd Mon Nov-Jun
800-896-3443 or 207-883-3443
Main Tpke Exit 45 to US 1 N or
6 mi S of Portland Via 295

UNION, ME
Maine Antiques Festival
350 dealers; Fri 2-7, $30
At the Fairgrounds in Union
Sat 9-5; Sun 9-4; adm $5, park free
207-563-1013
closed until August 30
I-95 Exit 30E (Augusta),
35 mi on Rte 17
2nd Sat/Sun in Aug
Coastal Promotion
PO Box 799
New Castle, ME 04553-0799

WELLS, ME 04090
Bo-Mar Hall Antiques
120 dealers
P.O. Box 308
Open daily 10-5 summer May 1 thru Oct
winter hours clsd Wed Nov-April
207-646-4116
I-95 Exit 19, N on US 1

WELLS, ME 04090
Wells Union Antique Center
9 adjacent shops in separate bldgs.
1755 Post Rd. (US 1)
Hours open varies from shop to shop,
most open 7 days
207-646-6996
I-95 Exit 19, N on US 1
There are 17 antique stores in Wells,
most on US 1.

WOOLWICH, ME
Monsweag Flea Market
100 dealers; 75% antiques & collectibles
On Rte 1 in Woolwich
Open 6:30-4; free parking
207-443-2809
35 mi N of Portland
Wed, Sat & Sun, May thru Oct,
also Fri Jun thru Aug
Norma Scopino
6 Hunnewell Lane
Woolwich, ME 04579

YORK, ME 03909
York Antique Gallery
70 dealers
746 Route 1 North, PO Box 303
Open daily 10-5 year round
207-363-5002
I-95 Exit 7, to Rte 1, at set of lights
turn L 1 mi. other antique stores in
York.

GREAT ANTIQUE GETAWAY TO COASTAL MAINE

WHEN: Anytime.

WHERE: All on US 1 Hwy, except auction

AUCTION: Houston -Brooks Auction, Antique & household items, every Sun at 7AM at Burnham, ME. I-95 Exit 138 N on Hwy 100. 80 miles N of Portland. 800-254-2214.

LODGING: Portland has a Fairfield Inn in the Scarborough suburb, a Courtyard, Doubletree, Comfort Inn and Holiday Inn in Portland.Portsmouth, NH has a Fairfield Inn, Holiday. Comfort, Hampton Inn & Courtyard. Many Bed and Breakfast Inns in Maine.

ANTIQUING: Northbound (If Southbound reverse this sequence)
1. I-95 N to Exit 7E to US1N to *York Gallery,* 70 dealers with quality antiques in a very nice antique mall at 746 US 1.

2. Continue N on US 1 to the *Blacksmith Mall* at 166 US 1 in Ogonquit.

RESTAURANT: A short distance North of the *Blacksmith Mall* on your right you will see a sign "To Perkins Cove". At that point turn toward the ocean, in a mile or so, you will come to a very quaint old fishing village at Perkins Cove, where we like to eat at "*Jackies*" or "Jackies Too."The food is good and the seascape is spectacular!

3. After lunch head N on US 1 to Wells, and 9 adjacent antique shops on W side of the Hwy. A really neat area to shop.

4. Next is *Bo-Mar Hall Antiques*, 120 dealers, just a little N of the 9 shops and across US 1.

5.Continuing N on US 1, you will come to *Antiques USA*, a large Mall with 300 dealers, in Kennebunk.

6. Across the street from *Antiques USA*, is another large antique mall, *Arundel Antiques* with 200 dealers.

7.Next continue N on US 1 to Scarborough, a suburb of Portland. At 200 US 1 you will find *Centervale Farm Antiques* with 20,000 sq. ft. of antiques and collectables.

LEISURE: In Portland, Taft House, built in 1755 is on Rte 22 and 9 near the Airport at 1270 Westbrook St. This 250 year old Georgian house has 18th century furniture which lends to it's London townhouse atmosphere. Wednesday afternoon tea is served in the 18th century garden. Adm $5.00, Seniors $4.00.

*Note: if you are planning on doing Vermont and New Hampshire too, our Getaway for New England is sequenced to start in Vermont, then New Hampshire & Maine.

MARYLAND

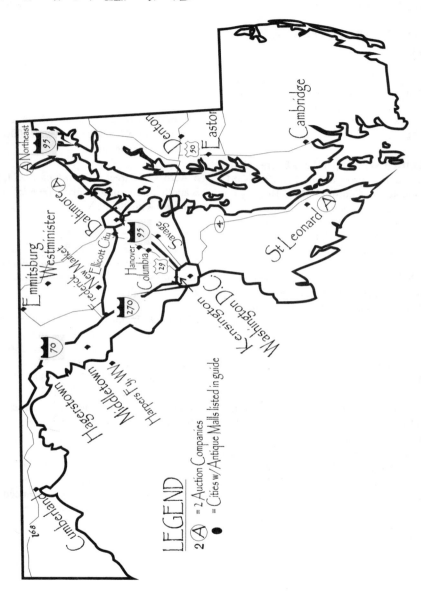

MARYLAND

WEEKEND ANTIQUE EVENTS
Baltimore Bazaar 500; 500 dealers,
Sat before Easter, last Sun in Oct, last Sat in Dec
Baltimore One Day Market, 125-275 dealers,
one Sun in Jan, Feb and Mar & Jun
Baltimore Howard County Fairground Market, 120 dealers,
generally last Sun & preceeding Sat in Mar & Oct
Baltimore Summer Antiques Fair-Baltimore Convention Center-450 dealers-
Sept.2-4th
Columbia Antique Market, 60-100 dealers,
every Sun from mid Apr thru mid Oct

AUCTION/ESTATE SALE CO'S

BALTIMORE/TOWSON MD 21204
Alex Cooper Auctioneers & Oriental
Rugs
Antique & collectible auctions
908 York Rd.
About every month, Mon-Fri 9-5
410-828-4838. call for dates

NORTHEAST,MD 21901
North East Auction Gallery
Auctions with some antiques
1995 Pulaski Hwy, PO Box 551
Every Tue evening
410-287-5588
I-95 Exit 100 S

ST. LEONARD, MD 20685
Chesapeake Auction House
Antique & collectible auction
P.O. Box 118
1st Fri Every month at 6 P.M.
800-286-0033 or 410-586-1161
35 Mi S of Wash. D.C. on Hwy 4

ANTIQUE MALLS, MARKETS/ SHOWS
ANNAPOLIS, MD 21401
Featherstone Square Antique Mall
165 dealers, plus 60 showcases
1550 Whitehall Rd & Rte 50
Sun-Thur 10-7, Fri & Sat 10-8
410-349-8317
At Exits 30 & 31 of US Hwy 50
Maryland's biggest mall

BALTIMORE, MD
One Day Antique & Collectors Market
125-275 dealers; antiques & collectibles
Fairgrounds;   Jan & Jun
Open Sunday 9-4; adm $1.50; $5 at 7am
410-583-5558 Call for exact dates
I-83 Exit 16A
One Sun in Jan, Mar
May, Nov and Dec
Holiday Promotions
P.O. Box 845
Abbington, MD 21009

MARYLAND

BALTIIMORE, MD
Baltimore Bazaar 500
350 dealers; antiques & collectibles
MD State Fairgrounds
Sun 9-4; adm $5; 7 A.M. adm $10
410-583-5558; call for exact dates
I-83 Exit 16
Usually Sat before Easter,
last Sun in Oct and at year end
Holiday Promotions
P.O. Box 845
Abbington, MD 21009

BALTIMORE, MD
Mid Atlantic Antique Market
120 dealers; all antiques & collectibles
Howard County Fairgrounds
Sat & Sun 10AM; $15 Sat at 8:30 A.M.-
5PM, Sun till 4 PM
410-228-8858 Call to confirm
I-70 Exit 80 S on Rte 32 to Rte 144 W
Generally the 1st weekend Sun in Apr
& Oct & preceeding Sat
Sims Rogers
P. O. Box 701
Cambridge, MD 21613,

BALTIMORE, MD 21201
Baltimore Summer Antiques Fair
450 antique dealers, plus 60 book
dealers
Baltimore Convention Center
Sept 2-4, 2005
1 West Pratt St.
adm $12 Fri 12-9, Sat 11-7, Sun 11-5 $8
Downtown in Inner Harbor area
Sha-Dor, Inc
301-933-6994
P.O. Box 12069
Silver Spring, MD 20908

BALTIMORE, MD 21201
Antique Row Stalls
One of 20 shops in an antique row
809-811 N. Howard St.
Open Mon-Sat 11-5; closed Tue (some
shops clsd Sun
410-728-6363
Downtown; from I-95 take M. L. King
Exit North 1.5 mi to traffic light
at Howard St and turn R

BALTIMORE/
ELLICOTT CITY, MD 21043
Taylor's Antique Mall
100 dealers
8197 Main St.
Open Mon-Sat 10:30-5, Sun 12-5
410-465-4444
Corner of Main St & Old Columbia
Pike

BALTIMORE/
ELLICOTT CITY, MD 21043
Antique Depot
100 dealers
3720 Maryland Ave.
Open Mon-Sat 10-5, Sun 12:30-5:30
410-750-2674
Across from the B & O Railroad
Station

CAMBRIDGE, MD 21613
Old Timer's Antique Mall
74 booths
2923 Ocean Gtwy (US 50)
Open Mon-Sat 10-6, Sun 12-6
410-221-1505
E of Cambridge on US 50
on the Eastern Shore

140

COLUMBIA, MD
Columbia Antique Market
60-100 vendors
At the Columbia Mall
Open Sun 10-4; indoors & out
1-800-676-2188
I-95 Exit 41, Rte 175 W
Every Sunday
mid-Apr to mid-Oct
Bellman Corp.
P. O. Box 330.
Parkton, MD 21120

DENTON, MD 21629
Denton Station Antique Mall
75 dealers
24690 Meeting House Rd.
Mon-Sun 10-5
410-479-2200
B.R. 404 Hwy, On the East Shore

EASTON, MD 21601
Foxwell's Antiques & Collectibles Mall
75 dealers
7793 Ocean Gateway
Open daily 10-6
410-820-9705
On US 50 Hwy, On the East Shore

EMMITSBURG, MD 21727
Emmitsburg Antique Mall
120 dealers
1 Chesapeake St.
Open 7 days 10-5
301-447-6471
On US 15 at Penn/MD state line
At traffic light in downtown turn E on
Lincoln Ave and you will see the mall.

In Frederick we had a great lunch
at *Frederick Coffee Co* at the corner of
Patrick and100 East St. Great Chicken
salad sandwich, and of course coffee,
open 24 hrs! 301-698-0039

FREDERICK, MD 21701
Frederick's Best Antiques
30 dealers
301 East 2nd St. (Corner of 2nd & East)
Daily 10-5; Sun 10-5
301-662-1597
I-70 Exit 56 , Rte 70 W 1.6 mi to East St
R to 2nd St

FREDERICK, MD 21701
Emporium Antiques
130 dealers
112 E. Patrick St.
Open 7 days 10-6, Sun 12-6
301-662-7099
I-70 Exit 56, W on Patrick St
to downtown Historic District
walk to 20 Antique shops

FREDERICK, MD 21701
Old Glory Antique Market
100 dealers
5862 Urbana Pike
Open 7 days 10-6, Thur 'til 8pm
301-662-9173
I-70 Exit 54, Rte 355 S 1/4 mi

HAGERSTOWN, MD 21740
Beaver Creek Antique Market (Mall)
150 dealers
20202 National Pike
Open 6 days 9-5, Closed Wed
301-739-8075
I-70 Exit 32-A, US 40 East 1 mi
www.beavercreek.com

141

MARYLAND

HANCOCK, MD 20895
Hancock Antiques Mall
300 dealers
266 N. Pennsylvania Ave.
Open 9-5,Clsd Wed, Sun 12-5
301-678-5959
I-70 Exit 3, Rte 144 w, 1.5 mi to
Pennsylvania Ave, R .75 mi

HANOVER, MD 21076
AAA Antiques Mall
400 dealers
2659 Annapolis Rd.
Open 10-6, 7 days
410-551-4101
I-295 Exit Hwy 175 E 1/4 mi
or I-95 Exit Hwy 175 E about 3 mi
Half way between D. C. & Baltimore)

KENSINGTON, MD 20895
Kensington Antique Market Center
35 dealers; Wash. D.C. area
3760 Howard Ave.
Open Mon-Sat 10-5:30, Sun 12-5:30
301-942-4440
I-495 Exit 33 CT Ave N to Knowles;
go N 1 more block to Howard Ave R
29 shops from 3700-4200 Howard Ave.

NEW MARKET, MD 21774
An antique district/ 1/2 open weekdays
9 E. Main St.
All shops open 10-5 Sat & Sun 12-5
I-70 Exit 62 to downtown
25 antique shops on and off
Main St in downtown New Market

SAVAGE, MD 20763
Antique Center I, II, III at Savage Mill
225 dealers
8600 Foundry Street
Open 7 days 10-6 Thur-Sat till 9
301-604-2077
S of Jct US 1 & Rte 32, 1/2 way
between D.C. & Baltimore; from US 1
go W on Groman Rd, R on Foundry St

WESTMINSTER, MD 21157
Westminster Antique Mall
150 dealers
433 Hahn Rd.
Open 7 days 10-6
410-857-4044
25 mi N of Baltimore on Rte 140(I-795
to 140) corner of Rte 27 N & Hahn Rd

TRAVEL NOTES

GREAT ANTIQUE GETAWAY TO FREDERICK, MD AND GETTYSBURG, PA

WHEN: Anytime

WHERE: Gettysburg, PA and Frederick MD

LODGING: In Gettysburg, the Brafferton Inn, B & B, on US 30 in a fieldstone 1786 home has a Confederate bullet lodged in the fireplace of one room. 717-337-3423.The Gettysburg Hotel, a perfectly restored historic hotel, in downtown, is a good choice. 1-800-528-1234. In addition, a Holiday Inn, Hampton and Days Inns.

RESTAURANT: We enjoyed our lunch in the Springhouse Tavern at the Dobbin House in town on US 15. Behind the fireplace was a hideaway for the under-ground railroad.

LEISURE: Visualize Pickets Charge from the top of the Battlefield, then go down to the Museum and see it dramatically portrayed with sound and lights on a canvas of the scenes that surrounds you on this enormous 1884 cyclorama painting of "Pickets Charge".

ANTIQUING:

1. *Antique Center of Gettysburg*, 100 showcases, 1/2 block S of the square and *Mels Antiques,* 80 dealers, across the street from the Lincoln Diner on Colorado St. Also, scattered shops in Gettysburg.

2. 10 Mi E on US 30 in New Oxford, are 4 malls and 25 antique shops.

3. Hanover, 3 mi S of New Oxford on Rte 94, has *Black Rose Antiques*, 160 dealers.

4.Next, head for Frederick, MD S on US 15. In Emmitsburg turn E at the traffic light on Lincoln Ave and right away you will see the Mall with 120 dealers.

5. Continue S on US 15 to I-70E to Market St. (I-70 Exit 54) N to Patrick St.,the Historic District and *Emporium Antiques,* 130 dealers at 112 E. Patrick St. Nearby we had a great lunch at the Frederick Coffee Co. on the corner of Patrick and Frederick, 100 East St. Great chicken salad sandwich.and of course, great coffee. Open 24 hours! Phone 301-698-0039

6. *Frederick's Best Antiques* at 200 East St. (Corner 2nd & East Sts.)

7. There are about 20 antique shops in the Historic District so inquire as you antique.

RESTAURANT: If you like Italian, you will love *Di Francesco's* at 26 Market St. in Frederick Historic District. We enjoyed the great Italian food served there.

8. Next is New Market, 10 mi E. of Frederick on I-70 with 25 antique shops downtown and off Main St.,an Antique District.

There is more antiquing to the west in Middletown, Hagerstown, Hancock & Berkeley Springs. Or to the south in Kensington and Alexandria.

Confederate buffs would surely like to continue on to Fredricksburg, VA for that Great Antique Getaway.

MASSACHUSETTS,
East

95

93

Rowley

Topsfield

128

Essex

95

Salem

Boston

Waltham

Cambridge

Holliston

3

Kingston

495

Provincetown
Plymouth

95

495

Buzzard's Bay

Seekonk

Taunton

Sandwich

Brewster

6

New Bedford

A

Hyannis

Dennis

LEGEND

2 (A) = 2 Auction Companies

● = Cities w/ Antique Malls listed in guide

MASSACHUSETTS - EAST

WEEKEND ANTIQUE EVENTS

Rowley-Todds Farm, 100-200 dealers, **Sun Apr thru Nov**
Topsfield-Indoor /Outdoor Antique Show, **4th weekend in Jun**
ANTIQUE DISTRICTS/ VILLAGES
Boston's St. Charles St., Cape Cod, Essex, Newburyport

ANTIQUE MALLS, MARKETS AND SHOWS

BOSTON, MA 02114
Boston Antique Co-op #1
One of 40 antique shops on Charles St.
119 Charles St., lower level
Open Mon-Sat 10-6; Sun 12-6
617-227-9810
Take L Exit from I-93, northbound, Storrow Dr. Exit, straight thru traffic light to Charles St. Park & walk

BOSTON/
CAMBRIDGE, MA 02141
Cambridge Antique Market (Mall)
150 dealers
201 Monsignor O'Brien Hwy.
Open Tue-Sun 11-6
617-868-9655
Take the Storrow Dr Cambridge Exit from I-93 follow Rte 28 N which is Msgr. O'Brien Hwy. Just a few blocks

BOSTON/
CAMBRIDGE, MA 02139
Antiques on Cambridge St.
100 dealers
1076 Cambridge St
Tu-Sun 11-6
617-234-0001
I-90 Exit 18, to Cambridge, cross river, take River St. (which changes to Prospect St.) to Cambridge St., R.

CAPE COD/ BREWSTER, MA
A dozen Antique Stores on Main St.
Most open 10-5 in season (Rte 6A).
Closed from Thanksgiving thru Memorial Day

CAPE COD/
BUZZARDS BAY, MA 02532
The Marketplace Antiques Co-op
30 dealer spaces
61 Main St.
Open Mon-Thur 10-4, 10-5 summer
508-759-2114
Rte 25 Exit 1, W 4 mi on US 6. There are 10 antique stores, all on Main St.

CAPE COD/
DENNIS, MA 02638
Antique Center of Cape Cod
250 dealers
243 Main St.
Open daily until 5 P.M. year round.
508-385-6400
Route 6A (Main St.)
13 shops on Main street
US Hwy 6 Exit 8 or 9 to Rte 6A.

MASSACHUSETTS - EAST

CAPE COD/
PROVINCETOWN, MA 02657
Scott Dinsmore Antiques
One of 8 shops on Commercial St.
179 Commercial St.
Open 7 days 11am-11pm in summer
508-487-2236
Downtown
In winter, after New Years, open Fri-Sun 11-5. Whalers Wharf has cluster of shops.

In Hyannis we enjoyed great Italian food at Alberto's Ristorante. The cannelloni especially exceptional. A favorite for 16 years at 360 Main St. 508-778-1770

CAPE COD/SANDWICH, MA 02563
Sandwich Antiques Center
150 dealers
131 Rte 6A
Open 7 days 10-5
508-833-3600
Downtown

ESSEX, MA 01929
Chebacco
One of 18 Antique Shops on Main St
38 Main St
Open 7 days, 10:30-4:30
978-768-7371
Rte 128 Exit 15, School St to Rte 133,

In Essex we enjoy the fine food and harbor view at *Tom Shea's Restaurant*, 122 Main St. 978-768-6931

HAVERHILL, MA 01832
Haverhill Antique Market
85 dealers
90 Washington St. (Rte 110)
Open Tue-Sun 10-5
978-374-6644
I-495 Exit 49 Rte 110 E to downtown
Historic District

HOLLISTON, MA 01746
Antiques Plus
30 dealers
Rte. 16
Mon-Sat 10-5; Sun 12-5
508-429-9165
I-95 Exit 22, Rte 16 S 10 mi.

HOLLISTON, MA 01746
Holliston Antiques
50 dealers, plus consignors
798 Washington St. Rte 16
Summer Tu-Fr 10-4, Sat 10-5, Sun 1-5
508-429-0428 Closed Mon
Winter Tu-Sat 10-5 Sun 1-5, Clsd Mon
I-95 Exit 22, Rte 16 S 10 mi

NEW BEDFORD, MA 02746
New Bedford Antique Company
250 dealers
85 Coggeshell Street
Open Mon-Sat 10-5; Sun 12-5
508-993-7600
Located on I-195, Eastbound exit 16, Westbound Exit 17

PLYMOUTH, MA 02360
Plymouth Antiques Trading Co.
125 dealers
8 Court St.
Open 10-5, clsd Tue in Jan-Feb
508-746-3450
Rte 3 Exit 6, US Hwy 44, E to downtown

PLYMOUTH, MA 02360
Main Street Antiques
100 dealers
46 Main St.
Open 7 days 10-5, clsd Tue in winter, Sun 12-5
508-747-8887
Rte 3 Exit 6, US Hwy 44 E to Main St.

PLYMOUTH, MA 02360
Main St. Marketplace
60 dealers
58 Main St.
Open 7 days 10-5, clsd Tue in winter, Sun 12-5
508-747-8875
Rte 3 Exit 6, US Hwy 44 E to Main St.

ROWLEY, MA 01969
Todd's Farm Antiques & Flea Market
100-200 dealers, Market opens Apr 3rd till Nov.
Rte 1A
Sun dawn to dusk; adm & park free
978-948-2217
Main St of Rowley
Dozen shops in the house & barn
Every Sun Apr thru Nov

SALEM, MA
Antique Gallery
35 dealers
Pickering Wharf, 69 Wharf St.
Open 7 days 11-5
978-741-3113
On the Salem waterfront, 6 shops nearby.

SEEKONK, MA 02771
Vinny's Antique Center
300 dealers
380 Fall River Avenue, Rte. 114A
Open Mon-Sat 10-5; Fri 'til 9
508-336-0800
I-195 Exit 1 to Rte 114A

Great food at the *Old Grist Mill Restaurant,* just down the red brick walk from Vinny's Antique Center in Seekonk by the duck pond. Open for lunch or dinner at 390 Fall River Ave. 508-336-8460

TAUNTON, MA 02780
Taunton Antique Center
300 spaces
19 Main Street Rte 44
Open Mon-Sat 10-5, Sun 12-5
508-821-3333
I-495 Exit 8, 4 mi S; or Rte 24 Exit 13, W on 44, 2 mi.

MASSACHUSETTS - EAST

TOPSFIELD, MA
The Great Indoor/Outdoor Antique
Show
Over 200 dealers
Topsfield Fairgrounds
Sat & Sun 9-4, $5.50 adm.
978-535-4811 to confirm
I-95 Exit 50, N 2 mi on US 1.
Generally 4th weekend in Jun (25th)
Also Ephemera City Show on June 4th
Drummer Boys Antique Shows
P.O. Box 2204
Peabody, MA 01960
wwwbornsteinshows.com

WALTHAM, MA 02453
Massachusetts Antiques Co-op
100 dealers
100 Felton Street
Open 6 days 10-5;Thur till 8, closed
Tues.
781-893-8893
www.massantiques.com
I-95 Exit 26 E to Main Street,
R on Moody, 1st light R onto Felton. In
the area 1 other antique mall.

MASSACHUSETTS - EAST

TRAVEL NOTES

MASSACHUSETTS,
West

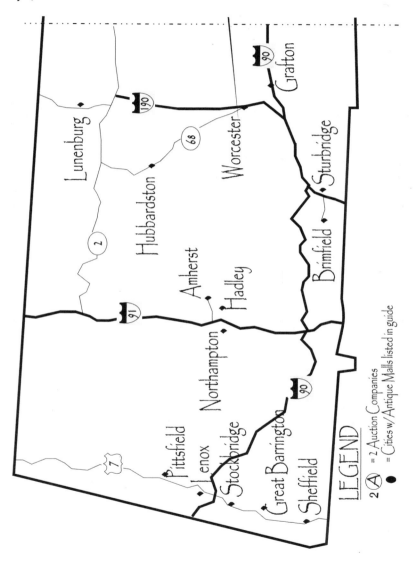

Grafton

90

190

Lunenburg

68

Worcester

Sturbridge

Hubbardston

2

Brimfield

Amherst

Hadley

91

Northampton

90

Pittsfield

Lenox

Stockbridge

Great Barrington

Sheffield

7

<u>LEGEND</u>

2Ⓐ = 2 Auction Companies
● = Cities w/Antique Malls listed in guide

MASSACHUSETTS - WEST

WEEKEND ANTIQUE EVENTS

Brimfield, 6 separate markets totalling 2000 dealers,
running simultaneously in mid May, **early Jul and mid Sep**
Grafton inside & out, **Sundays & Holidays   Mid-Mar thru Dec**
Hadley Flea Market, 200 dealers, **3rd Sun in April thru 1st Sun in Nov**
Hubbardston, Sundays, **Apr-Nov**

ANTIQUE DISTRICTS/VILLAGES
 Great Barrington, Sheffield
ANTIQUE MALLS, MARKETS/ SHOWS

BRIMFIELD, MA
**On US 20, half way between I-90
Exits 8 & 9 (6 separate antique
markets simultaneously, plus 12
other smaller markets.) Open 6 days
in the 1st half of May, Jul & Sept.
Check or call for dates which are
about the same every year. Some
markets start on Tue with additional
markets opening Wed, Thur & Fri.
Park & walk to all markets totaling
2,000-3,000 dealers.**

BRIMFIELD, MA 01010
Brimfield Meadows
250 exhibitors;all antiques & collectibles
P.O. Box 374
Open Tue-Sun 6-6; adm free; park $5.00
508-245-9427

BRIMFIELD, MA 01010
Shelton Antique Shows
175 dealers; antiques & collectibles
P.O. Box 124
Daybreak Tues-Sun; adm free
413-245-3591

BRIMFIELD, MA 01010
Heart-O-The-Mart
600 exhibitors; all antiques
P.O. Box 26
Open 9 A.M. Wed-Sun
413-245-9556
Mid May, Early July, Mid Sept
*homepage: www.brimfield-hotm.com
email: info@brimfield-hotm.com*

BRIMFIELD, MA 01010
Mays Antique Market
600 dealers; all antiques
P.O. Box 416
9 AM Thur-Sat; adm $5
413-245-9271

BRIMFIELD, MA 01566
New England Motel Antique Market
Brimfield Antiques & Collectibles Show
400 dealers; all antiques
30 Palmer Rd, Rte 20, parking $5
Open 6 A.M. Wed-Sun in Brimfield-2005
dates:
May 11-15, July 6-10, Sept 7-11
508-347-2179
Marie Doldoorian
P. O. Box 186
Sturbridge, MA 01566
www.antiques-brimfield.com

MASSACHUSETTS - WEST

BRIMFIELD, MA 01566
Brimfield Antique Center
80 dealers w/ 60 showcases
Rte 20
Open 7 days 10-5, Sun 11-5
413-245-9269 or 508-347-3929
**Rte 84 from Hartford W on Rte 20 for
6 mi Rte 91 E on Rte 20**

BRIMFIELD, MA 01010
J & J Promotions
500-750 exhibitors
Rt 20; P.O. Box 385
Fri 6am-5pm adm $5; Sat 9-5 adm $3
413-245-3436

GREAT BARRINGTON, MA 01230
Coffman's Antique Market (Mall)
200 dealers, 2 bldgs.
P.O. Box 592, Stockbridge Rd., Route 7
Open 7 days 10-5
413-528-9282
**I-90 Exit 2, Rte 102 W to Rte 7 S
In the yellow building and red barn.
May-Oct open till 6 PM Fri & Sat**

GREAT BARRINGTON, MA 01230
Olde Antiques Market(Mall)
75 dealers
Rte 7 Stockbridge Rd.
Open Daily 10-5
413–528-1840
Coffman's & Olde are neighbors.

GREAT BARRINGTON, MA 01230
Emporium
25 dealers
319 Main St.
Open Mon-Sat 10-5; Sun 11-4
413-528-1660
Downtown Great Barrington

There are 17 other single & multi-
dealer shops in Great Barrington,
and 19 more shops 6 mi S. on U.S.
Hwy 7 in Sheffield, also on Main St.
In Stockbridge is the centry-old
Red Lion Inn with its wrought iron
elevator, huge Oriental rugs and great
fireplace in the lobby. It is an interesting place to stay or just to stop in to
have a bite or drink and look it
over.413-298-5545

GRAFTON, MA
Grafton Flea Market
300 dealers; 30% antiques/collectibles
On Rte 140; indoors & out
Open 6-4; adm 1.00; park free
508-839-2217
**I-495 Exit 21B (Upton)
S 5 mi to Rte. 140, R 1 mi.
Sun & Holidays Apr-Dec**
Harry Peters
PO Box 206
Grafton, MA 01519

HADLEY, MA
Olde Hadley Flea Market
Up to 200 dealers; antiques & coll
On Rte 47
Open Sunday 6-4; adm & park free
413-586-0352
**I-91 Exit 19, E to Rte 47, S 2 mi.
3rd Sun in Apr thru 1st Sun in Nov
outdoors weather permitting**
Raymond Szala
45 Lawrence Plain Rd.
Hadley, MA 01035

HUBBARDSTON, MA
Rietta Ranch Flea Market
500 dealers, 35% antiques & collectibles
On Rte 68
Adm free; park free; indoors & out
978-632-0559
18 mi N of Worcester on Rte 68
Sundays Apr thru Nov,
rain or shine
John Kojiol & Ms Williams
P.O. Box 35
Hubbardston, MA 01452-0035

LUNENBURG, MA 01462
Jeffrey's Antique Co-op Mall
175 dealers
54 Chase Rd (Rte 13)
Open 7 days 10-5; Fri 10-6
978-582-7831
Rte 2 Exit Rte 13 N

NORTHHAMPTON, MA 01060
Antique Center of Northhampton
50 dealers
9 1/2 Market Street
Clsd Wed; Sun 12-5; Other days 10-5
413-584-3600
I-91 Exit 19, Rte 9, 1 mi W

STURBRIDGE, MA 01566
Showcase Antique Center
185 showcases with furniture
Entrance to Sturbridge Village
Mon, Wed-Sat 10-5, Sun 12-5; Closed Tue
508-347-7190
I-90 Exit 9, 1 mi W on Rte 20 At entrance to
Old Sturbridge Village

STURBRIDGE, MA 01566
Fairgrounds Antique Center
100 booths & showcases
362 Main St., Rte 20
 Open Mon-Sat 10-5, Sunm 12-5
508-347-3926

1/4 mi E. of Old Sturbridge Village
In Sturbridge our favorite restaurant
is *"The Whistling Swan"* at 502 Main
St. (Rte 20). Lunch & dinner Tue-Sun.
be sure to check out their great
homemade desserts. Upstairs is the
"Ugly Duckling Loft" in the
atmosphere of a rustic barn.

TRAVEL NOTES

GREAT GETAWAY TO ANTIQUE BRIMFIELD AND THE BEAUTIFUL BERKSHIRES IN MASS.

WHEN: 6 Days during 1st half of May, July, & Sept.Call one of the exhibitors listed in our text for exact dates.

WHERE: Brimfield Antique Market, near Sturbridge, 2000 dealers along both sides of US Hwy 20 just south of I-90 between Exits 8 & 9.Brimfield is one of the largest and finest antique markets in the country.

Due to the popularity of this Market it is advisable to make reservations far in advance.

LODGING: In Sturbridge, MA Public House Historic Inn and Country Lodge on 60 rolling acres with outdoor pool and tennis facilities, is our favorite. 1-800-PUBLICK.Or Hampton Inn, Holiday Inn Express, and Comfort Inn, are other possibilities in Sturbridge.

RESTAURANTS: In Sturbridge, we like to eat at the *Whistling Swan*, a charming restaurant at 502 Main St. or *The Ugly Duckling* located upstairs in the same building in an old barn atmosphere.

ANTIQUING:After doing the Brimfield Market, you will find Sturbridge I-90 Exit 9, 1 mi W on Rte 20 at entrance to Sturbridge Village is *Showcase Antique Center*, 185 showcases and *Fairgrounds Antique Center,* 100 dealers at 232 Main (Rte.20) There is more great antiquing in the beautiful Berkshires. Take I-90 W to Exit 2. Go W on Rte 8 to Stockbridge. Fans of Shaker furniture will be interested in Hancock Shaker Village with 21 Shaker bldgs. with original Shaker furniture, artifacts, weavers & woodworkers.This is 5 mi W of Pittsfield which is 12 mi N. of Stockbridge. Adm. $15.

LODGING: For this part of the Getaway you will want to stay in the century old Red Lion Inn, in Stockbridge. It's old iron elevator, and huge Oriental rugs and great fireplace make it a charming old world type atmosphere. 413-298-5545. The Red Lion Inn is at the corner of Main St and Rte 7.

ANTIQUING: The antiquing here is South on Rte 7, about 30 single and multi-dealer shops in Great Barrington and Sheffield with mostly quality antiques. There is a 25 dealer mall at 319 Main St., in downtown Great Barrington, otherwise the shops are on Rte 7.

This completes this Getaway, but if time allows there are 50 antiques stores in Woodbury, CT about 50 miles So of Sheffield, MA. Rte 7 S to Rte 63 S to US 6 W. Also, you could combine this with the Connecticut Getaway.

TRAVEL NOTES

MICHIGAN - North

LEGEND

2 (A) = 2 Auction Companies

● = Cities w/ Antique Malls listed in guide

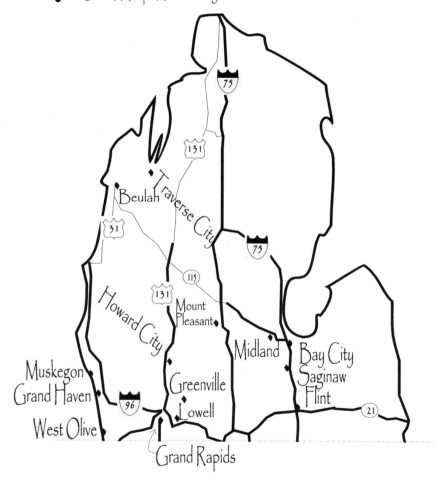

MICHIGAN - North

Howard City-Burley Park Antique & Collectible Market,
Memorial Day, Jul 4th, Labor Day, 1st Sun in Aug & Oct.
Midland Michigan Antique Festival, 1000 dealers,
1st weekend after Memorial Day & 4th weekend in Jul & Sep

ANTIQUE MALLS, MARKETS/ SHOWS

BAY CITY, MI 48708
Bay City Antiques Center
53,000 sq ft, 1oo dealers
1010 N. Water Street
Mon-Sat 10-5; Sun 12-5; Fri 'til 8
989-893-1116
**I-75 Exit 162A to downtown,
1st L after river, Saginaw St. to 3rd,
L 1 block to Water St
Will have auctions**

FLINT/
FLUSHING, MI 48433
R & J Needful Things Antique Center
150 dealers plus
6398 W. Pierson
Open 7 days 10-5
810-659-2663
I-75 Exit 122, W 2.5 mi

GRAND HAVEN, MI 49417
West Michigan Antique Mall
80 dealers
13279 168th Ave.
Open 7 daysMon-Sat 10-6, Sun 12:30-6
616-842-0370
**US 31 S (15 mi S Muskegon &
2.5 mi S Grand Haven)**

GRAND RAPIDS, MI 49508
Victoria's Warehouse
60 dealers
449 Century St.
Open Tue-Fri 10-6, Sat 10-6, Sun 12-5
616-235-929
**US 131 Exit Wealthy, turn R on
Granville, R on Century go S for 2
blks. 2 other malls in this warehouse.to
make 200 dealers total**

GREENVILLE, MI 48838
Greenville Antique Center
85 dealers
400 S. Lafayette
Open Mon-Thur 11:30-6; Fri 11:30-6, Sat
10-6, Sun 12-6
616-754-5540
**17 mi E of US 131 Exit 101,
north of Grand Rapids or corner of M-
57 East and M-91**

HOWARD CITY, MI
Burley Park Antiques & Collectibles
Market and Car Show
800 dealers
M-46 Howard City Heights
Open 8-4; adm $2
231-354-6354
**US 131 Exit 120 E 1 mi
Memorial Day, July 4, Labor Day,
1st Sun in Aug and Oct**
Burley Park, Ltd.
4540 Baily Rd
Coral, MI, 49322

MICHIGAN - North

LOWELL, MI 49331
Flat River Antique Mall
60 dealers
212 W. Main
Open 7 days 10-6, summer hours
extended
616-897-5360
**14 mi E of Grand Rapids on M-21,
or I-96 Exit 52, N 4 mi.**

MIDLAND, MI 48642
Michigan Antique Festival
100's of booths; antiques & collectibles
2156 Rudy Court
Sat 8-6; Sun 8-4pm , Adm $5, Fri $15
989-687-9001 7pm-9pm, Mon-Fri
7 buildings, & outdoor booths
**I-75 Exit 162 Bay City, W on US 10 to
Midland Fairgrounds. June 4 & 5, 1st
weekend after Memorial Day, & 4th
wkend Jul 23 &24 & Sep. 24 & 25th.**
Website: www.miantiquefestival.com

MOUNT PLEASANT, MI 48858
 Antique Center
50 dealers
1718 S. Mission St. (B.R.US 27)
Open daily 10-6 ; Sun 11-6
989-772-2672
On B. R. US 27 Hwy central Michigan

MUSKEGON, MI 49445
Memory Lane Antique Mall
40 dealers
2073 Holton Rd
Open 7 days,10-6 winter 11-6
231-744-8510
**In the Plaza at US 31 Exit for M 120
which is Holton Rd**

SAGINAW, MI 48604
Antique Warehouse Speciality Shoppes
75 dealers, 20,000 sq. ft.
1122 Tittabawassee Rd
Open Mon-Sat 10-6; Sun 12-6
989-755-4343
**I-675 Exit 4 (Tittabawassee Rd)
I-75 Exit 154 R at Exit on Adams 1/2 mi
to Tittabawassee take R.**

TRAVERSE CITY, MI 49684
Wilson Antiques Mall
50 dealers
123 S. Union
Open Mon-Sat 10-6; Sun 11-5, winter
10-5:30
231-946-4177
Downtown between Front St & State St.

WEST OLIVE, MI 49460
Lake Shore Antique Shop
80 dealers
10300 W. Olive Rd (on US 31)
Open Mon-Sat 10-6, Sun 12-5
616-847-2429
**11 mi N of Holland, on east side of
US 31.**

TRAVEL NOTES

MICHIGAN- South

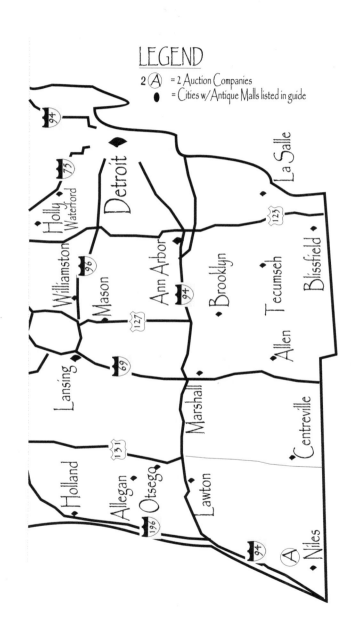

LEGEND

2 (A) = 2 Auction Companies
● = Cities w/ Antique Malls listed in guide

La Salle

94

75

Holly
Waterford

Detroit

123

Blissfield

Williamston

96

Mason

Ann Arbor

94

Brooklyn

Tecumseh

Allen

127

Lansing

69

Marshall

Centreville

131

Holland

Allegan

Otsego

196

Lawton

94

Niles

A

MICHIGAN - South

Allegan Antique Market, 300 dealers, **last Sun Apr thru Sep**
Ann Arbor Antique Market, 350 dealers, **3rd Sun Apr-Oct., 1st Sun in Nov**
Centreville Caravan Antique Market, 600 dealers,
      generally 1st Sun in May & Jun & 2nd Sun in Jul, Aug & Oct

ANTIQUE DISTRICTS/VILLAGES
    Allen, Blissfield, Marshall, Williamston

AUCTION/ESTATE SALE CO'S
NILES, MI 49120
AAA Straight-Up Auction
Antiques, furniture, & collectible auctions;
2725 Geyer Rd.
4 to 6 sales per month
616-695-7701

ANTIQUE MALLS, MARKETS AND SHOWS
ALLEN, MI 49227
Allen Antique Mall
427 Booths
9011 W. Chicago
Open 7 days 10-5
517-869-2788
I-69 Exit 13, (US Hwy 12) E 10 mi
Billed as Antique Capital of MI,
there are 4 malls and 12 shops here.

ALLEGAN, MI
Antique Market
400 dealers; antiques & collectibles
Fairgrounds, downtown Allegan
7:30-4; adm $3; park free
616-453-8780 or 616-735-3333
From US 131 Exit M-89W.
Allegan is 10 mi W of US 131 Exit 49.
Last Sun Apr, May, Jun, Jul, Aug, Sep
Larry Wood
2030 Blueberry Dr. NW
Grand Rapids MI 49504

ANN ARBOR, MI
Antique Market
350 dealers; all antiques
5055 Ann Arbor Saline Rd.
Open 6-4; adm $5
850-984-0122
3rd Sun in April thru Oct. & 1st Sun
in November. Also preceeding Sat in
April & Sept.
Nancy Straube
P. O. Box 1260
Panacea, Fla 32346

BLISSFIELD, MI 49228
Blissfield Antique Mall #1
125 dealers
105 W. Adrian
Open Tue-Sat 10-5; Sun 12-5
517-486-2236
US 23 Exit 5, W on US 223,
10 mi to downtown Blissfiled

In Blissfield we enjoyed a great meal
on the Sunday buffet of beef burgundy,
Oskar pancakes, veggie lasagne,
among numerous selections at the
"*Stable*"behind Hathaway House built
in 1851. Open 7 days a week, lunch &
dinner. In town on US 223.
517-486-2144

MICHIGAN - South

BLISSFIELD, MI 49228
Blissfield Antiques Mall #2
90 dealers
109 W. Adrian (US 223)
Open Tue-Sat 10-5; Sun 12-5
517-486-3544
US 23 Exit 5, W on US 223, 10 mi to
Downtown Blissfield
5 other shops in town

BLISSFIELD, MI 49228
Williams Crossroad Antiques
25 dealers
10003 E. US 223
Open Tue-Fr 10-5; Sat 10-6, Sun 10-6
517-486-3315
At the east edge of Blissfield on US 223

BROOKLYN, MI 49230
Pinetree Centre Antique Mall
50 dealers
129 N. Main
Open Mon-Sat 10-5; Sun 12-5
517-592-3808
On the Square; on M-50,
10 mi S of Jackson

CENTREVILLE
Centreville Antiques Market
300 dealers; all antiques & collectibles
Centreville Fairgrounds
Open 7-3; adm $4; park free
847-768-0298(call to confirm dates)
US 131 Exit M-86 E 6 mi; in S MI
Generally 1st Sun in May;
2nd Sun in Jun,Jul, Aug & Oct;
Centreville Antique Market
1510 N. Hoyne
Chicago, IL 60622-1804

In Detroit there is a 52 room mansion
with Tiffany stained glass windows
built in 1894 at a cost of $400,000.

It is now a restaurant called *The*
***Witney,* and is known for fine dining.**
Sunday Brunch is great. Open for
lunch Wed-Fri, dinner 7 days. 4421
Woodward Ave. 313-832-5700

DETROIT /
DEARBORN, MI 48124
Village Antiques
25 dealers
22630 Michigan Avenue
Mon-Sat 10:30-5:30,Thurs till 7:30, Sun
12-5
313-563-1230
US 12; between US 24 & M 39

DETROIT /
LIVONIA, MI 48150
Town & Country Antique Mall
48 dealers
31630 Plymouth Rd.
Th-Sat 11-8; other days 11-6
734-425-4344
I-96 Exit 175 S on Merriman,
W on Plymouth

DETROIT /
NORTHVILLE, MI 48167
Knightsbridge Antique Mall
200 plus dealers, 26,000 sq. ft.
42305 W. 7 Mile Rd.
Open daily 11-6, Wed til 8
248-344-7200
I-275 Exit 7 Mile Rd W 2 mi

HOLLAND, MI 49424
Harvest Antiques & Collectibles
100 booths
12330 James
Open 7 days 10-8
616-395-0823
US 31 at James
In the Holland Outlet Center

HOLLY, MI 48442
Arcade Antique Mall
25 dealers
108 Historic Battle Alley
Open Mon-Sat 10:30-5:30; Sun 12-5
248-634-8800
I-75 Exit 98, W 4 mi.

HOLLY, MI 48442
Water Tower Antique Mall
60 dealers
310 Broad Street
Open Tue-Sat 10-5; Sun 11-5
248-634-3500
Across from water tower;
US 23 Exit 79 E or I-75 Exit 101 W to
Holly

LASALLE, MI 48145
American Heritage Antique Mall
102 dealers
5228 S. Otter Creek Rd.
Open 7 days 10-6
734-242-3430
I-75 Exit 9, 9 mi N of Toledo

MARSHALL, MI 49068
J. H. Cronin Antique Center
35 dealers
101 W. Michigan
Open Mon-Sat 10-6; Sun 12-5
269-789-0077

Downtown, intersection of I-94 & 65
There are a half-dozen other antique
stores nearby on Michigan Ave.

When possible, we plan to eat lunch or
dinner in *Schuler's* Original 100 year
old restaurant in Marshall, Downtown.

NILES, MI 49120
Michiana Antique Mall
100 dealers
2423 M51/Bus.31
Open 7 days 10-6
269-684-7001 or 1-800-559-4694
5 mi N of I-80/90 Exit 77 (South Bend)

NILES, MI 49120
Pickers Paradise Antique Mall
100 dealers
2809 US 33 S
Open 7 days 10-6
269-683-6644
US 33 Hwy

NILES, MI 49120
Four Flags Antique Mall
50 dealers
218 N. 2nd St.
Open Mon- Sat 10-6; Sun 12-6 in
summer, starting end of May
(winter 10-5)
269-683-6681
Downtown

OTSEGO, MI 49078
Otsego Antiques Mall
35 dealers
114 W. Allegan St. (M-89)
Open Tue-Sat 10-6; Sun 1-5, clsd Mon
269-694-6440
US 131 Exit 49B, M89 W 5 mi

163

MICHIGAN - South

TECUMSEH, MI 49286
Hitching Post Antique Mall
40 dealers
1322 E. Monroe
Open daily 10-5:30
517-423-8277
**M50 near M52 about 23 mi S W of
Ann Arbor**

TRAVEL NOTES

WATERFORD, MI 48329
Great Midwestern Antique Emporium
50 dealers
5233 Dixie Hwy
Open 7 days 10-5, clsd major Holidays
248-623-7460
I-75 Exit 93 S 4 1/2 mi

WILLIAMSTON, MI 48895
Antiques Market of Williamston
75 dealers
2991 Williamston Rd.
Open 7 days 10-6
517-655-1350
I-96 Exit 117 N 1/3 mi

WILLIAMSTON, MI 48895
Williamston Village Mall
53 dealers
1435 Grand River Ave.
Open 10-6, Thur till 8, Sun 12-6
517-655-4321
**I-96 Exit 117 N 2 mi into downtown
About 5 shops downtown Williamston
at Grand River & Putnam**

TRAVEL NOTES

MINNESOTA

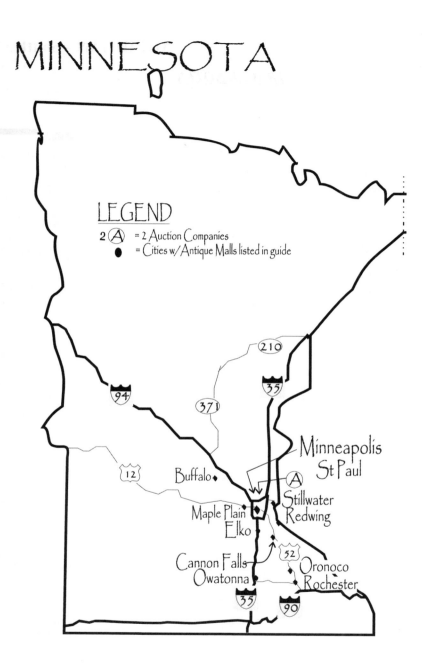

LEGEND

2 (A) = 2 Auction Companies
● = Cities w/ Antique Malls listed in guide

210

[35]

94

371

Minneapolis
St Paul

12 Buffalo ◆

(A)
Stillwater
Redwing

Maple Plain ◆
Elko

52

Cannon Falls
Owatonna ●

Oronoco
Rochester

[35]

[90]

MINNESOTA

WEEKEND ANTIQUE EVENTS

Minneapolis/Elko Extravaganza, 300 dealers,
Sat-Sun-Mon of Summer holidays
Minneapollis Star of the North Antique Show, 200-300 booths,
One Sat/Sun in Feb, Jul & Nov
Rochester Gold Rush, 1400 booths, **2nd W.E. in May, 3rd in Aug, 4th in Sep**
St. Paul, Prime Antiques Spectacular, Fairgrounds, 1000 dealers,
Generally 3rd weekend in April, and 2nd in June and Oct.
Oronoco, Gold Rush, 1000 dealers, **3rd Weekend in Aug**

ANTIQUE DISTRICTS/ VILLAGES
Stillwater

AUCTION/ESTATE SALE CO'S
St. Paul/Little Canada, Mn 55117
Rose Galleries
Antique Auction
3180 Country Dr.
every Wed at 6pm
I-694 to Rice St. S
651-484-1415
E on Country Rd C to Lincoln North.

**ANTIQUE MALLS, MARKETS/
SHOWS**
BUFFALO, MN 55313
Buffalo Nickel Antique Mall
65 dealers
Hwy 55
Open 10-6 daily
763-682-4735
I-94 Exit 193, S 11 mi.

CANNON FALLS, MN 55009
Country Side Antique Mall
45 dealers,
31752 65th Ave.
Mon-Sat 9:30-5:30, Sun 11-5
507-263-0352
**30 mi S of Mpls on US 52. On
frontage road behind Service Station**

MINNEAPOLIS, MN
Star of the North Antique Show
200-350 booths
Convention Center
Fri 10-8, Sat 10-6, Sun 10-5
507-288-0320 or 346-7530
Generally in Feb, July and Nov
Adm $5, Call for schedule dates
1300 block of 3rd Ave. South
Richard Townsend,
P.O. Box 726,
Rochester, MN 55903

MINNEAPOLIS
BURNSVILLE, MN 55337
Antiques Minnesota
325 dealers
191 River Ridge Circle
Mon-Fri 10-6, Sat 10-6, Sun 12-6
952-894-7200
**N.E. Corner of 35W & 13N
I-35 W Exit 3 A, left**

MINNESOTA

MINNEAPOLIS, MN 5511
Theatre Antiques
25 dealers
2934 Lyndale Ave
Mon-Sat 11-6, Sun 12-6
612-822-4884
Just N of Lake Ave, 6 blks E of Hinnepin

MINNEAPOLIS/ ANOKA, MN 55303
Antiques on Main
50 dealers
212 E. Main St.
Daily 9-6, Wed & Thur until 8pm
763-323-3990
I-94 Exit 29, N on US 169

MINNEAPOLIS/ ELKO, MN
The Great Minnesota Extravaganza
300 dealers, Adm $4.00, park free
I-35 and Country Rd 2
Open 1st day 8-5, other days 10-5
952-461-2400
I-35 Exit 76 W
Sat-Sun-Mon of 3 Summer holidays
Traders Promotions
7541 Bryant Ave
South Richfield, Mn 55423

MINNEAPOLIS/ HOPKINS, MN 55343
Hopkins Antiques Mall
70 dealers
1008 Main Street.
Open Mon-Sat 11-6, Sun 11-5
952-931-9748
I-494 Exit 16 E into Hopkins,
1 mi W of US 169

MINNEAPOLIS/ HOPKINS, MN 55344
Blake Antique Mall
45 dealers
901 Main Street
Mon-Sat 11-6, Sun 12-5
952-930-3283 or 952-930-0477
One mi W of US 169

MINNEAPOLIS/ MAPLE PLAIN, MN 55359
Country School House Shops
200 dealers
5300 Hwy 12
Mon-Sat 10-6, Sun 12-5
763-479-6353
20 mi W Minneapolis on US 12/I394

ORONOCO, MN 55960
Downtown Oronoco Gold Rush Market
1000 dealers, antiques & collectibles
P. O. Box 266
Dawn to Dusk
Phone: 507-367-2111
About 7 mi N of Rochester on US 52
Third weekend in Aug; Fri, Sat & Sun

OWATONNA, MN 55060
Uncle Tom's Antique Mall & Rock Shop
40 dealers
2923 US Hwy 14 West
Open Mon-Fri 10-5, Sat 10-4, Sun 12-4
507-451-2254
Closed Sundays Jan thru Apr15
I-35 Exit 42 W 3/4 mi on Hwy 14
ROCHESTER, MN

Gold Rush Show
1400 booths, Adm free; park $4
Olmsted County Fairgrounds; PO Box 726
Bldgs Fri 8-8pm, Sat/Sun 8-8
507-288-0320 or 346-7530
1400 Block S. Broadway just East of
US Hwy 63; 2nd full weekend in May,
3rd in Aug, 3rd every year in Sep
Richard Townsend
P.O. Box 726
Rochester, MN 55903

RED WING, MN 55066
Al's Antique Mall
12,000 sq. ft.
1314 Old West Main St.
Mon-Sat 9-6, Sun 10-6, winter clsd 5PM
651-388-0572
You can see it just off Hwy 61
on Old West Main going thru town

ST. PAUL, MN 55104
Antique Minnesota
80 dealers
1197 University Ave W.
Closed Tue, Sun 12-5 other days 10-5
651-646-0037
I-94 Exit 239 Lexington Ave.
N 2 blks, W on University, 3 blks

STILLWATER, MN 55082
Antiques St. Croix
65 dealers
124 2nd St. So.
Mon-Sat 10-5, Sun 1-5
651-351-2888
8 other shops on Main St.

ST. PAUL, MN

Prime Promotions Antiques Spectacular
1000 dealers
Mn State Fairgrounds
Sat 8-6, Sun 9-5, indoors & out
651-771-3476 Call for information
I-94 Exit 238, N 2 mi on Snelling Ave
Generally the 3rd weekend in
Apr, 2nd in Jun & Oct.
Prime Promotions, Attn: Rick
2097 E. Hawthorne
St. Paul, Mn 55119
www.mnantiqueshows.com

STILLWATER, MN 55082
American Gothic Antiques
45 dealers
236 S. Main.
Mon-Thur 10-5, Fri & Sat 10-8, Sun 11-6
651-439-7709
10 mi E of St. Paul on Hwy 36
then 1/2 mi N on Hwy 95

STILLWATER, MN 55082
Mill Antiques
75 dealers
410 N. Main Street
Open 7 days 10-6
651-430-1816

STILLWATER, MN 55082
Midtown Antique Mall
75 dealers
301 S. Main Street
Mon-Thur 10-5; Fri & Sat 10-7; Sun 11-6
summer hours extended
651-430-0808

MISSISSIPPI

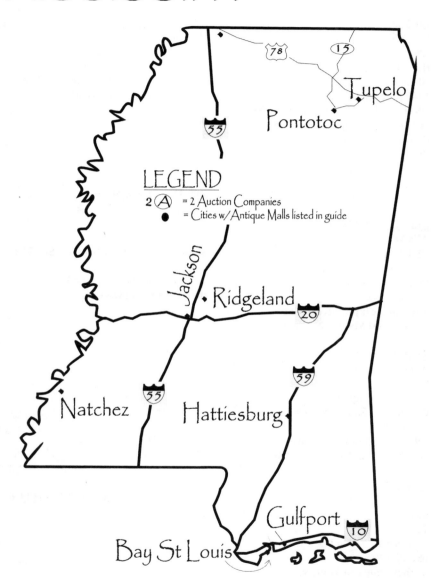

LEGEND

2Ⓐ = 2 Auction Companies
● = Cities w/ Antique Malls listed in guide

Tupelo

Pontotoc

Jackson

Ridgeland

Natchez

Hattiesburg

Gulfport

Bay St Louis

MISSISSIPPI

WEEKEND ANTIQUE EVENTS
Jackson Fairgrounds Market, **every Saturday and Sunday**

ANTIQUE DISTRICTS/ VILLAGES
Natchez

ANTIQUE MALLS, MARKETS/ SHOWS

BAY ST. LOUIS, MS 39520
Beach Antique Mall & Flea Market
20 booths
108 S. Beach Blvd
Open 7 days 10-5
228-467-7955
From US 90 go S on Main St. about 1
mi to Beach Mall at Main & Beach .
12 other antique shops nearby.

GULFPORT, MS 39507
Back in Time Antique Mall
30 dealers
205 Pass Rd.
Mon-Sat 10-5, Closed Sun
228-868-8246
Pass Rd. is parallel to and just N
of US 90, 6 other shops on Pass Rd
from 504 to 2170 E Pass Rd

HATTIESBURG MS 39401
Calico Mall
50 dealers
309 E. Pine St.
Mon-Fri 10-5; Sat 9-5; Sun 1-5
601-582-4351
Downtown

HATTIESBURG MS 39402
The Antique Mall
25 dealers
2103 W. Pine St
Mon-Sat 10-5; Sun 1-5
601-268-2511
Two mi W of Calico Mall

JACKSON, MS 39225-3579
Fairgrounds Antique Flea Market
180-200 dealers; antiques & coll
Fairgrounds at 900 High St.
Sat 8:00-6; Sun 10-5; adm. $1.00
601-353-5327
I-55 Exit 96B
Every Sat & Sun
Indoors
Frank Barnett
P.O. Box 23579
Jackson, MS, 39225-3579

JACKSON, MS 39202
High Street Collection
80 dealers
806 Larson
Open 6 days 10-5, clsd Sun
601-354-5222
I-55 Exit High St. to 1st light, R, next to
Days Inn

MISSISSIPPI

RIDGELAND, MS 39157
Antique Mall of the South
70 dealers
367 Hwy 51
Open Mon-Sat 10-6; Sun 12-6
601-853-4000
I-55 Exit 103; 1 mi North

NATCHEZ, MS 39120
Antique Mall
50 dealers
415 Franklin St
Mon-Sat 10-5; Sun 1-4
601-442-0885
**Downtown. Main St is 1-way W,
Franklin St is 1 block N of Main;
and 1-way E. 18 shops in Natchez**

PONTOTOC, MS 38863
Mason Jar Antique Mall
115 dealers
34 S. Liberty St
Mon-Sat 10-5
662-489-7420
15 mi W of Tupelo on Hwy 6

TUPELO, MS 38804
Olden Glow Antique Mall
20 dealers
624 W. Main
Mon-Sat 10-5; Closed Sun
662-840-1080
100 mi SE of Memphis on US 78 Hwy

TUPELO, MS 38801
The Antique Market
40 dealers
1469 N. Coley Rd.
Open Mon-Sat 10-5; Closed Sun
662-840-6777
**From US 78 Hwy takeW. Tupelo Exit
onto McCullough 1 mi to Coley Rd., R
17 scattered antique shops in Tupelo**

TRAVEL NOTES

172

MISSISSIPPI

TRAVEL NOTES

MISSOURI
East

LEGEND
2Ⓐ = 2 Auction Companies
● = Cities w/ Antique Malls listed in guide

Hannibal

{36}

Monroe City

{61}

Shipman Ⓐ

Williamsburg

Columbia

{70}

St. Charles

Maplewood

St Louis

Eureka

{144}

Sullivan

St Marys
Coffman

{55}

West Plains

{161}

Dexter

174

MISSOURI - East

WEEKEND ANTIQUE EVENTS

St. Louis, Monthly Antique Show and Sale,   **2nd Sun of Apr, Oct, & Dec**

ANTIQUE DISTRICTS/ VILLAGES
St. Louis Cherokee Antique Row and Clayton Rd., Eureka

AUCTION / ESTATE SALE CO'S
ST LOUIS/
Shipman, IL 62685
Harman Auction Center
Every Tue at 5:30 PM
Occasional antique/collectible auctions
P.O. Box 137
Shipman is north of Alton
618-836-7355
I-270 Exit 31A, N on Rte 367 and US
111 to Rte 16 E

ANTIQUE MALLS, MARKETS/ SHOWS

COFFMAN, MO 63670
Coffman Old School Antique
135 booths, 190 showcases
13326 State Rte F
Open 10-5 Mon-Fri, Sat, Sun 10-6
573-756-9700
Hwy 55 Exit 150 at St. Genevieve, W on
Hwy 32, immediate L on outer road B
14 mi then veer R on Rte F for 1 mile

COLUMBIA, MO 65202
Midway Antique Mall
40 dealers
6401 W. Hwy 40
I-70 & Hwy 40
Daily 10-6
573-445-6717
At I-70 Exit 121 in Truck Stop Plaza

COLUMBIA, MO 65201
Ice Chalet Antique Mall
200 plus dealers
3412 Grindstone Pkwy
Open Mon-Sat 10-7; Sun 11-6
573-442-6893
I-70 Exit 128, S 3 mi on
US Hwy 63, AC Exit R

DEXTER, MO 63841
Old Timers Mall
150 booths
Hwy 60 N. Outer Road
Open Mon-Sat 9-5; Sun 1-5
573-624-8288
I-55 Exit 66B, 20 mi W on Hwy 60
Behind Jerry Willis RV Sales

EUREKA - 63025
Great Midwest Antique Mall
400 dealers
530 N. Workman Rd
Mon-Sat 10-8, Sun 10-6
636-938-6760
Outer Rd. E. of Six Flags "next door"

MISSOURI - East

EUREKA, MO 63025
Eureka Antique Mall
30 dealers
107 E. 5th Ave.
Open 10-5 Mon-Sat, Sun 12-5
636-938-5600
N side of I-44 in town, Exit 264
Many single and multi-dealer shops
here, 30 min W of St. Louis.

FARMINGTON/LEADINGTON, MO
63640
Antique Treasures
255 booths, 75% collectibles
920 E. Woodlawn
Open daily 9-6
573-431-4866
Go S from St. Louis, N from Poplar
Bluff into Leadington. Located on side
road running next to Hwy 67.

HANNIBAL, MO 63401
Mrs. Clemens Antique Mall
40 dealers
305 N. Main St.
Open 7 days 9:30-5 summer; 10-4 winter
573-221-6427
Downtown in Historic district

HANNIBAL, MO 63401
Market Street Mall
30 dealers
1408 Market Street
Open Mon-Sat 10-5; Sun 1-5
573-221-3008
Hannibal is at the MS River & US 36;
Broadway to Market

MONROE CITY, MO 63456
Downtown Antique Mall
50 dealers
208 S. Main
Open Tue-Sat 10-5; Sun 12-5
573-735-4522
On US 24, 20 mi W of Hannibal

ST. CHARLES, MO 63303
St. Charles Antique Mall
450 dealers
#1 Charlestown Plaza
Open Mon-Fri 10-8; Sat 10-6 ,Sun 11-5
636-939-4178
I-70 Exit 228, S 3 mi on First
Capital Dr, L at Jung Station Rd, R into
shopping center, down from Mall off
Youngman Rd. In front of Kohl's in
that shopping center is Bandana's
BBQ. Great casual food.

ST. LOUIS, MO
Antique Show and Sale
90 dealers, all antiques & collectibles
2 Hearts Banquet Ctr, 4532 S. Lindberg
Open Sun 9-4; adm & park free
636-296-4803
I-44 Exit 270 S
(US Hwy 67) at Gravois
2nd Sun of Apr. Oct, & Dec
J. J. Promotions
4465 Lonedell Rd.
St. Louis, MO 63010

ST. LOUIS, MO 63128
South County Antique Mall
400 booths 450 showcases
13208 Tesson Ferry Rd.
Open Mon-Fri 10-6; Sat 10-8, Sun 11-5
314-842-5566
Exit off I-270 between I-44 & I-55,
S 2 mi on Tesson Ferry Rd.

176

ST. LOUIS, MO 63122
Warson Woods Antique Gallery
300 showcases, 65 booths
10091 Manchester Rd.
Open Mon-Fri 10-8; Sat 10-6, Sun 11-5
314-909-0123
I-64 Exit Kingshighway, S to Manchester, Exit off I-270, 3 1/2 mi east on Manchester

ST. LOUIS, MO 63118
Cherokee Antique Row
45 shops
2014 Cherokee SE
Open daily 11-4
314-664-7916 or 314-773-8810
**I-55 Exit Arsenal St,
S on Lemp, W on Cherokee**
*Cherokee Antique Row features
45 unique shops.*

ST. LOUIS/ MO 63124
Ladue Galleries Antique Mall
50 Gallery rooms, 200 showcases
8811 Ladue Rd.
Mon- Fri 10-5, Sat 10-6, Sun 12-5
314-726-6166
1/8 mi E I-170 on Ladue Rd

ST. LOUIS/ CREVE COEUR
Antique Mall of Creve Coeur
250 dealers, 60% collectibles
1275 Castillon Arcade
Mon- Sat 10-8, Sun 11-5
314-434-6566
**I-270 Exit 14, Olive Blvd . W 1 3/4 mi
at Fee Fee and Olive back in shopping
center**

ST. LOUIS, MO 63117
Finches Antiques
One of 5 shops in antique row
7729 Clayton Rd.
Open Mon - Sat 10-5, Closed Sun
314-725-2622

ST.LOUIS/ MAPLEWOOD, MO 63143
Treasure Aisles Antique Mall
100 booths, 60 showcases
2317 S. Big Bend Blvd.
Open Mon- Sat 10-7, Sun 11-5
314-647-6875
**I-64 Exit, Big Bend Blvd S,
or I-44 Exit 283 N**

ST. MARYS, MO 63673
St. Mary Antique Mall
485 booths, 200 showcases, 60%
collectibles
30 % antiques
77 7th St.
Open daily 9-6
573-543-2800
**This is tricky to find, possibly 2 hours
out of St. Louis, I-55 Exit 150 on 32
road. When you get to St. Mary look for
Pine on R, turn off Pine on 7th St., will
have to turn L uphill. Call for directions if you are coming I-55 Exit 141,
which is St. Mary exit. Left over
I-55, 4 mi to 1st stop sign, then L on 61.**

MISSOURI - East

SULLIVAN, MO 63080
Sullivan Antique Mall
50 booths, 30 dealers
201 N. Service Rd. W.
Open 7 days, 9-5pm
573-468-3943
I-44 Exit Hwy 185 N side of I-44

WEST PLAINS, MO 65775
Downtown Antique Mall
80 dealers
1 Court Square
Open Mon-Sat 9-5:30; Sun 1-5
417-256-6487
**West Plains is 1 mi approx from the jct
of US 160 & US 63 in S Central MO**

TRAVEL NOTES

MISSOURI - West

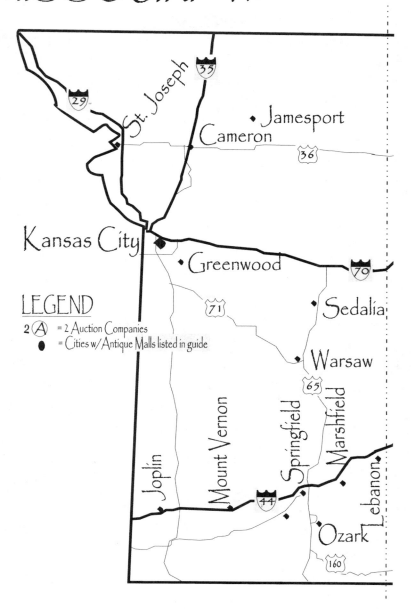

MISSOURI - West

WEEKEND ANTIQUE EVENTS
Kansas City Flea Market, **Sat once every month**

ANTIQUE DISTRICT/ VILLAGES
Jamesport, Ozark, in K.C. Stateline at 45th. In St. Louis, Cherokee St.

ANTIQUE MALLS, MARKETS/ SHOWS
CAMERON, MO 64429
Over the Hill Mall
90 dealers
Box 187, On Hwy 36 E
Open Mon-Fri 9-5:30, Sat 9-5, Sun 1-5
816-632-7807
I-35 Exit 54, 1/2 mi E

JAMESPORT, MO 64648
Warren House Antiques
27 booths
East of 4-way stop
Open Mon-Sat 9-5, Sun 1-5
660-684-6266
I-35 Jamesport Exit, E on Hwy 6 about 25 mi. Several shops near 4-way stop in Jamestown, the largest Amish community in MO.

JOPLIN, MO 64804
Southside Antique Mall
200 booths, 42,000 sq. ft.
4402 E. 32nd
Open Mon-Sat 9-6; Sun 10-5
417-623-1000
1 1/2 mi E of 32nd & Rangeline

JOPLIN, MO 64801
Connies Antiques
600 dealers, 50,000 sq. ft.
3421 N. Rangeline
Open Sun-Fri 9-6, Sat until 7 PM
417-781-2602
I-44 Exit 8B, US 71 N, down 5 mi .

KANSAS CITY/ GREENWOOD, MO 64034
Greenwood Antique Mall/Tea Room
70 dealers
502 Main
Open Mon-Sat 10-5, Sun 12-5
816-537-7172 or 7418
I-435 Exit 71 Hwy S to Hwy 150, E, 11 mi. Several other nearby antique shops. Outdoor market May & Mid-Sep

KANSAS CITY, MO
The Flea- Monthly Market
100 dealers
11730 N. Ambassador
Open 8-3 Sat
816-697-3830 or 800-252-1501 call for exact dates
Market once a month. At KCI Expo Center I-29 N Exit 13 R or I-435 N Exit 36 L
Dirk Soulis, Promoter

MISSOURI - West

One of our favorite restaurants is in surburban Kansas City. It is at the jct of US Hwy 40 and Lee's Summit Rd. **(I-70 Exit 14 S to US 40)** *Stephenson's Apple Farm Restaurant.* You will enjoy their apple fritters, and green rice casserole.

We also like *Andre's* (lunch only) Swiss Confiserie, 5018 Main St., near the Plaza. 816-561-3440. **Main Street angles into Brookside Dr. just below the Plaza, so you have to go right one block to get back on Main Street.**

KANSAS CITY, KS 66103
State Line Antique Mall
40 dealers
4510 State Line
Mon-Sat 10-5; Sun 12-5
913-362-2002
I-435 Exit 75-B, N on State Line; or I-435 Exit 16-A, W to State Line N. West of Country Club Plaza
You can walk to 10 other antique shops

KANSAS CITY/ GRAIN VALLEY
Brass Armadillo Antique Mall
550 dealers
1450 Golfview Dr.
Open 7 days 9-9
816-847-5260
I-70 Exit 21, So 100 yds to Coronado Dr., then L at light. It 's tricky because it is visable on frontage road, but you will need to backtrack to it.

KANSAS CITY /
INDEPENDENCE, MO 64055
Country Meadows
400 dealers
4621 Shrank Dr.
Mon-Sat 9-9, Sun 9-6
816-373-0410
I-70 Exit 14, S 1 mi on Lee's Summit Rd. to US 40, E 1/2 mi at Shrank intersection.
www.antiquelandusa.com

KANSAS CITY/ PLATTE CITY, MO 64079
W. D. Pickers Antique Mall
120 dealers w/ 200 showcases
16095 US Hwy 371
Open 10-6 daily
816-858-3100
Located at Exit 20 I-29, 7 mi north of KCI Airport

KANSAS CITY /
PRAIRIE VILLAGE, KS 66208
Mission Road Antique Mall
300 quality dealers, 50,000 sq. ft.
4101 W. 83rd
Open Mon-Sat 10-7; Sun 11-6
913-341-7577
SW corner 83rd & Mission, in Corinth Square Shopping Center.
I-435 Exit 77 N (Roe) to 83rd E 1/2 mi *The unique landmark location has been home to the areas finest antique dealers since 1994. Visit the Bloomsbury Bistro inside the mall, voted "Best New Lunch Spot" in town by* <u>*Squire Magazine.*</u>

MISSOURI - West

LEBANON, MO 65536
Heartland Antique Mall
200 dealers, 40,000 Sq. ft.
2500 Industrial Dr.
Open 7 days 8-8
417-532-9350
I-44 Exit 127
Russell Stovers candy, and Wisconsin cheese outlets and Knife Country ,Bear Cutlery, Victonnox, Custom-made knives, & Craft Haven. primitive furniture & rustic iron,, antique pottery, books, & collectibles.

LEBANON, MO 65536
Corner Antique Mall
75 dealers
25999 N. Hwy 5
Open Mon-Sat 9:30-5:30; Sun 12:30-5
417-588-3411
Quaint,small country store type setting, unique atmosphere for antiques
I-44 Exit 129 Hwy 5, N 4 mi through town, then 1 & 1/8 mi after Hwy divides to Hwy 5

LEBANON/ PHILLIPSBURG, MO 65536
Historic Route 66 Antique Mall
40 dealers, 5,000 sq. ft.
17711 Campground Rd.
417-532-7082
I-44 Exit 123, 5 mi W of Lebanon

MARSHFIELD, MO 65706
Antique Mercantile
150 dealers plus ahowcases-2 floors
1030 Spur Drive
Open 7 days 9-6
417-859-4961
I-44 Exit 100, So. 1/2 mile on R side.

In Marshfield, *Shiela's Place* Restaurant & Bakery is a great place for lunch. It is rigfht on the street by Walmart, with homemade pie and cobbler.

MT. VERNON, MO 65712
Nana's Antique Mall
100 plus dealers
1001 Daniel Dr.
Open M-Sat 9:30-5:30, Sun 12-5:30
417-466-2646
At I-44 Exit 46, on S Outer Rd

OZARK, MO 65721
Maine Street Antique Mall
125 dealers
Hwy 65 & 14
Open 7 days 9-5
417-581-2575
10 mi S of Springfield on US 65

OZARK, MO 65721
Crossroads Antique Mall
80 dealers
200 S. 20th St. (Hwy 65 & 14)
Open 7 days 9-6 summer; 9-5 winter
417-581-0428
10 mi S of Springfield on US 65

OZARK, MO 65721
Spring Creek Antiques & Tea Room
65 dealers
107 S. 3rd St.
M-Sat 9-5 winter, 9-6 summer, Sun 12-5
417-581-5914
Downtown on the main street

MISSOURI - West

OZARK, MO 65721
Ozark Antique Mall & Collectibles
150 dealers
Hwy 65 & 14
Open Sun-Fri 9-6, 9-5 winter; Sat 9-6
417-581-5233
10 mi S of Springfield on US 65

OZARK, MO 65721
Riverview Antique Center
100 dealers
909 W. Jackson
Mon-Sat 9:30-5:30, Sun 12-5
417-581-4426
1/2 mi E of Hwy 65 on Hwy 14

OZARK, MO 65721
Antique Emporium
150 dealers
1702 W. Boat St.
Open Mon-Sat 9-8; Sun 9-6 summer
hours
417-581-5555
**At Hwy 65 & CC, 1st Exit N of
Hwy 14, behind Lambert's Cafe
Winter hours are shorter**

SEDALIA, MO 65301
Mapleleaf Antique Mall
50 dealers
106 W. Main
Open Mon-Sat 10-5; Sun 11-5
660-826-8383
I-70 Exit 78 S 18 mi, downtown

SPRINGFIELD, MO 65802
Autumn Leaf Antique Mall
100 booths,70% collectibles
6537 W. Independence Dr.
Open 7 days 9-5:30
417-869-3660
2 mi W of Springfield at I-44 Exit 70

ST.JOSEPH, MO 64505
Jessie James Antique Mall
220 booths, 200 showcases
12777 Country Place Dr.
Open 7 days 9-6 Fri till 8
816-232-0099
**At I-29 Exit 53 at corner of I-29 &
Business 71 Hwy**

ST.JOSEPH, MO
St. Joseph Antique Show
60 dealers
Civic Arena at 4th & Felix
2nd weekend Feb, & Oct, Sat 9-6, Sun
11-4
Adm $3.00
Annette Weeks at 816-232-0099

WARSAW, MO 65355
Warsaw Antique Mall
40 dealers , 2 floors
245 W. Main
Open Mon-Sat 10-5; Sun 10-5, 11-4 in
winter
660-438-9759
**Downtown
50 mi So of I-70
Lake of the Ozarks area**

184

GREAT GETAWAY TO ANTIQUE THE SCENIC OZARKS

WHEN: Anytime; Spring/Fall most scenic.

WHERE: Branson is central to this Getaway.

LODGING: For luxury lodging, Chateau on the Lake, 1-888-333-5253. The Hampton Inn is near Andy Williams' - Moon River Theater. Every motel chain must be in Branson.

RESTAURANT: *McDuffy's* Restaurant on Rte 76W next to the Moon River Theater, we found to be among the best in Branson. Also, *Mary Jane's Fabulous Food*, 1 mi. S of Jct SR76 & 13, in a charming cottage at 17023 State Hwy 13. Lunch only 11-3, 417-272-8908.

In Springfield, outdoor enthuiasts would enjoy eating in the Bass Pro Shop's unique restaurant with its cascading waterfalls and 140,000 gallon game fish aquarium at 1935 S. Campbell St.

LEISURE: Andy Williams, 800-666-6094, and Shoji Tabuchi, 417-334-7469 are the two most popular shows in Branson. Reservations for all shows are made with www.ReserveBranson.com or 866-233-5535.

ANTIQUING: 10 mi S of Springfield, MO is Ozark with 600 dealers in a half-dozen malls. In Ozark at 107 S. 3rd St. is *Spring Creek Antiques* with a Tea Room, and 65 dealers. 4 antique malls in shopping center at Hwy 14 Exit of US 65, another is 1/2 mile E of US 65, and one at next Exit N, where you will also find Lambert's Restaurant, home of Throwed Rolls - an interesting place to eat.

2. Leaving Branson So. on US65 about 30 mi. to US62, W to Arkansas, to Eureka Springs thru the best of the Ozarks to *Yesteryear Antique Mall* on 62 E with another mall 6 blocks east.

3. Leave Eureka Springs , AR W on US62, 18 mi to Pea Ridge Battlefield with video reinactment of the battle.

Then into Rogers, AR and *Yesteryear Antique Mall*, 100 booths at 3704 Walnut, 1 mile E of I-540 on Bus. 71 Another 100 dealer mall at 3223 Hudson I-540 Exit 86 E, 1/2 mile.

4. Now, S. on I-540 and Exit US412, W to *Yesteryear Antique Mall* on 412 in Tontitown. Another 150 booth mall is 1/2 mi. W of Hwy 112, also several shops along this area.

RESTAURANT: If you like fried chicken, you will love "A Q Chicken" on Bus. 71-B in Springdale. I-540 Exit 72 E. on 412 to US 71-B, N 1.5 miles.

5. Downtown Springdale at 113 W. Emma, *Famous Hardware Co. Mall*, 20,000 sq.ft.

RESTAURANT: Heading N. on I-540 and US 71 you come to Jane, MO. and Stevenson Apple Farm Restaurant on US 71. Great food.

6. Continue N. on US 71 to Joplin Exit W. on 32nd to *Southside Antique Mall*, 200 booths at 4402 E. 32nd.

7. Continue W. on 32nd to Rangeline Rd. (BR 71) N. 5 mi. to *Connies Antiques*, 600 dealers at 3421 Rangeline Road.

8. *Nana's Antique Mall* with 100 dealers is 20 mi. E. on I-44 Exit 46, South outer road.

If headed further E. on I-44, Exit 100, then So 1/2 mi, is the *Antique Mercantile Mall* in Marshfield, MO with 150 dealers on Spur Drive. We found a great place to eat lunch there. *Sheila's Place* Restaurant & Bakery by Walmart, up from the mall.. Continue on I-44 E to Lebanon. Exits 123, 127 and 129 for 3 more antique malls - (See Lebanon listing for details).

There is a lot more antiquing in Kansas City, St. Louis, Little Rock, Tulsa and Oklahoma City - find these cities in our guide to the best antique malls.

185

MONTANA

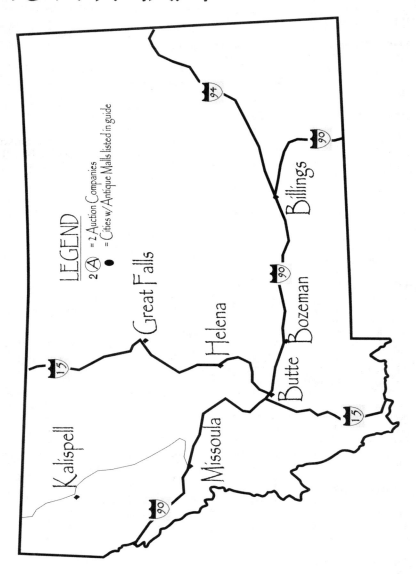

LEGEND

2Ⓐ = 2 Auction Companies

● = Cities w/Antique Malls listed in guide

Great Falls

Helena

Billings

Bozeman

Butte

Kalispell

Missoula

MONTANA

BILLINGS, MT 59101
Depot Antique Mall
60 dealers
2223 Montana Ave
Open 10-6, 7 days
406-245-5955
I-90 Exit 450 to Montana downtown then E on Montana

BILLINGS, MT 59101
Yesteryears Antique Mall
42 dealers
102 N. 29th St.
Open Mon-Sat 10-5:30; Sun 12-4
406-256-3567
Downtown Billings, I-90 Exit 450
There are a dozen shops in Billings.

BOZEMAN , MT 59715
Antique Mall Downtown Bozeman
25 dealers
1530 W Main
Mon-Sat 10-5; Sun 12-5
406-587-5281
I-90 Exit 306
There are a dozen antique shops in Bozeman, 5 on Main St

BOZEMAN, MT 59715
Country Mall Antiques
45 dealers
8350 Huffine Lane
Mon-Sat 10-5; Sun 12-5, extended summer hrs
406-587-7688
4 mi W of Bozeman on Hwy 205 next to Honda Auto

GREAT FALLS, MT 59401
Bull Market Antique Mall
63 dealers
202 2nd Street S
Mon-Sat 10-8; Sun 12-4
406-771-1869
I-15 Exit 278 or 280, E to 2nd St
6 other antique shops in Great Falls

HELENA, MT 59601
Rags to Riches. Antique Mall
20 plus dealers
4528 W. US Hwy 12
7 days 10-5:30
406-449-3334
On US Hwy 12 W

KALISPELL ,MT 59901
Kalispell Antique Mall
50 booths
48 Main St.
Open Mon-Sat 10-6; Sun 12-4
406-257-2800
Downtown

MISSOULA, MT 59802
Montana Antique Mall
40 dealers
331 Railroad St. W
Open 10-6 Mon-Sat; Sun 12-4
406-721-5366
I-90 Exit Orange St S to 1st legal L, then one block left to RR St L.
A dozen shops in Missoula.

NEBRASKA

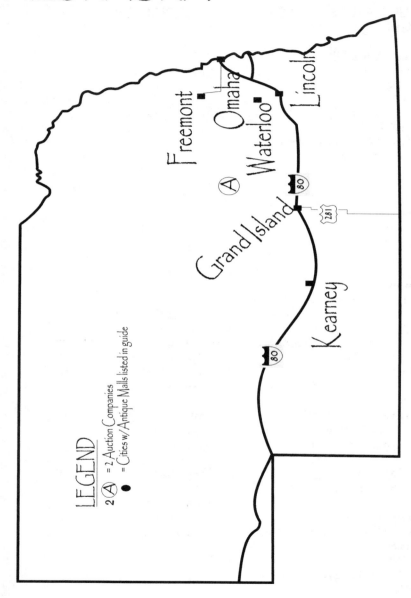

NEBRASKA

ANTIQUE DISTRICTS:

Downtown Fremont

ANTIQUE MALLS, MARKETS / SHOWS

FREMONT, NE 68025
Dime Store Days
40 dealers
109 E. 6th St.
Open Mon-sat 10-5; Sun 12-5
402-727-0580
Downtown
3 other 25 dealer malls and
7 shops in downtown Fremont.

GRAND ISLAND, NE 68801
Heartland Antique Mall
35 dealers
216 W. 3rd Street
Mon-Sat 10-5; Sun 1-5
308-384-6018
Downtown; I-80 Exit 312 N 5 mi

GREENWOOD, NE 68366
Platte Valley Antique Mall
200 dealers
13017-238th St
Open 9-8, 7 days
402-944-2949
I-80 Exit 420 Southside of I-80

KEARNEY, NE 68847
Kaufman's Antiques Emporium
150 dealers
2200 Central Ave.
Open Mon-Sat 10-5; Sun 1-5
308-237-4972
I-80 Exit 272 N to downtown

LINCOLN, NE 68517
Aardvark Antique Mall
270 booths, 250 showcases
5800 Arbor Rd.
Open 9-9, 7 days
402-464-5100
I-80 Exit 405 S 1 block
to Arbor Rd E

LINCOLN, NE 68508
Burlington Antique Mall
35 dealers
201 N 7th Street
Open 7 days
402-475-7502
In Historic Haymarket

LINCOLN, NE 68508
Q Street Mall
100 dealers
1835 Q street
Mon-Sat 10-6; Sun 12-5
402-435-3303
2 blocks N & 8 blocks E of 10th
& O-St.

In Omaha, for great food, our favorite is
***DiCoppa* for lunch or dinner. Closed**
on Sunday. I-680 Exit 2, Pacific St, 1/2
mi E to Regency Pwky, 1/2 mi. N to the
Regency Fashion Court Mall. We liked
the raspberry vinaigrette salad
dressing so much that we ordered a
quart to take home with us.

NEBRASKA

Grandmother's is also a favorite for homestyle cooking at 90th & Dodge, especially upholding Omaha's reputation for great steaks.

OMAHA, NE 68138
Brass Armadillo Antique Mall
360 dealers
10666 Sapp Brothers Drive
Open 7 days 9-9
1-800-896-9140, 402-896-9140
I-80 Exit 439 W to Sapp Brothers Dr then N on access Rd, or I-80 Exit 440

WATERLOO, NE 68089
Venice Antique Mall
68 dealers
26250 W. Center Rd
Tue-Fri -10-6;Sat 10-5 Sun 12-5, Mon clsd
402-359-5782
8 mi W of Omaha on Hwy 92

TRAVEL NOTES

NEVADA

LEGEND

2 (A) = 2 Auction Companies
● = Cities w/ Antique Malls listed in guide

Reno

Sparks

(A)

Las Vegas

NEVADA

AUCTION/ESTATE SALE CO'S

Reno/
Sparks, NV 89431
Lightning Auctions
Antique auction
870 S. Rock Blvd.
1st Sat of each month at 10 A.M.
775-331-4222
I-80 Exit Rock Blvd So.

ANTIQUE MALLS, MARKETS/ SHOWS

LAS VEGAS, NV 89103
Not Just Antiques
50 dealers
1422 Western Ave
702-384-4922
I-15 Exit Charleston west, take Martin Luther King, L on Wall, R on Western

LAS VEGAS, NV 89102
Antique Mall of America
180 dealers
9151 S. Las Vegas Blvd.
Open 7 days Mon-Sat 10-6, Sun 12-6
702-368-1170 subject to change
I-15 Exit Blue Diamond Rd E to Las Vegas Blvd. R

LAS VEGAS, NV 89102
Red Rooster Antique Mall
60 dealers
1109 Western
Mon-Sat 10-6; Sun 11-5
702-382-5253
I-15 Exit 41 W on Charleston to Western; Red Rooster Malls are at the corner of Charleston & Western & are connected.

For great food in Las Vegas it's hard to beat the buffets at the *Mirage* on the Strip or the *Golden Nugget* downtown. For French cuisine, however, we prefer the buffet at the *Paris*, which is our favorite pick.

There are 14 antique shops from 1626 to 3310 E Charleston Blvd.

RENO, NV 89502
Antique Center of Nevada
180 dealers
1251 S. Virginia Street
Open daily
775-324-4141
I-80 Exit 13, S
7 antique shops nearby on Virginia

RENO, NV 89502
All R Yesterday's Antique Mall
30 dealers
1215 So. Virginia
Mon-Sat 10-6, Sun 10-5

NEW HAMPSHIRE

LEGEND

2 (A) = 2 Auction Companies
● = Cities w/ Antique Malls listed in guide

North Conway

West Lebanon

93

16

Meredith

103

11

Wolfeboro

Laconia

89

4   Northwood

Keene

101

Concord

Amherst

Manchester

101

Hampton Falls

North Hampton

(A)

Milford

Nashua

NEW HAMPSHIRE

WEEKEND ANTIQUE EVENTS

Nashua Antiques Show, St. Stans Hall, **every Sun, Mid Oct thru Mid Apr**
Wolfboro Antique Fair, **last full weekend in Jul**

ANTIQUE DISTRICTS/VILLAGES

Amherst Rte 101-A, Claremont, Northwood Rte 4, North Conway Rte 16

AUCTION/ESTATE SALE CO'S

North Hampton , NH 03862
Paul McInnis, Inc.
Conducts antique & estate auctions
155 Lafayette Rd. #8
On US 1
800-242-8354, 603-964-1301
Call for dates

Keene/ West Swanzy 03469
Knotty Pine Auction Service
Antique Auctions Last Sun of mo. at 11 AM
Rte 10, 4 mi S of Keene
welcomes consignments
603-352-2313 or 800-352-5251

ANTIQUE MALLS, MARKETS/ SHOWS

AMHERST, NH 03031
101-A Antique & Collectible Center
175 dealers
#141 Rt 101-A
Open M-Sat 10-5; Sun 9-5, Thur till 8 pm
603-880-8422
Rte 101, Exit 8 off Rte 3

AMHERST, NH 03031
Needful Things
180 dealers
#112 Rte 101-A
Open 7 days 10-5, Sun 9-5, Thur till 8PM
603-889-1232
Rte 3 Exit 7, W on 101-A 6 mi

AMHERST, NH 03031
Antiques at Mayfair
200 dealers
119-121 Rte 101-A
Mon-Fri 10-5; Sat 10-6; Sun 8-5
603-595-7531
Rte 3 Exit 7, W on 101-A 6 mi
Open until 8 P.M. on Thur

**Rte 101-A through Amherst is known
as the Antique Trail and has many
single & multi-dealershops in addition
to the malls listed above.**

CONCORD, NH 03301
Concord Antique Gallery
150 booths
Stores at Depot St
Open Mon-Sat 10-6, Sun 12-4
603-225-2070
I-93 Exit 14 W to Main St, L to Depot St.

NEW HAMPSHIRE

HAMPTON FALLS, NH 03844
Antiques at Hampton Falls
55dealers
80 Lafayette Rd.
Open Mon-Sat 10-5; Sun 11-5
603-926-1971
I-95 Exit 1, 2 mi N on Rte. 1

KEENE, NH 03431
Antiques at Colony Mill
100 dealers
222 West Street
Open Mon-Sat 10-9; Sun 11-6
603-358-6343
I-91 Exit 3 in VT, E 15 mi on
Rte 9 on 2nd floor at Colony Mill
Marketplace

KEENE,
WEST SWANZEY, NH 03469
Knotty Pine Antique Market
250 dealers - Open to all
Route 10
Open 7 days 9-5
603-352-5252
4 mi S of Keene
Free tailgate show last Tue every
Month,From April- Oct 26 Monthly last
Sun auctions year around.

LACONIA, NH 03247
Country Tyme Antiques
170 dealer booths
Route 3
Open daily 9:30-5
\603-524-2686
I-93 Exit 20, US Hwy 3, N to Laconia

LEBANON /
WEST LEBANON, NH 03784
Colonial Antique Markets
75 dealers,
5 Airport Road
Open daily 9-5
603-298-7712
I-89 Exit 20, in Colonial Plaza.
Rte 12A to Airport Rd, first L
Outdoor flea market on Sundays

MANCHESTER, NH 03102
From Out of the Woods
50 dealers
465 Mast Rd..
Open daily 9-5
603-624-8668
101 W to 114N to 114 A -right

MEREDITH, NH 03253
Burlwood Antique Center
175 dealers
194 Daniel Webster Hwy (Route 3)
Open daily 10-5 May 1 thru Oct 31
603-279-6387
I-93 Exit 23 E
Jct Route 3 & Rte 104

MILFORD, NH 03055
N H Antique Co-op
280 dealers
P.O. Box 732, Rte 101 A Elm St
Open daily 10-5
603-673-8499
Rte 3, Exit 7, W on 101-A

We enjoyed the fine "country dining"at *Hannah Jacks Tavern* in Merrimack, NH. The part of the building where we ate dated back to Revolutionary War days. It's locaton is Exit 11, Rte 3, 5 mi N of Nashua.

For Italian food we loved Ya Mamma's. 75 Daniel Webster Hwy in Merrimack. **603-578-9201**

NORTHWOOD, NH 03261
Town Pump Antiques
70 dealers
295 First N.H. Tpke (Rte 4)
Mon-Sat 10-5, Sun 10-5
603-942-8612
23 mi. E of Concord on Rte 4. There are 18 antique stores on Rte 4, an antique alley.

NASHUA, NH
Nashua Antiques Show
45 dealers; all antiques & collectibles
St. Stans Hall
Adm $5, 9:30-10:30; $2. after 10:30-12
781-329-1192
Rte 3 Exit 6, E on Rte 130 E, 1st L onto Blue Hill Ave 1/4 mi on R. Sundays Mid Oct thru Early April
Nashua Antique Show
97 Richards St
Dedham, MA 02026

NORTHWOOD, NH 03261
Parker-French Antique Center
130 spaces
Rte 4
Open daily 10-5
603-942-8852
6 mi E of Epsom Circle
www.nhantiquealley.com

NORTHWOOD, NH 03261
Hearts Desire Antique Center
120 dealers
1190 1st NH Tpke
Open 7 days 10-5
603-942-5153
23 mi E of Concord on Rte 4

WOLFEBORO, NH
Wolfeboro Antique Fair
100 dealers
Kingswood High School on Rte 28
Open Fri & Sat 9-4, Adm $4, park free
603-569-0000
Last full week-end in July
Call for exact dates
Wolfeboro is on Lake Winnipesaukee
Antiquebug
P. O. Box 678
Wolfeboro, NH 03894

TRAVEL NOTES

ANTIQUE GETAWAY THROUGH SCENIC NEW HAMPSHIRE

WHEN: Anytime, but the first half of October is best for fall color.

ANTIQUE AUCTION: Last Sun of every month at West Swanzy Knotty Pine Auction at 11:00AM 1-800-352-2313.Rte 10, 4 mi S of Keene.

ANTIQUING: 1.Start in the SW corner of NH at Keene and W. Swanzy, *Knotty Pine Antique Mall,* 250 dealers, 4 mi S of Keene on Rte 10 and *Antiques at Colony Mall,* 100 dealers at 222 West St.. in Keene.

2. Next go E on Rte 101 from Keene about 38 mi to the *Antique Trail* of many shops and malls. *Milford, NH Co-op,* 280 dealers at Rte 101-A & Elm St.

3. Amherst -*Needful Things,* 180 dealers at 112 Rte 101-A.

4. Next *Antiques at Mayfair,* 200 dealers, at 191-121 Rte 101-A5. Then *101-A Antique & Collectible Center,* 175 dealers, 141 Rte 101-A.

LODGING: We have found the Fairfield Inn at Exit 11 W side of US3 in Merrimac, a hotel that Marriott converted to a Fairfield Inn, to be comfortable and convenient to antiquing and good restaurants.

RESTAURANTS: We enjoyed the fine "country dining"at Hanna Jacks Tavern,E side of US 3. The part of the restaurant we sat in dated back to Revolutionary days.

We also enjoyed delicious Italian food at *Ya Mamma's,* 3 mi S of Exit 11 on old US 3, Daniel Webster Hwy.

6. Go N on US 3 to Rte 101W to Rte 114 N to 114-A Right to 465 Mast Rd. *From Out Of The Woods Antique Mall,* 50 dealers in Manchester.

7. Next I-293 N to I-93 N Exit 14, W to Main, Left to Depot St., *Concord Antique Gallery,* 150 booths.

8. Get back on I-93 N to I-393 in Concord which is also US 202 & US 4 and continue E on US 202 to Northwood and *Hearts Desire Mall, & Parker-French Mall* each over 100 dealers.

9. Continue on US 202, 13 mi to Rte 11 at Rochester, N 35 mi on Rte 11 to US 3 South to Laconia and *Country Time Antiques,* 170 booths on US 3.

10. After Laconia, take US3 N 18 miles to Jct US3 and Rte 104 where *Burlwood Antique Center* with 175 dealers is located in Meredith.

11. After Meredith, continue on US 3 a short distance to Rte 25 E and N about 20 miles to Rte 16N to North Conway where you will find 10 antique stores on Rte 16.

This completes our New Hampshire Getaway, but if you have more time continue E on US 302 to Portland, Maine and enjoy a great "Getaway Antiquing Coastal Maine.

TRAVEL NOTES

NEW JERSEY

LEGEND

2 (A) = 2 Auction Companies
● = Cities w/ Antique Malls listed in guide

Stanhope
Morristown
Montclair
Dover
Chester
Far Hills
Summit
Raritan
Sommerville
Flemington
Lambertville
Somerset
Freehold
Red Bank
Point Pleasant Beach
Hainsport
Pemberton
Repaupo
Rancocas
Woods
Cherry Hill
Smithville
Mullica Hill
NJTpke
Atlantic City
Cape May

NEW JERSEY

WEEKEND ANTIQUE EVENTS

Atlantique , 1100 dealers, **4th weekend in Mar, 3rd weekend in Oct.**
Far Hills Antique Show, 100 dealers, **Second Sun in June**
Lambertville, 300 dealers, outdoors & in, **every Wed, Sat & Sun**
Stanhope - Waterloo Antiques Fair, 200 exhibitors,
    usually 2nd or 3rd weekend in May & Sept.

ANTIQUE DISTRICTS / VILLAGES
Cape May, Chester, Lambertville and Montclair, Cherry Hill/ Mullica Hill

ANTIQUE MALLS, MARKET/SHOWS

ATLANTIC CITY, NJ
Atlantique City
1600 booths , all antiques & collectibles
At the Convention center
Sat. 10-7 $17; Sun 10-5 $10
800-526-2724 for early admission tickets
Generally 4th weekend in March &
3rd weekend in Oct (Call to confirm)
Downtown at foot of AC Expressway
Ted Jones
P. O. Box 547
Mays Landing, NJ 08330

CAPE MAY
At South end of Garden State Parkway
one can walk to 14 antique shops, in
Cape May.

CHERRY HILL/
HAINSPORT, NJ 08060
Country Antique Center
100 dealers
Rte. 38, Hainesport
Open 7 days 10-5
609-261-1924
4.5 mi E of I-295 on Hwy 38

CHERRY HILL/
MULLICA HILL, NJ 08062
The Old Mill Antique Mall
50 dealers
1 So. Main St.
Open 11-5, 7 days
856-478-9810
NJ Tpke Exit 2 E 3 mi on US 322
Row of 24 antique shops here and
another 35 dealer antique mall

CHERRY HILL/
PEMBERTON BRGH, NJ 08068
Grist Mill Antique Center
125 dealers
127 Hanover Street (Route 530)
Open 7 days 10-5
609-726-1588
12. 5 mi E of I-295 Exit on Rte 38

CHESTER, NJ 07930
A dozen antique shops downtown
On Main
Most shops open Wed-Sun 10:30-5
I-80 Exit 27 S, 8 mi or
I-287 Exit 22 N 10 miles

NEW JERSEY

DOVER, NJ 07801
Iron Carriage Antique Center
40 individual shops
Corner of W. Blackwell & Sussex Sts
Open Wed 11-8; Sat 11-5; Sun 10-5
973-366-1440
**I-80 Exit 35A, S 2 mi to Dover; cross
Rte 46, 3 blocks to Blackwell St,
turn R to Sussex**

FAR HILLS
Far Hills Antique Show
100 Exihibtors; outdoors rain or shine
Fairgrounds
Sun 10-4; adm $6; park free
215-794-5009 or 215-862-5828
**2nd Sun in June
I-287 Exit 22
N 2mi on US 202**
David & Peter Mancuso
P.O. Box 667
New Hope, Pa 18938

FLEMINGTON, NJ 08822
Main Street Antique Center
85 dealers
156 Main Street
Open 7 days 10-5
908-788-6767
**I-287 Exit 17 S on US 202, 13 mi;
or I-78 Exit 17 S on Rte 31, 10 mi**

FREEHOLD, NJ 07728
Freehold Antique Gallery
65 dealers
2 Monmouth Ave
7 days 11-5
732-462-7900
**NJ Turnpike Exit 8; E 11 mi on Rte 33
Main Street to Throckmorton,
L on Monmouth**

LAMBERTVILLE, NJ 08530
Antiques on Union
14 dealers
32N Union
Mon-Fri 10-5 Sat & Sun 10-6
609-397-3300
From bridge 1st light Left 1 1/2 blocks

LAMBERTVILLE
Golden Nugget Antique Market
300 dealers; all antiques & collectibles
River Rd 1 mi S of Lambertville
Outdoors 6-4; mall 8:30-4; free
609-397-0811
**I-95 Exit 1, N on Rt 29 about 7 mi
Wed, Sat & Sun year round**
Golden Nugget Flea Market
Rte 29
Lambertville, NJ 08530

LAMBERTVILLE, NJ 08530
The Peoples Store
55 dealers
Corner Union & Church Sts.
Open 7 days 10-6
609-397-9808
**One block N of Bridge St.
downtown. 25 Antique shops
downtown in Lambertville.**

MONTCLAIR, NJ 07042
Ivory Bird Antiques
1 of 17 shops in antique district
555 Bloomfield Ave.
Hours vary shop to shop
973-744-5225
**Garden State Pkwy Exit 148
to Bloomfield Center then W on
Bloomfield to Montclair**

202

One of our favorite places to eat is here at the "Black Horse Tavern" about 8 milesW. of Morristown on Rte 24 in Mendham.

POINT PLEASANT BEACH, NJ 08742
Point Pleasant Antique Emporium
125 dealers
Bay Avenue at Trenton Avenue
Open 7 days 11-5
732-892-2222 or 800-322-8002
Garden State Pkwy; Exit 98 S on Rte 35, 7 mi then 2nd R on Trenton after drawbridge

POINT PLEASANT BEACH, NJ 08742
Shore Antique Center
30 dealers
300 Richmond Avenue
Open 7 days 11-5
732-295-5771
Rte 35 S

RARITAN, NJ 08869
Raritan Antique Village
40 dealers
44 W. Somerset St.
7 days 10-5
908-526-7920
I-287 Exit 17, S on US Hwy 206 to Rte 625 into Raritan

RED BANK, NJ 07701
Antique Center of Red Bank
100 dealers, 3 buildings
195 - 226 W. Front Street
Open Mon-Sat 11-5; Sun 12-5
732-842-4336 or 732-842-3393
Garden State Pkwy Exit 109 E on Rte 520, N Shrewsbury Ave 2 mi to Front St. turn R

In Red Bank we had great Italian food at *Basil T's Brew Pub & Italian Grill.*.**Down a side Street, Near Red Bank Antique Center**

SMITHVILLE, NJ 08201
Days of Olde
70 dealers, 16,000 sq. ft.
Rte 9 South
Open 7 days 10-5
609-652-7011
1 mi of S of Smithville on Rte 9 Garden State Parkway Exit 485, South 3 mi.

SOMERVILLE, NJ 08876
Antique Emporium
65 dealers
29 Division St.
Open 7 days 11-5
908-218-1234
I-287 Exit 17 S on US 206 to Rte 28 E into Somerville.

NEW JERSEY

STANHOPE, NJ
Waterloo Antiques Fair (Show/Sale)
200 exhibits in tents & outdoors
Waterloo Concert Field, Stanhope, N.J.
Open Sat-Sun 10-5; adm $6
212-255-0020, call to confirm
I-80 Exit 25
Generally the 2nd or 3rd weekend in
May and Sep
Stella Show Mgmt Co
151 W. 25th 2nd Fl.
New York, NY, 10001

SUMMIT, NJ 07901
Summit Antique Center
50 dealers
511 Morris Ave
Open 7 days 11-5
908-273-9373
W. of Newark Exit Rte 24 onto River
Rd.. S 1/2 mile to Morris Ave. then left.

NEW JERSEY

TRAVEL NOTES

NEW MEXICO

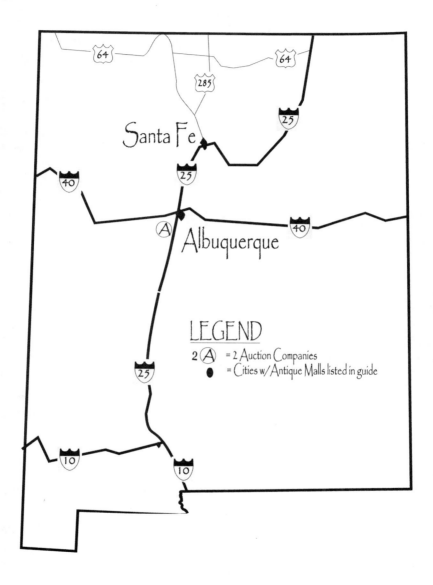

NEW MEXICO

WEEKEND ANTIQUE EVENTS
Albuquerque Open Air Flea Market, **every Sat & Sun except in Sep**
Santa Fe, Tesuque Flea Mkt., **every Fri, Sat & Sun, weather permitting.**
Santa Fe's Famous Indian Market **is 3rd weekend in Aug**

ANTIQUE VILLAGES & DISTRICTS
Many antique shops and malls on Central Ave in Albuquerque

AUCTION/ESTATE SALE CO'S
Albuquerque, NM 87107
Barry's Auction Service
Auction for household, antiques & coll
2820-A Richmond Dr.
Every Wed at 6:30 P.M.
505-875-1720

SANTA FE, NM
Allard Auctions
All Native American items
La Fonda Hotel on the Square
**2nd weekend in Aug which is the Wk-
end before Indian Market in Santa Fe**
Doug & Steve Allard 1-888-314-0343
#1 Museum Lane
St. Ignatius, MT 59865

ANTIQUE MALLS, MARKETS / SHOWS
ALBUQUERQUE, NM
New Mexico Open Air Flea Market
1100 spaces; Indian, new & used mdse.
Fairgrounds at Louisiana & Central NE
7 AM to 5 P.M. Sat & Sun; park $2.00
505-265-1791 or 304-2931
I-40 Exit 163,
S on LA 1 mi at Central
Every Sat & Sun except for Sep
NM Open Air Flea Market
PO Box 8546
Albuquerque, NM 87198

**Old Town Albuquerque has Indian
artifacts, jewelry and crafts
I-40 exit 157 Rio Grande Blvd, S 1/2 mi**

ALBUQUERQUE, NM 87123
Route 66 Antique Connection
70 dealers
12815 Central NE
Open Mon-Sat 10-5; Sun 12-5
505-296-2300
**I-40 Exit 165; S to Central, 15 yards NE
12 antique shops & malls on Central
from 519 NW to 1020 SE Central**

ALBUQUERQUE, NM 87108
Classic Century Square
70 shops
4616 Central SE
Mon-Sat 10-6; Sun 12-5
505-265-3161
I-40 Exit 166 S to Central, R

ALBUQUERQUE, NM 87108
Antique Specialty Mall
80 dealers
4516 Central SE
Mon-Sat 10-6; Sun 12-5
505-268-8080
I-40 Exit 166 S to Central, W 2 blocks

NEW MEXICO

Eating betweem Albuquerque and Flagstaff can be difficult, but in Grants, NM is a great solution. It is *La Ventana*, set back off Northside of old Route 66 (Main St.) downtown. Open 11AM-11PM 505-287-9393 at 110 1/2 Geis St.

Santa Fe's downtown square is good for Indian Jewelry and artifacts which may be bought direct from Native Americans or from the shops surrounding the Square.

In Santa Fe, our favorite place to eat is the *Little French Bakery & Creperie* off the lobby of La Fonda Hotel. Here you can get such things as Croque Monsieur, baked French pastries all at reasonable prices.
The dining room of the La Fonda is also a great place to eat.

For Southwest or Mexican food we found "Old Mexico Grill" at 2434 Cerrillos Rd to be outstanding with uniquely prepared dishes. It is in the L shaped shopping Center just South of Office Depot.

If you would like to eat a good homemade meal in a little hotel of the "Old West" then stop in Springer, NM at I-25 Exit 412 downtown Brown Hotel & Cafe. 505-483-2269

SANTA FE, NM
The famous Indian Market in Santa Fe is the 3rd weekend in Aug. every year. Hundreds of vendors all over Old Town Santa Fe.

SANTA FE, NM
Tesuque Flea Market
200+ dealers; antiques, Native American & SW mdse
By the Opera Grounds
Open 8-5; outdoors; adm & park free
505-988-3620
On US 285/84 N
Every Friday, Sat/Sun; Winter Sat/Sun weather permitting
Tesuque Pueblo
Rte 5, P.O. Box 360-T
Santa Fe, NM, 87501

TRAVEL NOTES

TRAVEL NOTES

NEW YORK

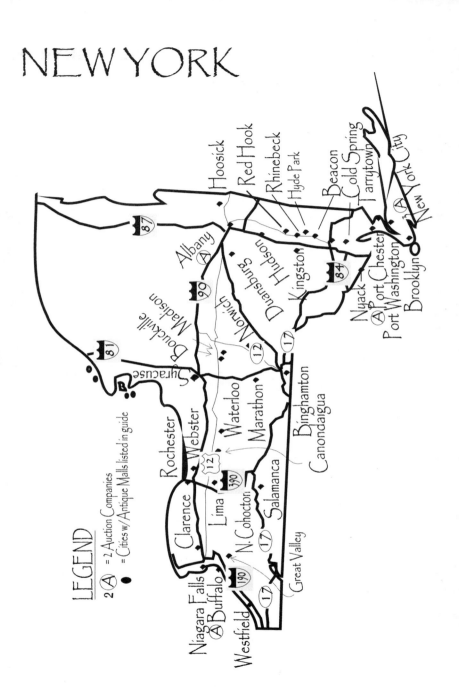

NEW YORK
WEEKEND ANTIQUE EVENTS

Bouckville Outdoor Antique Market and Antique Pavilion
Sun May thru Nov 1; special shows **1st Sat & Sun in June &**
3rd weekend in Aug. have 1000 dealers
Buffalo/Clarence, Antique World , 100's of dealers,
every Sun
New York City, Annex Antiques Fair on the Avenue of the America's between
24th & 25th Sts, 100 dealers, **every Sat**
New York City, Triple Pier;
usually 2nd & 3rd weekends in Jan & Mar
Rhinebeck Antique Fair, **Memorial & Columbus Day   weekends,**
and 4th Sat in July
Syracuse/Liverpool, Antiques, 500 dealers, **Third weekend in July.**

ANTIQUE DISTRICTS/ VILLAGES
Binghampton, Bouckville/ Madison US 20, Brooklyn, Buffalo, Clarence,
Hudson, NYC, Nyack, Port Washington

AUCTION/ESTATE SALE CO'S

Buffalo/
Batavia, NY 14020
Page Auction Gallery
Auctions antiques, collectibles & toys
5596 E Main St.
I-90 Exit 486
Auctions about everySat
585-343-2934 Call for dates

New York City, NY 10020
Christie's
Conducts collectible auctions here
20 Rockefeller Plaza
Call for information on next sale
212-636-2000

ANTIQUE MALLS, MARKETS / SHOWS

BEACON, NY 12508
Back In Time Antiques
One of 15 antique shops on Main St.
432 Main St.
Open 11-5; closed Tue & Wed; Sun 12-5
845-838-0623
I-84 Exit 11 S.(Beacon) Downtown

BINGHAMTON, NY
10 shops in this antique row
99 Clinton St.
Open Mon-Sat, usually not on Sunday.
Fwy 17 W to Mygatt St. Exit,
L on Mygatt St to Clinton Antique Row

NEW YORK

BOUCKVILLE, NY 13310
The Depot
50 dealers
Box 57
Open 7 days 10-5; Jan & Feb clsd M,T, W
315-893-7676
40 mi SE of Syracuse via
Rte 92 and US 20 East

BOUCKVILLE, NY
Bouckville Antique Pavilion
50 vendors; no new merchandise
On US 20
Open 7-4; adm & park free
315-893-7483; call for exact dates
Antique Market Sun May 1-Nov 1
1st Sat-Sun in June & 3rd wkend in Aug
Up to 1000 vendors
Steve Bono
RR #1, Box 111
Bouckville, NY 13310

BOUCKVILLE/
MADISON, NY 13310
Madison Bouckville Antique Dlrs Assoc.
100 dealers in 37 shops on US 20
P.O. Box 3
Hours vary
No phone
Madison & Bouckville are only
3 mi apart on US 20 Hwy

BROOKLYN, NY 11217
In Days of Old, Ltd.
One of 18 shops in this antique row
357 Atlantic Ave.
Open Wed-Sun 11-5
718-858-4233
I-278 Exit 27 Atlantic Ave E 5 blocks

BROOKLYN, NY 11230
Once Upon a Time Antiques
One of 18 shops on Coney Island Ave.
1053 Coney Island Ave.
Open 10-5 Mon-Sat.; closed Sun
718-859-6295
Coney Island Ave is parallel to
and E of Ocean Pwky.

BUFFALO, NY
There are a dozen antique stores on
Elmwood Ave in the 00 & 100 blocks,
plus others on adjacent Allen &
Franklin Sts. in downtown Buffalo.
Also, a half dozen more in the 1400-
1500 blocks of Hertel Ave. In Clarence
we like to eat at the *Old Red Mill Inn*
on Rte 5, 1/2 mi E of Rte 78 at 8326
Main St. Closed Mondays. 716-633-
7878.
We also like to eat at the *Original*
***Pancake House*, 3 mi E of the Red**
Mill at 5479 Main St. 716-634-1025

BUFFALO/
CLARENCE, NY 14031
Antique World
100's of dealers; antiques & collectibles
10995 Main
Open Sunrise to 4 PM every Sun; adm
$1 per car. 716-759-8483
I-290 Exit 47, 10 mi E on Rte 5;
or I-90 Exit 48A, 7 mi W on Rte 5
Extravaganzas May & Sept; adm $6
Long recognized for Sunday Flea
Markets. With the largest con-
centration of antiques and col-
lectibles dealers, it's the antique
Capital of Western New York.

212

BUFFALO/
CLARENCE, NY 14031
Courtyard Antique Center
50 dealers, 10,000 sq. ft.
10255 Main St.
Open 7 days 10-5
716-759-1726
In Clarence Courtyard
Clarence has 4 multi-dealer malls

CANANDAIGUA, NY 14424
Antiques Unlimited
50 dealers
168 Niagara
Mon-Sat 10-5; Sun 12-5
585-394-7255
I-90 Exit 43, S 6 mi ; or I-90
Exit 44, S 7 mi on Rt 332 down Main St,
then 1st L after RR Tracks on Niagara

CANANDAIGUA, NY 14424
Antique Center
30 dealers
47 Saltonstal St.
Open 7 days 10-5
585-394-2297
Downtown, just off Main

COLD SPRING NY 10516
Dew Drop Inn Antique Center
40 dealers
Route 9
Closed Tue, otherwise open 11-5
845-265-4358
I-84 Exit 13 S, about 5 mi
9 antique shops in Cold Springs
38 Main St. to 290 Main St.

DUANESBURG NY 12056
Black Sheep Antique Center
70 dealers
US Route 20
7 days 10-5; cl Tue & Wed Jan & Feb
518-895-2983
I-88 Exit 24, W 3 mi on US 20

FARMINGTON, NY 14425
Ontario Mall Antiques
1000 dealers
1740 Rte 332
7 days 10-6
585-398-3030
3 mi So. of NY S Thruway exit 44

GREAT VALLEY, NY 14741
Green Gable Village
14,000 sq. ft. mall plus barn
Rte 219
Open 7 days 10-5, Thur till 6
716-945-3600
60 miles S of Buffalo on US 219, on Rte
17 Exit 21 N 3 mi

HOOSICK, NY 12089
Hoosick Antique Center
65 dealers
Route 7, P. O. Box 203
Open 10-4:30, Clsd Wed, Sun 11:30-5
518-686-4700
7 mi E of Bennington, VT. 30 miles east
of Albany by state line on Rte 7

213

NEW YORK

HUDSON, NY 12534
Armory Art & Antique Gallery
65 dealers
State at N. 5th St., P.O. Box 352
Open 11-5, Clsd Tue & Wed
518-822-1477
I-87 Exit 21 to downtown Hudson
State is 2 blocks N. of Warren St.
60 shops in 5 historic walking blocks

LIMA, NY 14485
Crossroads Country Mall
45 dealers
7348 E. Main
Open 11-5 daily
585-624-1993
I-390 Exit 10

HYDE PARK, NY 12538
Hyde Park Antique Center
45 dealers
4192 Albany Post Road
Open daily 10-5
845-229-8200
6 mi N of Poughkeepsie on US 9

MARATHON, NY 13803
Riverbend Antique Center
40 dealers
Route 11
Open 10-6; closed Mon & holidays
607-849-6305
At I-81 Exit 9

HYDE PARK, NY 12538
Village Antique Center
40 dealers
4321 Albany Post Road
Open daily 10-5
845-229-6600
US 9 Hwy

NEW YORK CITY, NY
Annex and Garage Antiques Show
Up to 700 vendors; outdoors & indoors
On the Avenue of the Americas (6th Ave)
Open 6:30 to 5 pm; adm $1
212-243-5343
Between 24th & 25th Sts in garage and
on lots every Sat antiques & col-
lectibles only,
on Sun 200 vendors of everything.
Annex Antiques Fair, Alan Boss
P. O. Box 7010
NY NY 10116-4627

KINGSTON, NY 12401
Shillypot Antique Center
26 plus dealers
41 Broadway
11-5 weekends, clsd Wed
845-338-6779
Jan-Mar 11-5, Fri-Mon only
5 other antique stores in Kingston

214

NEW YORK CITY, NY
Triple Pier Expo
600 different antique dealers each
weekend
Piers 88, 90, 92
Open Sat 9-6; Sun 11-6; adm $15
212-255-0020 Call for exact dates
55th St & 12th Ave
Usually 2nd & 3rd weekends in Jan,
Feb & Mar, 3rd or 4th weekend in Jan
for Piers 88 & 90, 300 dealers
Stella Show Mgmt Co.
151 W 25th 2nd Fl
NY NY, 10001
www.stellashows.com

NEW YORK CITY, NY 10010
Antique Showplace
135 dealers
40 W. 25th St.
Mon-Fri 10-6; Sat & Sun 8:30-5:30
212-633-6063
www.nyshowplace.com

NEW YORK CITY, NY 10022
Manhattan Art and Antique Center
104 galleries
1050 Second Avenue
Mon-Sat 10:30-6; Sun 12-6
212-355-4400

NEW YORK CITY, NY 10022
Ann Morris Antiques- To Trade only
One of a dozen nearby shops
239 E. 60th
Mon-Fri 9-6; closed Sat & Sun
212-755-3308
Many shops on 61st, 62nd, 63rd, &
64th Sts in this antique district.

NEW YORK CITY, NY 10003
Big Apple Antiques
One of 8 antique shops in one block
52 E.11th St.
Mon-Fri 9-5, Closed Sat-Sun
212-260-5110
Lower Manhattan

NEW YORK CITY, NY 10022
Lillian Nassau, Ltd.
One of 15 antique shops in area
220 E. 57th St.
Tue-Thur10-5; Sat 10:30-5, clsd Sun &
Mon
212-759-6062
57th St. from # 11 to #301 E. 57th St.

NEW YORK CITY, NY 10014
Old Japan,Inc.
One of 6 antique shops on Bleecker St.
382 Bleecker St.
Open 1-7 Tue-Sun; closed Mon
212-633-0922
In Greenwich Village between
7th & 8th Ave below 14th St
Tue-Sat 1-7pm; Sun 12-5; clsd Mon

NEW YORK CITY, NY 10003
10 antique shops in 800 block Broadway
Mon-Fri 10-5; closed Sat & Sun

NYACK, NY 10960
Franklin Antique Center
30 shops
142 Main St.
Open Wed-Sun 11-5
845-353-1130
I-87 Exit 11 to Main St. Walk to a dozen
shops on Main & Broadway.

NEW YORK

PORT WASHINGTON, NY 11050
Port Antique Center
15 dealers
289 Main St.
Open Tue-Sat 11:30-5:30; Sun 12-5
516-767-3313
One of 10 antique shops on Main St. downtown Port Washington, Long Island, I-495 Exit 35 N

REDHOOK, NY 12571
Annex Antique Center
30 dealers
23 E. Market St.
Open 7 days 11-5
845-758-2843
5 mi N of Rhinebeck on US 9, Downtown Walk to 3 other antique shops.

RHINEBECK, NY
Rhinebeck Antiques Fair
175 dealers
Fairgrounds, on US 9, N of town
Sat 10-5, Sun 11-4; adm $9, park free
845-876-1989
Sat/Sun of Memorial Day weekend, Always 4th Sat in July, Sat/Sun of Columbus Day week in Oct
Bruce Garrett Manager
PO Box 838
Rhinebeck, NY 12572
www.rhinebeckantiquesfair.com

RHINEBECK, NY 12572
Beekman Arms Antique Market
35 dealers
6387 Mill St
Open daily 11-5
845-876-3477
Downtown
Beekman Square behind the hotel

SALAMANCA, NY 14779
Salamanca Mall Antiques
1000 plus dealers
1000 Main St.
7 days 10-6
716-945-5532
Rte 17, Exit 21 N to stop sign, L on Clinton St. Rte 417 to Main St. Turn right

SARATOGA SPRINGS, NY 12866
Regent Street Antique Center
20 dealers, 72,000 sq.ft.
163 Regent Street
Open 7 days 10-5
518-584-0107
I-87, Exit 14W, on Union Ave, R on Regent Street.

SYRACUSE, NY 13208
Syracuse Antiques Exchange
50 dealers
1629 N. Salina
Mon-Sat 10:30-5; Sun 12-4
315-471-1841
From I-81 S exit Court St., go straight 1 block to Salina. From I-81 north-bound. Exit Hiawatha straight ahead to Salina.

216

NEW YORK

SYRACUSE/
LIVERPOOL, NY
Great American Antiquefest
350 dealers; all antiques & collectibles
Onondaga Lake Park
Fri 10-4, $20; Sat 8-6, Sun 9-4, $6
315-457-6954
I-90 Exit 38 or 39
Third weekend in July
every year
Antiquefest Inc.
PO Box 264
Liverpool, NY 13088

TARRYTOWN, NY 10591
Belkind Biji
One of 12 antique shops on Main
21 Main St.
Shops closed Mon
 otherwise 11:30-5:30 PM
914-524-9626
I-87/287 Exit 1 & 119 before Tappan
Zee Bridge (from NYC) Downtown.

TRAVEL NOTES

NORTH CAROLINA
East

NORTH CAROLINA - East

WEEKEND ANTIQUE EVENTS
Raleigh Antique Extravaganza,175 dealers, **3rd week-end in Jan & July**

ANTIQUE DISTRICTS/VILLAGES
Hillsborough, Wilmington

ANTIQUE MALLS, MARKETS / SHOWS

BURLINGTON, NC 27215
Granddaddy's Antique Mall
300 dealers, 80,000 sq. ft.
2316 Maple Ave.
Open Mon-Sat 10-6, Sun 1-6
800-494-1919 or 336-570-1997
At I-85/ 40 Exit 145

FAYETTEVILLE, NC 28301
Eastover Trading Co. Antique Mall
60 dealers
3551 Dunn Rd
Open Mon-Sat 9-5; closed Sun
910-323-1121
Hwy 301 N., I-95 Exit 55 W to 301 N

HILLSBOROUGH, NC 27278
The Antique Mall, Inc.
25 dealers
387 JaMax Drive
Mon-Sat 10-5; Sun 1-5
919-732-8882
At I-85 Exit 164
There are 6 other malls here
with a total of about 200 dealers

RALEIGH, NC 27605
Carolina Antique Mall
74 dealer spaces
2050 Clark Avenue
Mon-Sat 10-5:30
919-833-8227
I-440/US 1 Exit 7, Glenwood Ave
(US 70) S to Oberlin Rd, then left on
Clark

RALEIGH, NC 27616
Gresham Lake Antique Mall
45 dealers
6917 Capitol Blvd.
Open Mon-Sat 10-5:30; Sun 1-5
919-878-9381
US Hwy 1 N from I-440 Exit 11

RALEIGH, NC 27604
Oakwood Antique Mall
63 dealers
1653 Old Louisburg Rd.
Tue-Sat 10-6; Sun 1-5
919-834-5255
I-440 Beltline to Exit 11, 401 S
toCapital Blvd 1 mi, R on Tillery Place

NORTH CAROLINA - East

RALEIGH, NC
Antique Extravaganza (Show)
175 dealers; all antiques
Raleigh Convention Center
Fri 10-7; Sat 10-6; Sun 11-5; adm $5.
336-924-4359
At Lenoir & Salisbury Sts., downtown
Twice a year; 3rd weekend
Jan & Jul every year
Antiques Extravaganza of NC
P.O. Box 11565
Winston-Salem, NC 27116

WILMINGTON/
SOUTHPORT, NC 28461
Northrop Antique Mall
38 dealers, 2 stories
111 E. Moore Street.
Mon-Sat 10-5; Sun 12-5
910-457-9569
Downtown

25 mi N of Southport in Wilmington
is a cluster of 18 antique stores
Wilmington is at the east end of I-40

WILSON, NC 27894
Fulford's Antique Warehouse
67,000 sq. ft.
320 Barnes St. South
Open Mon-Fri 8-5; Sat 8-3; closed Sun
252-243-7727
E on U.S. 264 to Lodge St., L to Barnes

WILSON, NC 27894
Boone's Antiques
Direct Antique Importer
2014 U.S. Hwy 301 S W
Mon-Fri 9-5; Sat 10-5; closed Sun
252-237-1508
I-95 Exit 121 E to US Hwy 301 S
There are 3 antique stores by Boone's

WILSON, NC 27895
Greater Wilson Antique Market
35 spaces
2610 Hwy 301 S
P.O. Box 3574
Open Mon-Sat 10-5; Sun closed
252-237-0402
I-95 Exit 119 then Exit 43 on US 301

TRAVEL NOTES

TRAVEL NOTES

NORTH CAROLINA
West

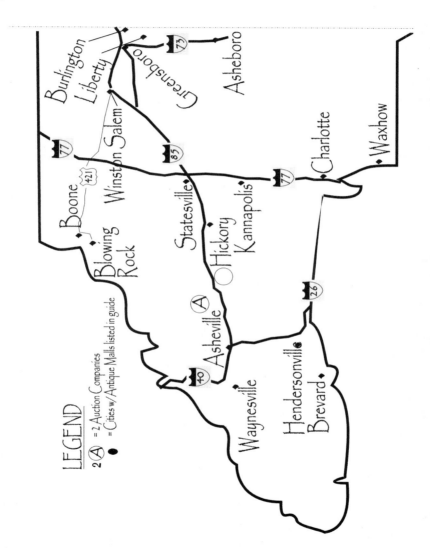

LEGEND

2Ⓐ = 2 Auction Companies

● = Cities w/Antique Malls listed in guide

Burlington
Liberty
Greensboro
Asheboro
Charlotte
Waxhow
Winston Salem
Boone
421
77
85
77
73
Blowing Rock
Statesville
Hickory
Kannapolis
26
Asheville
Ⓐ
40
Waynesville
Hendersonville
Brevard

NORTH CAROLINA - WEST

WEEKEND ANTIQUE EVENTS

Charlotte Antique & Collectibles Show, 700-1200 dealers,
1st Sat weekend of every month, Apr, July & Nov are "Spectaculars"-2000 dealers
Greensboro, Super Flea Market, up to 200 dealers,
2nd weekend of each month
Winston-Salem Antique Extravaganza,175 dealers, **last week-end in Nov.**
Liberty Antique Festival- 350 dealers, **last Fri & Sat in Sept and April**

AUCTION/ESTATE SALE CO'S

Asheville, NC, 28805
Tommy Tuten Auction
Antique auction
155 Craven St.
Every Fri at 6 P.M.
828-253-7712

ANTIQUE MALLS, MARKETS / SHOWS

ASHEBORO, NC 27203
Collectors Antique Mall
135 dealers
211 Sunset Avenue
Open Mon 10-8; Tue-Sat 10-6; Sun 1-5
336-629-8105
24 mi S of Greensboro on US 220;
Downtown
Sunset is the main street of town

ASHEVILLE, NC 28805
Antique Tobacco Barn (Mall)
92 dealers, 70,000 sq. ft.
75 Swannanoa River Rd.
Open Mon-Thu 10-5; Fri-Sat 9-5
828-252-7291
I-40 Exit 50, N 1/2 mi to Wendy's, R
then turn left to mall

ASHEVILLE, NC 28801
Asheville Antique Mall
30 dealers
43 Rankin Ave.
Open Mon-Sat 10-5; Sun 1-5
828-253-3634
Downtown

ASHEVILLE/ FLETCHER, NC 28732
Smiley's Antique Mall
50 dealers
P. O. Box 458, US Hwy 25
Open 7 days 10-5
828-684-3515
12 mi S of Asheville
I-26 Exit 13 N, 1/2 mi on US 28

BLOWING ROCK, NC 28605
Blowing Rock Antique Center
40 dealers.
US Hwy 321 Bypass
Open Mon-Sat 10-5; Sun 1-5
828-295-4950
40 mi N of Hickory on US 321
10 antique shops in town,
6 on Main St. #1157 S to #999 N

NORTH CAROLINA - West

BOONE, NC 28607
Boone Antique Mall
40 dealers
805 W. King St.
Open Mon-Sat 10-6; Sun 1-6
828-262-0521
US Hwy 421 - King Street,
Center of Business District

BREVARD, NC 28712
Brevard Antique Mall
70 dealers
57 E. Main St.
Open Mon-Sat 9:30-5:30; Sun 1-5
828-885-2744
I-26 Exit 18, S, US 64, 22 mi to Brevard

CHARLOTTE, NC
Charlotte Antique & Collectibles Show
1000-1500 dealers; Fri, Sat & Sun
7100 Statesville Road
Open 9-5; park free
704-596-4643
I-77 Exit 16A, every 1st Sat weekend
Apr July and Nov are Spectaculars
with 2,000 dealers; $7 adm. Thur. $12
Charlottle Antique & Collectibles Show
P. O. Box 26652
Charlotte, NC 28261

GREENSBORO, NC
"Super Flea" Market
Up to 200 dealers; 80% antiques & coll
Greensboro Coliseum Exhibit Hall
Sat 8-5; Sun 10-5; park $3, adm $3.00
336-373-8515
I-40/85 Exit 217, N to 1921 W. Lee St.
Generally second weekend of each
month. Call to confirm
Smith-Tomlinson Co.
P.O. Box 16122
Greensboro, NC 27416

GREENSBORO, NC 27420
Replacements, Ltd.
225,000 sq. ft. of crystal, china & antiques
1089 Knox Rd.
Open daily 8-9
1-800-737-5223 or 336-697-3000
At I-40 Exit 132 N side
www.replacements.com

GREENSBORO, NC 27401
Antique Marketplace
150 dealers
6428 Burnt Poplar.
Open M-Wed 10-6;Thur-Sat 10-8, Sun 1-6
336-273-1767 or 336-662-0544
Near intersection of I-40 & NC 68
There are 8 antique shops on So. Elm St.
200-600 blocks

HENDERSONVILLE, NC 28739
Hendersonville Antique Mall
50 dealers
670 Spartanburg Hwy.(US 176 S)
Open Mon-Sat 10-5; Sun 1-5
828-692-5125
I-26 Exit 18 S on US Hwy 176, 2 mi

HENDERSONVILLE, NC 28739
Jane Asher's Antiques & Fine Traditions
25 dealers
344 N. Main St.
Open Mon-Sat 10-5; Sun closed
828-698-0018
I 26 Exit 18 to downtown.
8 other shops on Main St & 7 nearby.

NORTH CAROLINA - West

HICKORY, NC 28602
Hickory Antiques Mall
85 booths
348 US Hwy 70 SW
Open Mon-Sat 10-6; Sun 1:30-6
828-322-4004
I-40 Exit 123 N to US 70 W, take a R
www.hickoryantiquesmall.com

KANNAPOLIS, NC 28081
Antique Malls at Cannon Village
45 dealers
104 S. Main Street
Mon-Sat 10-6; Sun 1-6
704-932-2529
I-85 Exit 68 or 58 to downtown

LIBERTY, NC
Liberty Antique Festival
350 dealers (Walk several acres on a farm)
Off 421 Liberty/Staley Exit, 2 mi South of Liberty. Adm $5
Open 8-6 PM Rain or shine Fri-Sat
336-622-3040
Last Fri & Sat in Sept & April .
20 min from Greensboro or Burlington
Mary & Vito Sico
P.O. Box 939
Liberty, NC 27298

WAYNESVILLE, NC 28786
Barber's Orchard Antique Mall
50 booths
36 Providence Place (Old Balsam Rd.)
Open 7 days 10-5
828-456-7229
Across from Thad Wood's
Antique Mall on US 23-74,
Bypass West.

WAYNESVILLE, NC 28786
Thad Wood's Antique Mall
100 booths
US Hwy 23-74 Bypass West
Open Mon-Sat 9:30-5:30; Sun 1-5
828-456-3298, or 453-3759
I-40 Exit US 23-74 S about
20 mi W of Asheville

WAXHAW, NC 28173
20 antique stores in Waxhow
A turn-of-the-century village
at Jct of Hwy 16 & 75
14 mi S of Charlotte
closed Tue, Mon-Sat 10-5, Sun 1-5

WINSTON-SALEM, NC 27101
Antique Extravaganza of NC
175 dealers all antiques
LJVM Colliseum Annex on Deacon Blvd.
Fri 10-7, Sat 10-6, Sun 11-5, Adm $5.00
336-924-4359 call to confirm
From I40 Bus, take Cherry St. to
Deacon Blvd.
Last weekend in Nov.
Antiques Extravaganza of NC
P.O. Box 11565
Winston Salem, N. C. 27116

WINSTON-SALEM, NC 27101
Lost In Time Antique Mall
80 dealers, 16,000 sq. ft.
2101 Peters Creek Pkwy
Mon-Sat 10-6, Sun 1-6
336-725-5829
I-40 Exit 192 N on Peters Creek Pkwy

225

NORTH DAKOTA

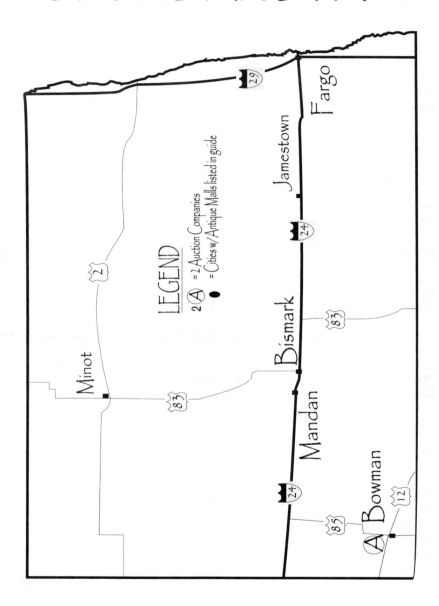

NORTH DAKOTA

WEEKEND ANTIQUE EVENTS
Minot, Magic City Flea Market, 75 dealers;
2nd Sat every month except Jan
Mandan, Dakota Midwest Market,
1st weekend of every month except Jan

AUCTION/ESTATE SALE CO'S
Bowman, ND 58623
Penfield Auction
Estate, household & antique auctions
P.O. Box 111
Held every 2nd Sat of the month
701-523-3652

ANTIQUE MALLS, MARKETS/ SHOWS

BISMARK, ND 58501
Third Floor Antique Mall
28 dealers
200 W Main Avenue
Mon-Sat 10:30-5; closed Sun
701-221-2594
Downtown

MANDAN, ND
Dakota Antique Show & Flea Mkt
70 dealers; 80% antiques & collectibles
Mandan Community Center, 901
Division
Fri 4-9, Sat 9-5; adm $1; indoors
701-223-6185
**I-94 Exit 152, S on 6th Ave to Division
First full weekend of every month
except Jan**
Bruce Skogen
2512-93 St. SE
Bismark, ND 58504

MINOT, ND
Magic City Flea Market
75 dealers; antiques, collectibles, crafts
State Fairgrounds
Open Sat 8-4 & Sun 10-4; adm $1 & park
free. Call to confirm date
701-852-1289 or 701-838-1150
**On Business US 2 Hwy E of US 83.
Second Sat every month Feb thru Dec.**
Richard Timboe
PO Box 1672
Minot, ND 58701

MINOT, ND 58701
Downtown Mall
15 dealers
108 S. Main St.
Mon-Sat 9-5;Sat 9-4, closed Sun
701-852-9084
**Downtown, off Hwy 83
North of Bismark**

OHIO

Toledo

Ashtabula

Alvon ³Ⓐ Cleveland

90

11

Burton

Brookfield

80

Findley

Medina

76

Ravenna

Akron

Wapakoneta 75

Columbiana

Youngstown

71

East
Liverpool

New
Philadelphia

Urbana

Sunbury

Tipp City

Springfield

Cambridge

Zannesville

Lawrenceburg, In

70

Ⓐ Columbus

Dayton

Waynesville

77

Lebanon

Logan

Marietta

Blanchester

Cincinnati

Jackson 33

Ⓐ

Newport,
Ky

35

LEGEND

2Ⓐ = 2 Auction Companies

● = Cities w/ Antique Malls listed in guide

OHIO

WEEKEND ANTIQUE EVENTS

Cleveland-Pappabello Antique Show, 120 dealers
   mid July
Burton Great Geauga Antique Market,
   twice a year, usually 1st Sat in Jun & 3rd Sat in Sept.
Cincinnati - See Burlington, KY for Antique Market
   every 3rd Sun Apr thru Oct,
Lawrenceburg, IN for Antique Market, **first Sun May thru Oct.**
Columbus, Scott Antique Market,
   usually 3rd or 4th weekend of month.   Nov-Apr.
Medina Fairgrounds Antique Show, **every 1st Sun except Jan, Jun & Aug.**
Springfield Antique Show & Flea Market,
   usually 3rd weekends, except Jul & Dec,   600-1500 dealers.
Extravaganzas in May,   July & Sept.
Urbana Antiques & Flea Market, 150 dealers,
   every 1st full weekend except Aug

ANTIQUE DISTRICTS/VILLAGES

Cleveland/ Avon/ Shaker Heights, Columbus/ Powell, Lebanon, Marietta, Sunbury, Waynesville, Columbia

AUCTION/ESTATE SALE CO'S

COLUMBUS/ PLAIN CITY, OH 43064
Plain City Auction Service
Antique & collectibles auction
145 E. Main
Usually Last Fri of every month at 3pm
614-873-5622

ANTIQUE MALLS, MARKETS/ SHOWS

AKRON, OH 44303
Stage Coach Antiques
One of 3 shops in 400 block W. Market
449 W. Market
Mon - Sat 10-6, Sun 12-5
330-762-5422
From I-77 take the Market St Exit
(Hwy 18) to downtown Akron

ASHTABULA, OH 44004
Moses Antique Mall
Dozens of booths
4135 State St.
Open Mon-Sat 10-5, Sun 12-4
440-992-5556
I-90 Exit 229 Hwy 11 N to US Hwy 20,
W to first light then L

BLANCHESTER. OH 45107
Broadway Antique Mall II
85 booths
Corner Broadway & Main
Open Mon- Sat 10-5, Sun 12:30-5
937-783-2271
I-275 Exit 57, Hwy 28, 13 mi NE

OHIO

BURTON, OH
The Great Geauga Antique Market
500 dealers twice a year
Fairgrounds Racetrack
Daybreak adm $20; 9:30-5pm, adm $5
440-834-0213
25 mi E of Cleveland on Hwy 87
Usually the 1st Sat in Jun, and 2nd Sat
after Labor Day. Call to confirm.
Antique Market
P.O. Box 370
Burton,OH 44021

BROOKFIELD, OH 44403
Valley View Antique mall
350 booths & showcases
7281 Warren Sharon Rd
Open Sun-Thur 10-6, Fri & Sat 10-8
800-587-2535 or 330-448-6866
I-80 Exit 234, N 3 mi on
Rte 7 to Brookfield Center;
turn R on Warren Sharon Rd

CAMBRIDGE, OH 43725
Penny Court Antique Mall
100 booths, 56 dealers
637 Wheeling Avenue (US 40)
Open Mon-Sat 10-6; Sun 12-5, Call on
holiday hours
740-432-4369
Downtown, I-70 Exit 178 N
or I-77 Exit 46 Wat the I-70/ I77
interchange on US 40

CAMBRIDGE, OH 43725
Guernsey Antique Mall
20 dealers
623 Wheeling Ave.
Open Mon-Sat 10-5
740-432-2570
Downtown

CINCINNATI/MT HEALTHY, OH 45231
Covered Bridge Antique Mall
30 dealers
7508 Hamilton Ave. (US 127)
Mon-Sat 10-6; Sun 12-6
513-521-5739
I-275 Exit 36 S, North of Mt Healthy
Exit. There are 2 other shops nearby.

CINCINNATI, OH 45209
Duck Creek Antique Market
150 dealers
3715 Madison Rd
Open Mon-Sat 10-5; Sun 12-5
513-321-0900
I-71 Exit 3 E.

CINCINNATI/ READING , OH 45215
Grand Antique Mall
175 dealers
9701 Reading Rd.(US 42)
Mon-Sat 10-6, Sun 12-6
513-554-1919
I-75 Exit 14, E 1 mi.,
R turn on US 42, 1 mi.

CINCINNATI, /
FLORENCE, KY 41042
Florence Antique Mall
40,000 sq. ft.
8145 Mall Rd.
Open Tue-thru Sat- 10, Sun at 12, clsd
Mon
859-371-0600
I-75 Exit 180 W 1/4 mi to Mall Rd, R
1/2 mi

CINCINNATI, /
MIAMITOWN, OH 45041
 12 antique shops in 3 blocks
 State Rte 128
 Most open 7 days
 I-74/ I-275 Exit 7, 15 mi W of
 Cincinnati on State Rte 128.

CINCINNATI /
ROSS, OH 45061
Venice Pavillion Antique Mall
80 dealers
At corner of Rte 128 & 126
Open daily 11-7
513-738-8180
Take I-275 Exit 35, N on US 27, 6 mi to
Rte 128, 1 mi S. 2 other malls in area.

CLEVELAND/
AVON, OH 44011
Jameson Homestead
30 dealers
36675 Detroit Road
Open Mon-Sat 11-5; Sun 12-5
440-934-6977
Alt US 56 & Rte 254 W
Off I-90 (Avon) Exit Rte 83

CLEVELAND /
AVON, OH 44011
The Williams House
25 dealers
37300 Detroit Road, Rte 254
Open Tue-Sat 10-5; Sun 12-5
440-934-1800
Rte 254 Just W. of rte 611, S of I-90
a dozen antique shops in
Avon on Detroit Rd #35800-37300

CLEVELAND/
N. RIDGEVILLE, OH 44039
Hatchery Antique Mall
38 dealers
7474 Avon Belden Rd. (Rte 83)
Open 7 days 11-5
440-327-9808
Ohio Tpke Exit 9 A, N on Rte 83

CLEVELAND/
SHAKER HGTS, OH 44120
Bischoff Galleries
1 of 25 shops in antique district
12910 Larchmere Blvd.
Open Tue-Sat 11-5
216-231-8313
12600 to 12900 Larchmere Blvd

CLEVELAND OH 44135
Pappabello Antique Show
100 plus dealers
IX Center
6200 Riverside Dr.
Fri 12-8, Sat 11-6, Sun 11-5 $6
301-933-9433
Mid-July
Call for dates
 Pappabello Shows Inc.
P.O. Box 12069
Silver Spring, MD 20908

COLUMBIANA, OH 44408
Columbiana Antique Gallery
25 dealers
103 S. Main St.
Open Mon-Fri, 10-4:30, Sat/Sun 12-5
330-482-2240
Exit Hwy 11 Freeway at Hwy 164
E to downtown. Walk to 5 other shops

OHIO

COLUMBUS, OH
Scott Antique Market
800 inside/outside booths
Ohio State Fairgrounds
Sat 9-6; Sun 10-4; adm free; park $4
740-569-4112; call for exact dates
I-71 Exit 111, 17th Ave to Fairgrounds
3rd or 4th weekend of each month,
Nov-Apr.
Scott Antique Markets
P.O. Box 60
Bremen, OH 43107

COLUMBUS, OH 43206
Greater Columbus Antique Mall
70 dealers
1045 S. High Street
Open 7 days 10-6
614-443-7858
I-70 Exit 100 S, 3/4 mi from I-70 on
South High St, 1 block N of Greenlawn,
Exit I-71 Greenlawn Ave S. I-270 Exit
22 N to Powell Rd, W.
5 shops downtown.

DAYTON, OH 45409
Treasure Barn Antique Mall
50 dealers
1043 S. Main St.
Open Tue-Sat 11-5; Sun 12-5
937-222-4400
Inside Montgomery County Fairgrounds
South of downtown City Center.

EAST LIVERPOOL, OH 43920
Pottery City Antique Mall
200 dealers
409 Washington St.
Open Mon-Sat 10-6; Sun 12-6
330-385-6933
Downtown at 4th & Washington
1/2 block from clock tower

FINDLAY, OH 45840
Jeffreys Antique Mall
250 dealers
11326 Township Rd 99
Open 7 days 10-6
419-423-7500
At I-75 Exit 161 on NW corner

LEBANON, OH 45036
Shoe Factory Antique Mall
70 dealers, 4 floors
120 E. South Street
Open Mon-Sat 10-6; Sun 12-5
513-932-8300
Lebanon is 7 mi E of I-75 Exit 29
or 3 mi W of I-71 Exits 28 or 32
Park and walk to malls downtown

LEBANON, OH 45036
Broadway Antique Mall
85 booths
15-17 S. Broadway
Open Mon-Sat 10-5; Sun 12-5
513-932-1410
Downtown

LEBANON, OH 45306
Millers Antique Market
80 dealers plus
201 S. Broadway
Open Mon-Sat 10-5; Sun 12-5
513-932-8710
Downtown

LEBANON, OH 45306
Hunters Horn Antique Center
70 dealers
35 E. Main
Open Mon-Sat 10-5'; Sun 12-5
513-932-5688
Downtown
Walk to a dozen other shops

LOGAN, OH 43138
Logan Antique Mall
100 dealers
12795 State Rte 664
Open Mon-Sat 10-8; Sun 11-6
740-385-2061
US Hwy 33, 45 mi SE of Columbus

LOGAN/ROCKBRIDGE, OH 43149
Spring Street Antique Mall
12,000 sq ft , 120 dealers
26782 us Hwy 33
Open Mon-Sat 10-8; Sun 12-5
740-385-1816
Right on US Hwy 33

MARIETTA, OH 45750
Tin Rabbit Antiques
15 dealers
204 Front St.
Open Mon-Sat 10-5; Sun 12-5
740-373-1152
**I-77 Exit 1 to downtown
5 other nearby antique shops.**

MARIETTA, OH 45750
Antique Mall of Marietta
70 dealers
135 2nd St.
Open Mon-Sat 10-6, Sun 11-5
740-376-0038
I-77 Exit 1 to downtown

MEDINA, OH 44256
Medina Antique Mall
500 dealers
2797 Medina Rd.
Open 7 days 10-6, Sat & Sun 10-8
330-722-0017 or 800-677-0177
I-71 Exit 218 E 1/4 mi
Huge variety of antique items for anyone's collection from French to Victorian, refined to primitive. Plan to spend some time to see all the showcases plus booths. One of the largest malls in the Midwest.

MEDINA, OH 44256
Brothers Antique Mall
50 dealers
6132 Wooster Pike
Open daily 10-5; Sun 12-5
330-723-7580
I-76 Exit 2, 5 mi N

MEDINA, OH 44256
Fairgrounds Antique Show
150 dealers; antiques & collectibles
735 Lafayette Rd, US Hwy 42
Early bird 7-10 A.M. $3; 10-3 $2
330-723-8249 call to confirm
**20 mi East of Akron;
I-71 Exit 218, W 4 mi
1st Sun except Jan, Jun & Aug**
Conrad & Dowdell
775 W. Smith Rd.
Medina, OH 44256

OHIO

NEW PHILADELPHIA, OH 44663
Riverfront Antique Mall
350 dealers
1203 Front Ave SW
Open 9-8; Sun 9-6
1-800-926-9806 or 330-339-4448
I-77 Exit 81, Rte 39E to first light then R to mall

RAVENNA, OH 44372
AAA I-76 Antique Mall
400 dealers, 50,000 sq. ft.
I-76 Hwy
Open 7 days 10-6
330-325-9776
At I-76 Exit 38N
Our 50,000 sq. ft. mall on I-76 has quality antiques & collectibles (No crafts, no new items & No repros). The newly constructed building with 250 booths & 200 locked showcases enjoys air -conditioning, & is fully carpeted.

SPRINGFIELD, OH
Springfield Antique Show & Flea Market
600-1200 dealers
Clark County Fairgrounds, in & outdoors
Sat 8-5; Sun 9-4; $2; Fri 8 A.M. $10
937-325-0053 or 937-427-7501
At I-70 Exit 59
May, July, & Sept Extravaganzas
Fri noon $3
Usually 3rd weekend, except July & Dec, call to confirm
Bruce Knight
P.O. Box 2429
Springfield, OH 45501
jenkinsshows.com

SPRINGFIELD, OH 45502
I-70 Antique Mall
150 dealers
4700 S. Charleston Pike
Open daily 10-6
937-324-8448
At I-70 Exit 59

SPRINGFIELD, OH 45502
Springfield Antique Center
450 dealers
1735 Titus Rd
Open 7 days 10-6
937-322-8868
S side of I-70 at Exit 59

SPRINGFIELD, OH 45505
Heart of Ohio Antique Centre
650 dealers
4785 E. National Rd.
Open 7 days 9:30-6
937-324-2188
I-70 Exit 62 & US 40

SUNBURY, OH 43074
Village Square Antique Mall
25 dealers
31 E. Granville
Mon-Sat 10-6, Sun 11-6, clsd 5 in winter
740-965-4377
I-71 Exit 131, E 4 mi on Hwy 37, on the Square 10 antique shops on the Square

234

TIPP CITY, OH 45371
Benkin Antique Gallery
40 dealers
14 E. Main St.
Open Mon-Sat 10-5; Sun 1-5
937-667-5526
I-75 Exit 68 at 14 E. Main.
4 other antique shops nearby

TOLEDO, OH 43606
Old Orchard Antique Mall
130 dealers
2635 W. Central Ave.
Open Mon-Sat 10-5, Thur & Fri 10-6,
 Sun 12-5
419-475-4561
I-475 Exit 13. E on Central Ave. 2
other shops in same block

TOLEDO/
PERRYSBURG, OH 43551
Perrysburg Antique Market (Mall)
30 dealers
116 Louisiana Avenue
Open Mon-Sat 10:30-5:30; Sun 11-4
419-872-0231
Downtown; I-75 Exit 193 (US Hwy 20)
or I-475 Exit 2 N

TOLEDO AREA, see LaSalle, MI
for 45 dealer mall I-75 Exit 9;
and Blissfield, MI for over 150
dealers in 4 malls and 2 large
shops, 20 mi on US 223

URBANA, OH
Urbana Antiques Show & Flea Market
150 indoor & 100-200 outdoor dealers
Champaign Cnty Fairgrounds on Park Av
 Sat/Sun 9-4; park free, $1 adm
937-788-2058
12 mi N of Springfield on US Hwy 68.
Every first full weekend except Aug.
Summer: Sat 9-5, Sun 10-5
 Steve Goddard
5890 Valley Pike.
Urbana, OH 43078

WAPAKONETA, OH 45895
Auglaize Antique Mall
80 dealers
116 W. Auglaize Street
Open Mon-Sat 10-6; Sun 12-6
419-738-8004
Downtown; I-75 Exit 111
Walk to 5 other antique shops
on Auglaize St.

WAYNESVILLE, OH 45068
Waynesville Antique Mall
55 dealers
69 S. Main, Box 697
Open 7 days 10-5
513-897-6937
I-75 Exit 38, E 10 mi or
I-71 Exit 45, W 9 mi
20 antique shops on Main downtown.

OHIO

YOUNGSTOWN/
BROOKFIELD, OH 44403
Valley View Antique mall
350 booths & showcases
7281 Warren Sharon Rd
Open Mon-Thur 10-6; Fri & Sat 10-8,
 Sun 10-6
800-587-2535 or 330-448-6866
**I-80 Exit 234, N 3 mi on
Rte 7 to Brookfield Center;
turn R on Warren Sharon Rd**

ZANESVILLE, OH 43701
Olde Towne Antique Mall
80 dealers
527 Main Street
Open Mon-Fri 10-5; Sat 10-5; Sun 12-5
740-453-8694
**I-70 Exit 154 to Downtown, from East,
155 exit, 3 blocks So.**

TRAVEL NOTES

TRAVEL NOTES

GREAT ANTIQUING GETAWAY TO S. W . OHIO

WHEN: 3rd weekend in May, July & Sept for Extravaganza with 1200 dealers. July can change. Call 937-325-0053 or 937-427-7501.

3rd weekends other months, 600 dealers, but call about Dec. (See text for details)

WHERE: Springfield Antique Show and Flea Market at Clark County Fairgrounds, I-70 Exit 59, for Extravaganza, Fri at 8 AM $10 adm, noon $3, Sat 8-5 & Sun 9-4 is $2.

ANTIQUING:

1. After the Market go under I-70 to the South side where at the same exit as the Market you will find the *AAA I-70 Antique Mall* with 150 dealers and on up the road aways at the same exit, is the *Springfield Antique Mall* with 450 dealers.

2. Next, go E on I-70 for 3 miles to Exit 62 for the *Heart of Ohio Antique Mall* with 650 dealers. It might take the rest of the day to look through all the aisles as the building is divided up in corriders. It has a good cafe which will help for a tasty lunch.

Lodging: Dayton, Springfield, Cinncinati and the area in between, harbor practically every lodging chain, so call your preference.

Leisure: Casino at Lawrenceburg, IN, I-275 Exit 16. Phone 888-274-6797.

ANTIQUE MARKETS:

Lawrenceburg also has a 250 dealer Antique Market 1st Sundays, May-Oct. (see text). Burlington, KY has a 350 dealer Antique Market 1st Sundays, April-Oct.(See text)

3. Take I-70 Exit 52, US Hwy 68 S to Xenia where you take US 42 S to Waynesville and it's 20 or so shops on Main Street.

4. Now continue S on US 42 to Lebanon and four 75 dealer malls all on, or just off Broadway and all very walkable.

Restaurant: In the middle of these malls in Lebanon you will see the *Golden Lamb Dining Room* at 27 S. Broadway. Built in 1803 as a Stage coach Inn, it has an extensive collection of Shaker furniture and 1890's toys. Good family style dinners including leg of lamb. 513-932-5065.Mark Twain, Charles Dickens, and many US Presidents have dined at this restaurant.

5. Next take Rte 63 W from Lebanon to I-75 S into Cincinnati to I-75 Exit 14E 1 mile, R on US 42, 1 mi to *Grand Antique Mall*, 9701 Reading Rd (US 42) 175 dealers.

6. Now continue S on US 42 to Rte 562 E to I-71S to I-71 Exit 3 E on Madison Rd. to *Duck Creek Antique Mall,* 150 dealers at 3715 Madison.

GREAT ANTIQUING GETAWAY TO S. W . OHIO cont'd

Restaurant: At the next Exit of I-71S, Exit 2, take Art Museum Dr,which eventually becomes Celestial St. At 1077 Celestial St., you will find *Rookwood Pottery Restaurant* at the top of Mt. Adams where one can dine in one of the huge kilns of the *Old* Rookwood Pottery Co. Trendy shops and night spots in area. 513-721-5456.

7.*Florence Antique Mall*, **closed Mondays,** 40,000 sq. ft., I-71S to KY Exit 180 W, 1/4 mi to mall R in shopping Center.

8.Return to I-71/ I-75 N to I-74/275 Exit 7, Miamitown, a dozen shops in 3 blocks of Rte 128.

9. Now take I-275N to Rte 126E to Mt. Healthy and US 127N to 7508 Hamilton (US127), the *Covered Bridge Antique Mall*, 30 dealers and 2 nearby antique stores.

10. Return to 126 W to US 27N to Ross and *Venice Pavilion Antique Mall*, 80 dealers at Jct US 27 and Rte

This ends this Getaway, but if you are headed north or east, you should plan to visit the *Medina Mall* with 500 dealers on your way home. It is one of the largest and best antique malls in the country at I-71 Exit 218 W 4 mi.

OKLAHOMA

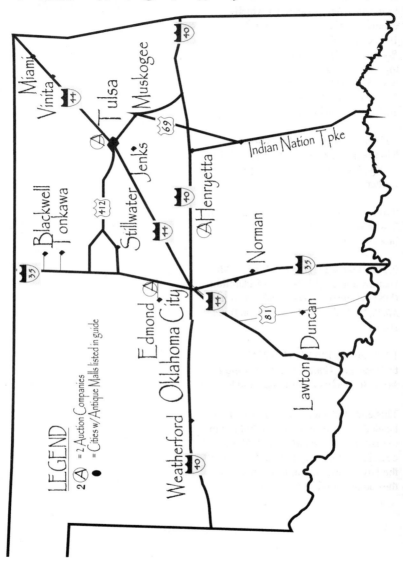

LEGEND

2Ⓐ = 2 Auction Companies
● = Cities w/ Antique Malls listed in guide

OKLAHOMA

WEEKEND ANTIQUE EVENTS
Tulsa Flea Market, Fairgrounds,
every Sat. except late Sep & early Oct (those 4 Saturdays)
Oklahoma City, Buchanan's Antique Flea Market, Fairgrounds,
usually 3rd weekend, call to confirm.
ANTIQUE DISTRICTS/VILLAGES
Oklahoma City's May Ave, Tulsa's E 15th St, & Persimmon Hollow, Claremore & Jenks

AUCTION/ESTATE SALE CO'S
Oklahoma City, OK 73107
Danny's Oklahoma City Auction
Antique auction
2728 NW 10th St.
Every Fri at 7 P.M.
Also at Colonies Mall in Okla. City
every Wed at 9AM
405-942-5865

ANTIQUE MALLS, MARKETS/
SHOWS
BLACKWELL, OK 74631
Ashby's Antique Mall
80 dealers
110 N. Main
Open Mon-Sat 10-5; Sun 11-5
580-363-4410
I-35 Exit 22 to downtown
Walk to 3 other malls on that street

DUNCAN, OK 73533
Antique Mall of Duncan
30 dealers
920 Main
Open Mon-Sat 10-5:30, Sun 1-5
580-255-2552
Downtown

DUNCAN, OK 73533
Antique Market Place & Tea Room
40 dealers
726 W. Main
Open Mon-Sat 10-6
580-255-2499
60 mi SW Oklahoma City, via I-44 &
US 81

EDMOND, OK 73034
Courtyard Antique Market (Mall)
15 dealers
3314 S. Broadway
Mon-Sat 10-5:30, closed Sun
405-359-2719
I-35 Edmond Exit W to Broadway S.
Other mini-malls & shops on Broadway.

EL RENO, OK 73036
Route 66 Antique Mall
100 dealers
1629 E. US 66
Tue-Sat 10-6; Thu 'til 8 P.M.; Sun 1-5
405-262-9366
I-40 Exit 125; 34 mi W of Okla City

HENRYETTA, OK 74437
2nd Street Mall
35 dealers
115 N. 2nd
Open Mon-Sat 9-5; Sun 12-5
918-652-2484
I-40 Exit 240 to downtown

OKLAHOMA

At *Miss Addies Tea Room* in
Muskogee we had a delightful lunch of
homemade Minestroni soup, King
Ranch chicken casserole & cinnamon
bread pudding with a tasty sauce.
Fantastic baked fudge! It's downtown at
821 Broadway. 918-682-1506
Closed Sundays

MUSKOGEE, OK 74401
Old America Antique Mall
100 dealers
2720 S. 32nd
Open Mon-Sat 10-6, Sun 1-5
918-687-8600
S 69 Hwy
I-40 Exit US 69 N

NORMAN, OK 73069
Company Store Antique Mall
100 dealers, 60%collectibles, 30% new
300 E. Main St.
Mon-10-5:30; Sat 10-5;Sun closed
405-360-5959
I-35 Exit Main Street E.
2 mi into Norman, 6 other stores with
antiques.

NORMAN, OK 73069
S & J Marketplace Antiques
30 dealers
219 E. Gray
Mon-Fri 10-6, Sat 10-5, Sun 1-5
405-321-1242
Downtown to Gray St.

In Oklahoma City, if you enjoy cafete-
rias, you will like the *Queen Anne*
Cafeteria on the ground floor of the
tall cylindrical Founder's Building
behind & west of Home Depot. On N
May Avenue, turn west on NW 59th St
to Drexel, then turn L through parking
lot area . Some really good food.

OKLAHOMA CITY, OK 73013
Buchanan's Antique Flea Market
300 dealer spaces
Oklahoma State Fairgrounds,I-40 &
May Av
Sat 9-5, Sun 11-5; adm $2; park free
405-478-4050
I-40 Exit 147, at May or
I-44 Exit 124, S on May
Usually 3rd weekend, but call for dates
Buchanan Productions
P.O. Box 6534
Edmond, OK 73083-6534

OKLAHOMA CITY, OK 73107
Antique Co-op
65 dealers
1227 N. May
Mon-Sat 10-6; Sun 1-6
405-942-1214
I-40 Exit 147 N on May

OKLAHOMA CITY ,OK 73107
23RD St. Antique Mall
85 dealers
3023 N. W. 23rd St.
Mon-Sat 10-5:30. No Sun
405-947-3800
1-40 Exit 122, E on NW 23rd St.

OKLAHOMA

OKLAHOMA CITY, OK 73107
May Antique Centre
80 dealers
1515 N.May Ave.
Mon-Sat 10-6, Sun 1-5
405-947-4447
I-40 Exit May Ave North

OKLAHOMA CITY, OK 73112
Villa Antique Mall
45 dealers
3132 N. May
Open Mon-Sat 10-6; Sun 1-5
405-949-1185
I-40 Exit 147 N on May

OKLAHOMA CITY, OK 73118
The Colonies (Mall)
40 dealers
1116 NW 51st St.
Open Mon-Fri 11-5; Sat 10-5, clsd Sun
405-842-3477
I-44 Exit 126, Western Ave
S to 51st St
Auction every Wed at 9AM

STILLWATER, OK 74074
Antique Mall of Stillwater
100 dealers
116 E. 9th off Main & 9th
Mon-Fri 10-5:30; Sat 10-5; Sun 1-5
405-372-2322
15 mi E of I-35 Exit 174

TULSA, OK 74159
Tulsa Flea Market
200 dealers; 90 % antiques/collectibles
Fairgrounds, 21st St. & Yale
Open 8-4 every Sat; adm $1 & park free
918-744-1386
I-244 Exit 10 S to 21st St;
or I-44 Exit 229 N to 21st St
Not late Sep to early Oct (4 wks)
Patsy Larry
P. O. Box 4511
Tulsa, OK 74159

TULSA, OK 74105
I-44 Antique & Collectible Mall
70 dealers
2235 E. 51st St
Mon-Sat 10-5, Sun 1-5
918-712-2222
I-44- Exit 227

TULSA, OK 74012
Persimmon Hollow Antique Village
10 shops at 70th St & Garnett
6927 S. 115th E Ave (mail)
Open Sat & Sun 9-5
918-252-7113
US 64/169 S to 71st St., then 1 block
east of Garnett, then one block N

OKLAHOMA

TULSA/
CLAREMORE, OK 74017
Hoover's Have All Mall
45 dealers
714 W. Will Rogers Blvd.
Open 7 days 10 -6
918-341-7878
15 mi N Tulsa on Hwy 66

TULSA/
CLAREMORE, OK 74017
Antique Peddler Mall
50 dealers
420 W. Will Rogers Blvd.
Open Mon-Sat 10-5; Sun 12-5
918-341-8615
Downtown.
**12 antique shops and malls
on Will Rogers Rd.**

TULSA/
JENKS, OK 74037
**4 mi S on US 75 and 1/2 Mi E;
Tulsa's 96th Street S.
Walk to 30 shops and malls.**

VINITA, OK 74301
Vinita Antique Mall
60 dealers
127 S. Wilson
Mon,Thur-Sat 9:30-5:30; Sun 1-5:30
Closed Tue & Wed
918-256-5754
Downtown; I-44 Exit 289

WEATHERFORD, OK 73096
Southwestern Antique Mall
60 dealers
1225 E. Main
Open Mon-Sat 10-6; Sun 1-5
580-772-1535
I-40 Exit 82

TRAVEL NOTES

244

OKLAHOMA

TRAVEL NOTES

OREGON

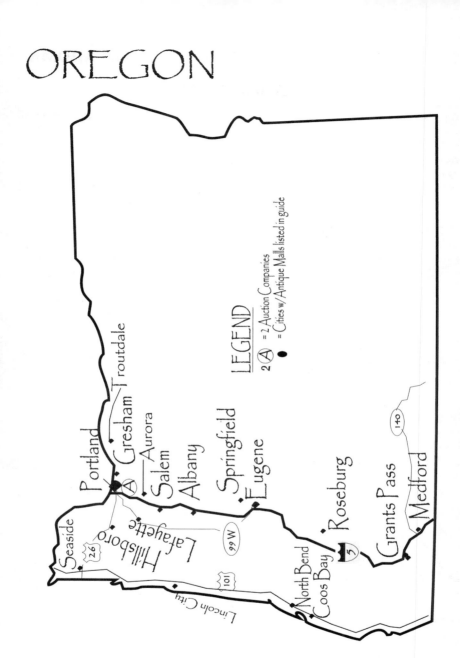

OREGON

WEEKEND ANTIQUE EVENTS

Portland Antique and Collectible Show, 1350-1600 booths;
generally 1st weekend in Mar, 3rd in Jul, 4th in Oct
Salem Collectors Market, 300-500 dealers,
One Sunday of per month, Sept thru June

ANTIQUE DISTRICTS/VILLAGES

Portland, Sellwood, Grant's Pass & Coos Bay/Northbend

AUCTION/ESTATE SALE CO'S

Portland/
Clackamas, Or 97015
Ralph Alsman Auctions
Furniture and estate auctions
15050 SE 91st Ave
Mondays at 6:30 P.M.
503-656-9966
I-205 Exit 13

COOS BAY/
NORTH BEND, OR 97459
Fat Cat Antique Mall
25 dealers
2005 Sherman Ave
Open 10-5, Clsd Sun summer(Sun 11-4)
541-756-5751
US 101 Southbound at Virginia
4 antique shops on Sherman
(US 101) in North Bend

ANTIQUE MALLS, MARKETS/
SHOWS

AURORA, OR 97002
Main Street Merchantile
65 dealers
At 2nd & Main, P.O.Box 287
Open Mon-Sat 9-5, Sun 11-5
503-678-1044
I-5 Exit 278 E to downtown Aurora Exit
16 antique shops on Main & Hwy 99E
Street Fair Mid Aug, Sat & Sun

GRANTS PASS, OR 97526
Sixth Street Antique Mall
35 dealers
328 SW 6th St.
Mon-Sat, 9:30-5, Sun 12-4
541-479-6491
I-5 Exit 58 on 6th St
You can walk to 10 shops from
this mall.

OREGON

LAFAYETTE, OR 97217
Lafayette Schoolhouse Antique Mall
100 dealers
748 Third, P.O. Box 698
Open 7 days 10-5
503-864-2720
www.myAntiqueMall.com
30 mi SW of Portland on Hwy 99 W

LINCOLN CITY, OR 97367
Little Antique Mall
82 dealers, 15,000 sq. ft.
3128 N E Hwy 101
Mon-Sat 10-6; Sun 11-5
541-994-8572
www.littleantiquemall.com
On US Hwy 101

MEDFORD, OR 97501
Main Antique Mall
200 shops, 30,000 sq. ft.
30 N. Riverside Avenue
Mon-Sat 10-5; Sun 10-4
541-779-9490
1/2 block S of Red Lion Inn

PORTLAND, OR
Antique & Collectibles Show
1350 -1600 booths
Portland Expo Center
Sat 9-6; Sun 10-5; adm $7; park $7
503-282-0877, call to confirm
At I-5 Exit 306B; 1st weekend in Mar,
3rd in Jul, last weekend in Oct.
Palmer Wirtfs & Assoc.
4001 NE Halsey
Portland, OR 97232
www.palmerwirfs.com

PORTLAND, OR 97213
Antique Alley
80 dealers
2000 NE 42nd St.
M-F 9:30-5:30; Sat 9:30-5; Sun 12-5
503-287-9848
I-5 Exit 301, Sandy Blvd NE,
1 block N of 42nd & Sandy

PORTLAND, OR 97213
Hollywood Antique Showcase
60 dealers
1969 NE 42nd St.
503-288-1051
1 1/2 block N of 42nd & Sandy

PORTLAND, OR 97202
Sellwood Antique Mall
100 dealers
7875 SE 13th
Open 7 days 10-6
503-232-3755
I-5 Exit 295, N, Hwy 99 to McAdam,
E over Sellwood Bridge L on 13th
25 shops in Historic Old Sellwood

PORTLAND, OR 97202
Stars An Antique Mall
75 dealers
7027 SE Milwaukee
Open Mon-Sat 11-6; Sun 12-5
503-239-0346
I-5 Exit 299A to Ross Island Bridge
Exit Milwaukee Ave S

PORTLAND, OR 97202
Stars & Splendid Antique Mall
75 dealers
7030 SE Milwaukie
Open Mon-Sat 11-6; Sun 12-5
503-235-5990
I-5 Exit 299A to Ross Island Bridge
Exit Milwaukie Ave S

PORTLAND, OR 97213
More Stars Antique Mall
75 dealers
6717 S. E.Milwaukee
503-235-9142
Same Exit as Stars Mall

Portland is where the first *Original*
***Pancake House* opened many years**
ago at 8601 SW 24th (just off I-5
Exit 296-A Southbound, Barber Blvd.
at SW 24th). Everything here is great
and our favorite is the Cinnamon
Apple Pancake. It's huge!

PORTLAND /
HILLSBORO, OR 97124
 Snider's Hill Theatre Antique Mall
70 dealers
127 NE 3rd
Open Mon-Sat 10-5; Sun 12-4
503-693-1686
Downtown; US 26 W to Airport Exit

ROSEBURG OR 97470
From Days Gone By
6000 sq. ft.
630 S. E. Rose St
Mon-Sat 10-5
541-673-7325
Off I-5, 3 blocks north from Eugene
Harvard exit cross river bridge

SALEM, OR
Salem Collectors Market
300-500 dealers; antiques & collectibles
Oregon State Fairgrounds, 2770 17th St.
Sun 9:30-3:30; adm $2; 7 A.M. $10, park $3
503-769-8042
I-5 Exit 256, W on Market to 17th N
One Sunday/month, except July & Aug
Karen Haley Huston
P.O. Box 20805,
Salem,OR 97307-0805

SPRINGFIELD, OR 97477
Glory Days Antique Mall
70 dealers
2020 Main, corner 21st & Main
Open Mon -Sat 10-5, Sun 12-5
541-744-1112
I-5 Exit 191, N to Main
Located at the corner of 21st & Main

SPRINGFIELD, OR 97477
Antique Peddlers
25 dealers
612 Main St
Mon-Sat 10-5; Sun 12-5
541-747-1259
Downtown

TROUTDALE, OR 97060
Troutdale Antique Mall
80 dealers
359 E. Historic Columbia River Hwy
Open Mon-Fri 11-5:30, Sat 10-5:30, Sun
12-5
503-674-6820
I-84 Exit 17 E on frontage Rd. toN E
257th, S to Columbia River Hwy, E to

GREAT ANTIQUE GETAWAY TO PORTLAND

WHEN: 1st Weekend in March, 3rd in July and 4th in Oct. Call 503-282-0877 for exact dates.

WHERE: Portland Expo Center at I-5 Exit 307, over 1000 booths, antiques and collectables. Sat 9-6, Sun 10-5; Adm $7, Parking $7.

Auction: Ralph Alsman Furniture and Estate Auctions, 15050 SE 91st Ave. Mondays at 6:30pm in Clackamas, I-205 Exit 13. Phone 503-656-9966.

Lodging: The Fairfield Inn in Lake Oswego, suburban Portland is conveniently located at I-5 Exit 292-B, South on Bangy Rd, then just E at 6100 SW Meadows Rd. Other motels also in the area.

ANTIQUING:

After the *Portland Expo Market* or anytime, Aurora, which bills itself as the "Antique Capital of Oregon." is a good place to start.

1. I-5 Exit 278 to downtown Aurora, *Main Merchantile Antique Mall*, 65 dealers, at 2nd & Main.

2. There are 16 single and multi-dealer antique stores on Main St. and Hwy 99E in Aurora. If you are there in Mid-August, you could also enjoy a Street Fair.

3. After Aurora, go N on I-5 to Exit 295 N on Hwy 99 to McAdam E over the Sellwood Bridge then L on 13th to *Sellwood Antique Mall* with 100 dealers, 7875 SE 13th.

4. There are 25 antique shops in Historic Old Sellwood - inquire as you go.

5. Continue N on SE 13th which turns into SE Milwaukee and you will come to *Stars Antique Mall*, 75 dealers at 7027 SE Milwaukee and *Stars and Splendid Antique Mall* at 7030 SE Milwakee with 100 dealers.

Restaurant: Caprial's Bistro: Creative American dishes by renowned chef who has her own TV show on PBS, 7015 SE Milwaukee, phone 503-236-6457.

6. Continue N on SE Milwaukee to #6717, for *More Stars Antique Mall*, 75 dealers.

Restaurant: If it is a nice day, you can eat some great food in a garden courtyard setting at *Sala*, an Italian Bistro, 3200 SE Milwaukee, phone 503-235-6665.

7. After the *Stars Mall*, go N on SE Milwaukee to US Hwy 26 W across the Ross Island Bridge to I-5 N to Exit 301, Sandy Blvd NE to 42nd St N to #1969 NE 42nd St. is the *Hollywood Antique Showcase* with 60 dealers. Across the street at #2000 42nd St is the *Antique Alley* with 80 dealers.

8. Next return on Sandy Blvd to I-84 E to Exit 17E on frontage Rd to NE 257th, South to Columbia River Hwy, E to the *Troutdale Antique Mall* with 80 dealers. There are 5 other antique stores in the area.

250

GREAT ANTIQUE GETAWAY TO PORTLAND cont'd

9. After, *Troutdale Antique Mall,* you could go to Vancouver, WA. Take I-84 to I-5 N across the Columbia River to Vancouver City Center then N on Main St. to 2000 Main, *Old Glory Antique Mall,* and 2 antique stores across the street.

Leisure: At I-205 Exit 10, then 1726 Washington St. is the End of the Oregon Trail Center with exhibits, artifiacts and displays. Adm $6.50.

This ends the Portland Getaway, however, if you are on an extended trip, you are only 150 miles from the start of the Seattle Getaway.

TRAVEL NOTES

PENNSYLVANIA
East

PENNSYLVANIA - EAST

WEEKEND ANTIQUE EVENTS

Adamstown every Sunday, 1000 dealers along and just off Rte 272.;
Extravaganzas last Sun in Apr, Jun & Sep
Kutztown, Renningers #2, 250 dealers, 1200 dealer extravaganza in
last Thur, Fri and Sat in Apr, Jun & Sep.
Kutztown is a Saturday market town, every weekend
Middletown, Saturdays Market, 400 dealers, **every Saturda**
New Oxford-Annual Antique Market-**100's of dealers-3rd Sat in June**
Philadelphia/King of Prussia, 500 dealers, **4th weekend in Feb every year**

ANTIQUE DISTRICTS/VILLAGES
Adamstown, Carlisle, New Hope/
Lambertville area, Philadelphia's Pine St.

AUCTION/ESTATE SALE CO'S
ADAMSTOWN/
DENVER, PA 17517
Renningers No. 1 Extravaganzas
1,000 dealers, Adm/park free
Rte 272, 2500 Reading Rd.
Sundays only 7:30-4
717-336-2177 or 570-385-0104
1/2 mi N of Tpke Exit 286.
Extravaganzas last Sun in Apr, Jun
& Sep, other Sundays, 250 dealers
www.renningers.com
If you like BBQ, right up from
Renniger's is *Pig Newton*, **a great**
place to eat right on Rte 272

ADAMSTOWN, PA 19501
Stoudsburg Antique Mall
500 dealers; 1,000 at extravaganza
Rte 272
Open Sun only 7:30-4; indoors & out
717-484-4385
Extravaganzas last Sun in Apr,
Jun & Sep, Adm and park free

ANTIQUE MALLS, MARKETS/
SHOWS

ADAMSTOWN, PA 19501
Shupp's Grove Antique Market
175 dealers Sat., 275 Sun
Rte 897 at Willow St.
Open Sat. & Sun 7 AM-5PM
717-484-4115
PA Tpke Exit 286, N on 272 to Rte 897
R 1 mi; Apr - Oct; Park free
Picturesque shopping under large
shade trees.
Shupp's Grove
P. O. Box 892
Adamstown, PA 19501

ADAMSTOWN, PA 19501
South Point Antiques
100 dealers
Rte 272 and Denver Rd., P. O. Box 811
Mon -Thur 9-5; Fri , Sat & Sun 9-6
717-484-1026
PA Tpke, Exit 21, N on 272

PENNSYLVANIA -EAST

Fantastic Sundays are the last Sunday in Apr, Jun & Sep. During Spring, Summer & Fall there are many outdoor & indoor markets on and off Rte 272 at Adamstown, literally thousands of dealers. If you are in range it's the place to be on Sundays.

ADAMSTOWN / DENVER, PA 17517
Adamstown Antique Gallery
300 dealers
2000 N. Reading Rd.
Closed Wed, Wkdays 9-4, Sat & Sun 9-4
717-335-3435
PA Tpke Exit 286, S 1/4 mi on Rte 272

ADAMSTOWN /
DENVER, PA 17517
Antiques Showcase
300 dealers
2222 N. Reading Rd.
Open 7 days 10-5
717-335-3300
Rte 272; PA Tpke Exit 286

ADAMSTOWN /
DENVER, PA 17517
Adams Antique Annex
200 dealers
2400 N Reading Rd. (Rte 272)
Open 7 days 10-5
717-335-0001
PA Turnpike Exit 286, N on Rte 272

ADAMSTOWN /
STEVENS, PA 17578
272 Antiques
100 dealers
Rte 272, 1300 N. Reading Rd.
Open 7 days M-Fri 10-5; Sat & Sun 10-6
717-336-0888 or 717-484-4646
2 mi S of PA Tpke Exit 286 Rte 272
Another Heritage Antique Center
w/100 dealers 2 mi N on Rte 272

CARLISLE, PA 17013
Northgate Antique Malls
200 dealers
725 & 726 N. Hanover Street
Open 7 days 10-5
717-243-5802
I-81 Exit 52 N on Rte 11or PA Tpke
Exit 226, go S 2 1/2 miles
8 nearby shops on Hanover St.

CHADDS FORD, PA 19317
Pennsbury Chadds Ford Antique Mall
125 dealers
640 Baltimore Pike (US 1)
Thurs-Sun 10- 5pm: Clsd M, Tue & Wed
610-388-1620
12 mi W of I-476 on US 1

CHADDS FORD, PA 19317
Brandywine River Antiques Market
40 dealers
878 Baltimore Pike (US 1)
Open Wed-Sun 10-5, Clsd Mon & Tue
610-388-2000
5 1/2 mi South of US 202, several other
antique shops on US 1

DILLSBURG , PA 17019
B & J's Antique Mall
75 spaces
14 Franklin Church Rd
Closed Tue, Other days 10-5.
717-432-7353
20 mi S of Harrisburg on US Hwy 15

In Gettysburg, the *Brafferton Inn* has a Civil War Bullet imbedded in the fireplace in one of it's bedrooms. Down the road is the *Dobbin House* where in the *Spring House Tavern* we enjoyed food and drink. Behind the fireplace was a hideaway for the historic underground ralroad.

GETTYSBURG PA 17325
Mel's Antiques & Collectibles
80 dealers
32 Foth Alley
winter -Fri, Sat, Sun 9-5, summer M, & Thur 10-4:30, Fr - Sun 9-5, clsd Tue & Wed
717-334-9387
**32 mi W of York on US 30,
Across street from Lincoln Diner on Colorado St.**

GETTYSBURG PA 17325
Antique Center of Gettysburg
100 showcases
30 Baltimore St.
M, W, Th, Sat 10-6; Fri 10-8; Sun 12-6
717-337-3669
1/2 Block S of the Square

GETTYSBURG/
NEW OXFORD, PA 17350
New Oxford Antique Center
70 dealers
333 Lincoln Way W (US Hwy 30)
Open Mon-Sat 10-5; Sun 10-5
717-624-3703, or 1-866-333-NOAC
There are many antique shops on US 30 between York & Gettysburg; 30 shops in New Oxford and 15 in Gettysburg. (See New Oxford Listings)

GETTYSBURG/
NEW OXFORD, PA 17350
Collector's Choice Antique Gallery
80 dealers
330 Golden Lane
Open 7 days
717-624-3440
From US 30 go N 1blk on Tracy Ave you will see Collector's Choice Street Fair 3rd Sat in June

GETTYSBURG/ NEW OXFORD, PA 17350
New Oxford Annual Antique Market
100's of dealers on the streets of New Oxford-717-624-2800
3rd Sat in June
Chamber of Commerce
P.O.Box 152, New Oxford, PA17350

GETTYSBURG/ NEW OXFORD, PA 17350
Golden Lane Antique Gallery
75 dealers
11 Water St.
Open 7 days 10-5
717-624-3800

PENNSYLVANIA -EAST

GETTYSBURG/ NEW OXFORD, PA 17350
New Oxford Antique Mall
50 dealers
214-B W Golden Lane
Open 7 days 10-5
717-624-1419
Mall is just off US 30 on W. Golden Lane

GREENCASTLE, PA 17225
Greencastle Antique Mall
100 dealers
R-345 S. Washington Street
Open 6 days 9-5; closed Wed.
717-597-9198
I-81 Exit 5, W 3/4 mi to traffic light, left 2 blocks

HANOVER, PA 17331
Black Rose Antiques & Collectibles
160 dealers
1155 Carlisle St. Rte 94
Mon-Thur 10-9,Fri-Sat 10-9:30, Sun 11-5
717-632-0589
3 mi S of Rte 30 between Gettysburg & York

HERSHEY, PA 17033
Crossroads Antique Mall
100 dealers
825 Cocoa Avenue
Th-M 10-5:30 in winter; 7 days summer
717-520-1600
Corner Rte 322 & 743

HERSHEY, PA 17033
Ziegler's in the Country
100 dealers
2975 Elizabethtown Rd.
Thur-Mon 9-5, Closed Tue & Wed
717-533- 1662
3 mi S on Rte 743

In Hershey, we always enjoy lunch at *Hershey's Pantry*, which is 1/2 mile or so East of downtown.

KUTZTOWN, PA 19530
Renninger's No. 2 Extravaganzas
1200 dealers,
Thur 10-5, $15 per person
740 Noble Street
Fri adm $6, Sat $4, 8:00-4
610-683-6848 Adm free other Sats
Off Rte 222; Extravagenzas starts on Thur of last Weekend in Apr, Jun & Sep. 250 dealers every Sat.
www.renningers.com

LEWISBURG, PA 17837
Roller Mills Marketplace I & II
300 dealers
517 St. Mary St.
Open 7 days 10-5
570-524-5733
I-80 Exit 30 S. 7 mi on US 15
The II mall is at 100 N. Water St. with 100 dealers

MIDDLETOWN, PA 17057
Saturday's Market
400 dealers indoors, 100's Outdoors
3751 E. Harrisburg Pike
Open every Sat 8-4; inside & out
717-944-2555
**Market is SE of Harrisburg just off
Rte 283, Exit Toll House Road,
left on Rte 230 1 mi**

NEW HOPE, PA
**4 shops up on Rte 202.
Then there are 5 shops 5 mi West on
202 in Lahaska, where we usually
enjoy lunch or dinner at *Jenny's* in
Peddler's Village. Cross the bridge at
New Hope and you are in Lambertville,
NJ with 2 antique malls and 20 shops.**

NEW OXFORD (SEE GETTYSBURG)

PHILADELPHIA, PA 19106
12 Shops on Pine St,
Mon-Sat 10-5:30, Closed Sun
**Downtown; take I-76 Exit 41 South St,
E to 1100 block, then N to Pine.**

PHILADELPHIA/
KING OF PRUSIA -
Renninger's Mid-Winter Classic
500 booths, Admission (see below)
Valley Forge Convention Center
Sat 8-10AM, $20,10-6, $6.00
Sun 10-5, $6.00
570-385-0104
**The 4th weekend in Feb
PA Tpke Exit 326, 1st Ave to Gulf Rd N**
Rennninger's
27 Bensinger Drive #31
Schuylkill Haven, PA 17972

QUAKERTOWN - 18951
Quaker Antique Mall
100 dealers
70 Tollgate Rd
Mon, Thu, Fri 10-8, Sat 10-6; Sun 10-5
215-538-9445
**About 10 mi. S of Allentown, PA Tpk
Quakertown Exit, L on 663 to 309, R**

REEDSVILLE, PA 17084
Dairyland Antique Center
60 dealers
Jct. Rte 322 & Rte 665
Open Wed-Sat 10-5, Sun 12-5
717-667-9093
**55 mi NW of Harrisburg. 30 mi SE of
State College.**

SHREWSBURY, PA 17361
Shrewsbury Antique Center
50 dealers
65 N. Highland Dr.
Open 7 days, 10-5
717-235-6637
**I-83 Exit 4 into town
5 antique shops downtown Main St.**

PENNSYLVANIA -EAST

STROUDSBURG, PA 18360
Olde Engine Works Market Place
125 dealers
62 N. 3rd Street
Open 7 days, 10-5, Sat 10-6
570-421-4340
I-80 Exit 307to Main St to 3rd St
www.oldeengineworks.com

YORK, PA 17404
Antique Center of York
70 dealers
161 E. 10th Ave.
Open daily 10-5
717-846-1994
**From US 30, 1/2 block W of I-83, turn
S on George St., 1 block to left on 11th
to stop sign, then R to 10th.**

**In York we had a great lunch at
the Rooseveldt Tavern, 400 W. Philadelphia St. Rte 462 W, 717-854-7725
Lunch & dinner 7 days.**

258

TRAVEL NOTES

GREAT ANTIQUE GETAWAY TO BUCKS COUNTY, PA
AND NORTHERN NEW JERSEY

WHEN: Any weekend year round,
Oct. for vivid fall color.

WHERE: Golden Nugget Antique Market,
Sat, 300 dealers, 6AM-4PM, FreeAdm. I-95
Exit 1 N on Rt 29. In about 3 mi you will
pass the site where George Washington
crossed the Delaware River .Another 3 mi
to the Market for picturesque antique
shopping under trees and some shelter.

ANTIQUING:

1. After the Market,go into quaint old
Lambertville, 1.5 mi N of Market to the 25
antique shops on Bridge, Union, Church
and other nearby streets. The largest store
is *Peoples Store,* 55 dealers at the corner of
Union and Church St., which is one block N
of Bridge St. and the smaller *Antiques on
Union a*t 32 N. Union. There are many
single and multi-dealer shopsin area.

2. After visiting the shops in Lambertville,
cross over the bridge to New Hope with
antique shops along the main road and on
US 202 for about 5 miles to Lahaska. Here
there is a typical flea market and a popular
Peddlers Village,a 42 acres shopping &
dining complex. (No antiques).

Restaurant: We enjoy eating at "Jenny's"
which is at the main entrance to Peddler's
Village.

LODGING: There is a Courtyard at
Somerset and Red Bank; A Hampton Inn
and Ramada Inn in Flemington. Many B &
B's in Bucks County and motels of all types
in North New Jersey.

1. After completing the Bucks County part
of the Getaway return on US 202 thru
Lambertville to Flemington , *Main Street
Antique Center,* 50 dealers at 156 Main St.

2. Continue on US 202 to Raritan to*Village
Antique Center,* 50 dealers at 44 W. Somerset
St.

3. From Raritan follow signs to nearby
Somerville, *Antique Emporium*, 65 dealers at
29 Division St.

4. Get on I-287 N to Exit 22 N on US 206
to Chester and it's dozen antique stores all
on Main St. Only open Wed- Sun.

Restaurant: About 6 mi E of Chester on
Rte 510 is the *Black Horse Tavern* with
great food.

5. From Chester or *Black Horse Tavern* take
Rte 510 E past 287 to Expwy 24 to River
Rd Exit, 5 1/2 mi to Morris Ave. Left to
Summit Antique Center at 511 Morris Ave
with 50 dealers.

6. Return to Expwy 24 E to I-78E to
Garden State Pkwy. North to Exit 148 to
Bloomfield Center then W on Bloomfield
Ave to the Antique District in Montclair
with about 15 antique shops.

7. Next, south about 30 minutes on the
Garden State Parkway is the *Red Bank
Antique Center,* 100 dealers in 3 large
buildings.G.S. Pkwy S to Exit 109 E on Rte
520, N on Shrewsbury Ave 2 mi to Front St.
turn R.

Restaurant: From the *Antique Center of
Redbank* you can walk or drive down a
side-street for great Italian food.at *Basil
T's Brew Pub and Italian Grill.* Get
directions from the *Antique Center.*

GREAT ANTIQUE MARKET TO MARKET GETAWAY TO
PA DUTCH COUNTRY

WHEN: Extravaganza on the last weekend in April, June and Sept. enjoy picturesque antique shopping under shade trees to air-conditioned inside shopping.

WHERE: Kutztown on Saturday and Adamstown on Sunday.

Sat: Kutztown, *Renninger's #2 Extravaganza,* 1200 dealers, last weekend in April, June & Sept., (250 every Sat.), 8:30-4pm. 740 Noble St. off Rte 222 about 15mi. SW of Allentown. From Kutztown to Adamstown take Rte 222 S. to Rte 272 S. Altogether, about 25 mi. to Adamstown , many antique malls open on Saturday afternoons.

Sun: Adamstown, 7000+ dealers for extravaganza, mostly on Rte 272 (Reading Rd). Additionally, *Shupp's Grove Market* opens first at 7am. It is N of *Renninger's* on Rte 272 to Rte 897 R, 1 mile. You will enjoy the great, clean atmosphere to antique under a grove of large trees. The markets at *Renninger's* and *Stroutsburg* open at 7:30am as do most other markets in the Adamstown area. We generally prefer to do the outdoor shopping first.

Restaurants: When it's time for lunch, *Zinn's Dutch Cooking* serves very good Amish food and is right on Rte 272, among the markets. If crowded, ask to sit at the counter for a quick turnaround meal. If you like BBQ, there is a good location N of *Renningers,* on Rte 272, called "Pig-Newton."

Lodging: Opposite *Zinn's Dutch Cooking* is the Pennsylvania Dutch Motel, 2275 N Reading Road, reasonabily priced.
Phone 717-336-5559

ANTIQUING:
1. If you get tired of walking the Markets, there are many antique malls with high quality antiques on Rte 272, with hundreds of dealers (See text for individual malls). There are 2 very good antique malls in Hershey if you're headed West.

Leisure: If you wish to visit the heart of the Pennsylvaina Dutch country, head S on Rte 272 or Rte 222 to US 30 in Lancaster to Rte 340 S.E. to "Bird-in-Hand and Intercourse" which was founded in 1754, and is less than 10mi. E. of Lancaster and the heart of Amish country. The Bird-in-Hand Farmer's Market offers souse, schmiercase, cup cheese, schnitz, shoofly pie and other Amish delicasies.

Lodging: There is a Comfort Inn and Holiday Inn in Denver, PA near Adamstown. Make reservations!

Time permiting, you can do the Gettysburg and Fredrick, MD Antique Getaway. Just go E on the PA Tpke, I-76 to the Exit for US Hwy 222, South to Lancaster and US 30, W to York, New Oxford and Gettysburg.

PENNSYLVANIA
West

Northeast

West Middlesex

LEGEND

2 (A) = 2 Auction Companies

● = Cities w/Antique Malls listed in guide

Beaver Falls

Pittsburgh

Canonsburg

Somerset

PENNSYLVANIA - WEST

ANTIQUE DISTRICTS/VILLAGES
Cannonsburg, Pittsburg/ Blanox

ANTIQUE MALLS, MARKETS/ SHOWS
BEAVER FALLS, PA 15010
Riverfront Antique Mall
300 dealers, 68,000 sq. ft.
2586 Constitution Blvd.
Open Mon-Sat 9-8, Sun 9-6
1-800-443-5052, or 724-847-2304
Off Shenago Rd in shopping Center

BEAVER FALLS, PA 15010
Antique Emporium
65 dealers
818 7th Ave
Open Mon-Sat 10-5, Sun 12-5
724-847-1919
PA Tpke Exit 13, S 5 mi.

CANONSBURG, PA 15317
Cannonsburg Antique Mall #2
50 dealers
99 Weaverton Rd.
Open 7 days 10-5
724-745-1050
I-79 Exit 45 for Cannonsburg;
Mall #1 is at 145 Adams Ave
220 dealers in 7 malls in town

NORTH EAST, PA 16428
Interstate Antique Mall
7000 sq ft; antiques & collectibles
5446 Station Rd (Rte 89)
Mon-Fri 10:30-5, Sat & Sun 12-5
814-725-1603
1/3 of mi N of I-90 Exit 41 on Rte 89

PITTSBURGH, PA 15234
Pittsburgh Antique Mall
20,000 sq ft, 26 dealers
1116 Castle Shannon Blvd
Open 7 days 10-5, Tue until 8
412-561-6331
I-279 Exit 7, S Rte 51 to Library Rd,
(Rte 88) W to Castle Shannon Blvd N
Ask for map to the shops in the area.

PITTSBURGH/
BLANOX, PA 15238
Cottage Antiques
A dozen Shops on Freeport Rd.
231 Freeport Rd.
Tue-Sat 10-4:30, closed Sun & Mon.
412-828-9201
PA Tpke Exit 48, W on Freeport Rd 5
mi. or, from Pittsburgh take Rte 28
North along river to Blanox.

SOMERSET, PA 15501
Somerset Antique Mall
35 dealers
113 E. Main St.
Open Tue-Sat 10-5, Sun 12-5
814-445-9690
PA Tpke, I-70/76 Exit 110 into town.
Take R turn off Center St because of 1
way St. Go around 2 blocks on R

RHODE ISLAND

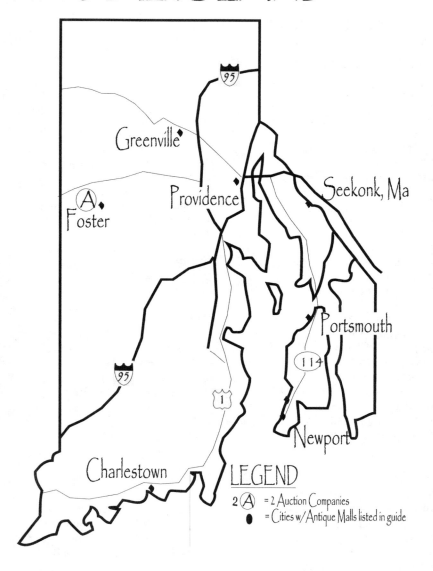

Greenville

Providence

Seekonk, Ma

Ⓐ.
Foster

Portsmouth

114

95

1

Newport

Charlestown

LEGEND

2Ⓐ = 2 Auction Companies
● = Cities w/ Antique Malls listed in guide

RHODE ISLAND

WEEKEND ANTIQUE EVENTS

Charlestown, General Stanton Flea Market, up to 200 dealers, outdoors **every Sat, Sun & Mon holidays Apr thru Oct 15.**

ANTIQUE DISTRICTS/ VILLAGES

Newport's Thames, Spring & Franklin Sts. Providence's Wickenden St.

AUCTIONS

FOSTER, RI 02825
Marty's Olde Tyme Country Auction
Estate & country auction
Danielson Pike (US Hwy 6)
Every Tue at 7 PM & alternate Fri
401-568-7196 Call for details

ANTIQUE MALLS, MARKETS/ SHOWS

BRISTOL, RI 02809
Jenkins & Stickney Antiques
One of 8 antique shops on Rte 114
295 Hope St.
Mon- Sat 11-5, closed Sun
401-254-1114
I-95 E 2 mi to Rte 114S to Bristol

CHARLESTOWN, RI 02813
General Stanton Flea Market
Up to 200 dealers
4115 A&B Old Post Rd, PO Box 1169
Sat, Sun & Mon Holidays 7-4; park $1
401-364-8888
Entrance off US 1, 20 mi E of
CT-RI border; Apr Sun only,
May-Oct 15- Sat, Sun & Holidays

GREENVILLE, RI 02828
Greenville Antique Center
140 dealer spaces
711 Putnam Pike
Open 6 days (Closed Tue) 10-5
401-949-4999
I-295 Exit 7B, W on US 44, 3 mi

NEWPORT, RI 02840
Armory Antiques & Fine Art Center
125 dealers
365 Thames St.
Open daily
401-848-2398
I-195 Exit Rte 114 S near Seekonk
Newport has 25 antique shops
on Franklin, Spring & Thames St

PORTSMOUTH, RI 02871
Eagles Nest Antique Center
125 dealers
310 E. Main Rd (Rte 138)
Mon-Sat 10-5, Sun 12-5
401-683-3500
I-195 , Rte 24 S to Rte 138
3 shops on E. Main Rd (Rte 138)

PROVIDENCE, RI 09203
This and That Shop
45 dealers
236 Wickenden St.
Open Mon-Sat 10-5; Sun 12-5
401-861-1394
I-95 Exit 2, Wickenden St E.
7 shops 140 to 466 Wickenden St.

PROVIDENCE/
SEEKONK, MA 02771
Vinny's Antique Center
300 dealers
380 Fall River Ave., Rte 114A
Open Mon-Sat 10-5; Fri 'til 9
508-336-0800
I-195 Exit 1 to Rte 114A
Great food at the Grist Mill across pond
from *Vinny's Antique Center.*

SOUTH CAROLINA

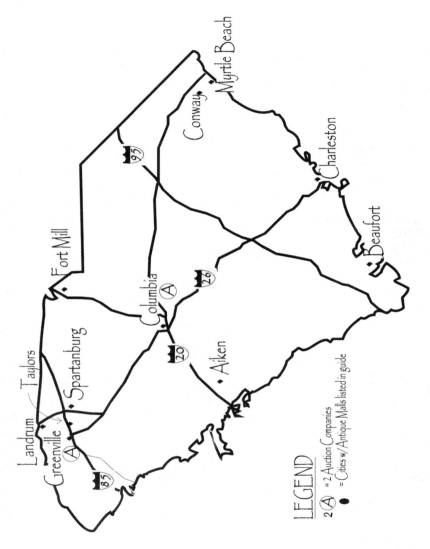

SOUTH CAROLINA

ANTIQUE DISTRICTS / VILLAGES
Charleston, Columbia

ANTIQUE MALLS, MARKETS & SHOWS

AIKEN, SC 29801
Aiken Antique Mall
50 dealers
112-114 Laurens St. S. W.
Open Mon-Sat 10-6, Sun 1:30-6
803-648-6700
At US Hwy 1 & US Hwy 19 from I-20, Exit 18, S on US 19 to downtown
5 other shops downtown

AIKEN, SC 29801
Swan Antique Mall
150 + dealers
321 Richland Ave W.
Mon-Sat 10-5:30, Sun 1-5
803-643-9922
I-20 Exit 22, S on US 1, 1/4 mi

AIKEN, SC 29801
Marketplace Antique Mall
55 dealers
343 Park Ave. S. W.
Mon-Sat 10-5:30, closed Sun
803-648-9696
Downtown

In Charleston, *Joseph's Diner* for breakfast was recommended, along with *Jestine's Kitchen* for authentic Low Country cooking in the "Deep South." Also, the *Middleton Place Plantation* Restaurant.

BEAUFORT, SC 29902
The Antique Mall of Beaufort
28 dealers 200 consignors
913 Port Republic St.
Open Mon-Sat 10-5, Closed Sun
843-521-0660
Downtown

CHARLESTON, SC
Low Country Flea & Collectibles Market
100 dealers; antiques and collectibles
Giallard Auditorium
Sat & Sun 9-6; Adm $2.00
843-849-1949
Year round, indoors;
3rd full weekend of each month,
except 2nd weekends in Nov & Dec.
Nelson Garrett
513 Pelzer Dr.
Mt. Pleasant, SC 29071

SOUTH CAROLINA

CHARLESTON, SC 29412
Terrace Oaks Antique Mall
40 Dealers
2037 Maybank (Hwy 700)
Open Mon-Sat 10-5:30, Sun clsd
843-795-9689
I-26 Exit 221 (US 17), W to Hwy 700 S.

There are 50 antique shops in Charleston, 30 in 3 blocks of King St. downtown.

CHARLESTON/
MT PLEASANT, SC 29464
Antiques Market
104 booths, 20,000 sq. ft.
634 Coleman Blvd.
Open Mon-Sat 10-6, Sun 1-5
843-849-8850
Coleman Blvd is the main Blvd thru Mt. Pleasant

COLUMBIA, SC 29201
City Market Antiques
100 dealers
705 & 709 Gervais Street
Open Mon-Sat 10-5:30, Sun 1:30-5:50
803-799-7722 or 803-252-1589
Downtown in the Vista

COLUMBIA, SC 29201
Columbia Antique Mall
25,000 sq. ft.
602 Hugar at Blossom
Open Mon-Sat 10-6, Sun 1:30-5:30
803-765-1584
Downtown, take Gervais St W across bridge to 1st traffic light, L on Hugar St.

COLUMBIA, SC 29169
Old Mill Antique Mall
75 dealers
310 State St., W. Columbia
Open Mon-Sat 10-5:30, Sun 1:30-5:30
803-796-4229
Downtown in the West Vista

CONWAY, SC 29526-5108
Hidden Attic Antique Mall
200 dealers and consignors
1014 4th Ave
Open 10-4 Tue-Fri, Closed Wed & Sun
843-248-6262
14 mi NW of Myrtle Beach at 4th & Main St., downtown

FORT MILL, SC 29715
Antique Mall of the Carolinas
40 dealers
3700 Avenue of the Carolinas
Open Mon-Sat 10-9, Sun 1-6
803-548-6255
At I-77 Exit 90. W side

GREENVILLE/ TAYLORS, SC 29687
Buncombe Antique Mall
100 dealer spaces
5000 Wade Hampton Blvd
Open Mon- Sat 10-5:30, Sun 1:15-5
864-268-4498
Take US 29, 7mi N. of Greenville

GREENVILLE/ TAYLORS, SC 29687
Old Faithful Antique Mall
40 dealers, 8000 sq. ft.
5111 Wade Hampton Blvd
Open Mon, Tue,Thur -Sat 10-6, Sun 1-6,
clsd Wed
864-879-2577
Take US 29, 7 mi N of Greenville

LANDRUM, SC 29356
Landrum Antique Mall
50 dealer spaces
221 Rutherford Rd
Open Mon-Sat 10-6, Sun 1-5
864-457-4000
I-26 Exit 1 into Landrum 2 mi.

MYRTLE BEACH, SC 29579
Fox and Hounds Antique Mall
65 dealers
4357 Hwy 501
Open daily 10-5
843-236-1027
About 8 mi W of the beach on US 501

SPARTANBURG, SC 29302
South Pine Antique Mall
6,000 sq. ft.
856 S. Pine Street
Open Mon-Sat 10-5:30, Closed Sun
864-542-2975
I-85 B.R. Exit 23
I-585 (also Pine St.) S about 5 mi

SOUTH DAKOTA

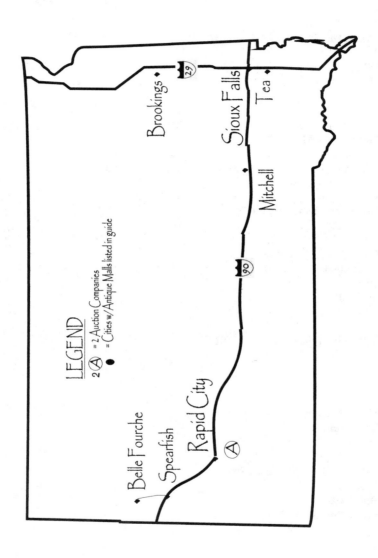

SOUTH DAKOTA

Sioux Falls Flea Market, up to 250 dealers,
1st weekend of every month. None in May, Jun, Jul & Aug

ANTIQUE MALLS, MARKETS/SHOWS

BELLE FOURCHE, SD 57717
Love That Shop
50 dealers
515 State Street
Open Mon-Sat 9-5; Sun clsd
605-892-4006
I-90 Exit 10 N 10 mi
In Downtown Belle Fourche
at Jct of US Hwys 85 and 212

BROOKINGS, SD 57006
Threads of Memories Antique Mall
25 dealers
411 Fourth St.
Open Mon-Sat 10-5; Sun 1-4
605-697-7377
I-29 Exit 132 to Downtown

MITCHELL, SD 57301
Second Impression Palace
40 dealers, 50 consigners
412 N. Main St.
Mon-Sat; summer 8:00-7:00, Sun 8-6;
winter 10-5
605-996-1948
I-90 Exit 332 N to 1st St W to Main N

RAPID CITY, SD 57701
St. Joe Antique Mall
40 dealers
615-A St. Joseph Street
Open Mon-Sat 9:30-5
605-341-1073
Downtown, more antique shops nearby

SIOUX FALLS, SD 57101
Benson's Flea Market
Up to 250 dealers; 75% antiques, col-
lectibles
Expo Bldg at 12th & Fairgrounds
Open Sat 9-5; Sun 11-4; indoors,
Adm. $1.00
605-483-3111
I-29 Exit 79
1st weekend of every month
except none in Mar, Jun, Jul & Aug
Benson's Flea Market
6753 Wicklow Hills Lane
Wentworth, SD 57075

SIOUX FALLS, SD 57103
Proud Panda Antique Mall
170 dealers, 24, 000 sq. ft.
2121 E. 10th St.
Mon-Sat 10-6:00, Sun 12-5
605-338-0000
I-229 Exit 6, W 3 blocks to Downtown
www.proudpanda.com

SIOUX FALLS/
TEA, SD 57064
I-29 Antiques & Collectibles
110 dealers
46990 271st
Mon 9-9; Tue-Sat 9-5; Sun 12-5
605-368-5810
I-29 Exit 73 W 1/4 mi

TENNESSEE
East

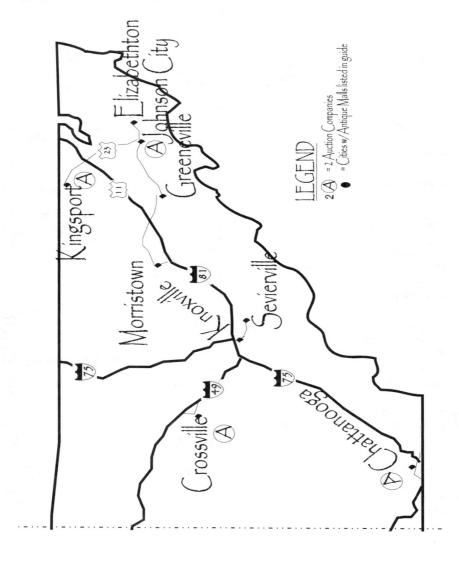

LEGEND

2 (A) = 2 Auction Companies

● = Cities w/Antique Malls listed in guide

TENNESSEE - East

ANTIQUE DISTRICTS/ VILLAGES
Chattanooga Slater Rd, Knoxville
Kingston Pike, Morristown, Sevierville

AUCTIONS /ESTATE SALE CO'S
CHATTANOOGA, TN 37343
Lawson Auction
Antique auction two Mon per month
5393 Wilbanks Dr.
At 6 P.M.
423-847-1076 Call for dates

CROSSVILLE, TN 38555
Page Auction Co.
Antique and collectible auctions
2085 Old Jamestown Hwy, P.O. Box 896
Every 2nd & 4th Tue of the month.
931-484-2805
Hwy 127 N
I-40 Exit 317 S

JOHNSON CITY, TN 37604
Kimball Sterling Auctions
Antique & collectible auctions
125 W. Market
Call for time & dates
423-928-1471 or 773-4075

KINGSPORT, TN 37660
Olde Tyme Auctions
Antique & collectibles
318 Cumberland St.
Every Tue at 5 P.M., box lots at noon
423-392-0726.

ANTIQUE MALLS, MARKETS/ SHOWS

CHATTANOOGA, TN
**Several single and multi-dealer
shops on historic Broad Street.
Railorad buffs will be interested
in seeing an engine and car from
the 1880 Chattanooga Choo Choo
train and the model railroad exhibit
museum in the restored railroad
terminal now called** *Chatanagooa
Choo Choo* **at 1400 Market St.,
I-24 Market St, Exit South.**

CHATTANOOGA, TN 37412
East Town Antique Mall
200 booths & 110 showcases
6503 Slater Road
7 days 10-6
423-899-5498
**I-75 Exit 1, behind Cracker Barrel
Marie's Antique Mall and several other
antique shops here.**

CHATTANOOGA, TN 37412
Marie's Antique Mall
70 dealers
6503 Slater Road
Open 7 days 10-6
423-899-4607
**I-75 Exit 1, behind Cracker Barrel.
See Ft. Oglethorpe, GA for 200
dealer mall at I-75 Exit 142 W**

TENNESSEE - East

<u>GREENEVILLE, TN 37744</u>
Greeneville Antique Market
55 dealers
177 W. Depot Street
Mon-Sat 10-5:30; Sun 1:30-5:30
423-638-2773
I-81 Exit 23, 11 mi E on Hwy 11E

<u>JOHNSON CITY/</u>
<u>ELIZABETHTON, TN 37643</u>
Duck Crossing Antique Mall
45 dealers
515 E. Elk Avenue
Mon-Sat 10-5, Sun clsd
423-542-3055
6 mi E of Johnson City on Hwy 91

<u>KINGSPORT, TN 37660</u>
Haggle Shops Antique Mall
100 dealers
147 Broad St.
Mon-Sat 10-5:30, Sun 1-5:30
423-230-1090
**I-81 Exit 59 and follow directions on
signs.**

<u>KINGSPORT, TN 37660</u>
Nooks & Crannies Antiques
100 dealers
146 Broad Street
Mon-Sat 10-5:30; Sun 1-5
423-246-8002
**I-81 Exit 59, follow the signs.
2 smaller malls on Broad Street in the
200 block**

<u>KNOXVILLE, TN 37917</u>
Antiques Plus
30 dealers
4500 Walker Blvd
Tue-Fri 11-5,-Sat 10-5; Sun & Mon
closed
865-687-6536
I-640 exit 6 (Hwy 441, L 1 block)

<u>KNOXVILLE, TN 37919</u>
Bearden Antique Mall
90 booths
Off 5200 Kingston Pike (US Hwy 11 &
70)
Open Mon-Sat 10-5:30; no Sun
865-584-1521
**I-40/75 Exit 383, S to Kingston Pike W
at 310 Mohican.**

<u>KNOXVILLE, TN 37922</u>
Kingston Pike Antique Mall
35 dealers
223 N. Seven Oaks Dr.
Open Mon-Sat 10-5:30; Sun 1-5:30
865-769-0040
**I-40/75 Exit 378, S to Kingston Pike W
1/4 mi in Windsor Sq. 10 shops on
Kingston Pike #4612**

**In Knoxville, we like the *Regas
Restuarnt* You can see their sign atop
their building from I-40 Exit at James
White Pkwy, R at Summit Hill, then R
at Gay St. We like their health con-
scious menu 865-637-9805.
Closed Sun**

274

MORRISTOWN, TN 37814
Olde Town Antique Mall
30 dealers
181 W. Main Street
Mon - Sat 10-5, Sun 1-5
423-581-6423
I-81 Exit 8, N to downtown
5 other antique stores nearby.

SEVIERVILLE, TN 37864
Riverside Antique & Collectors Mall
100 dealers, 200 showcases
1442 Winfield Dunn Pkwy, P.O. Box 4425
Open 7 days 10-6
865-429-0100
I-40 Exit 407, S 5 mi
5 other shops on Windfield.

TENNESSEE
West

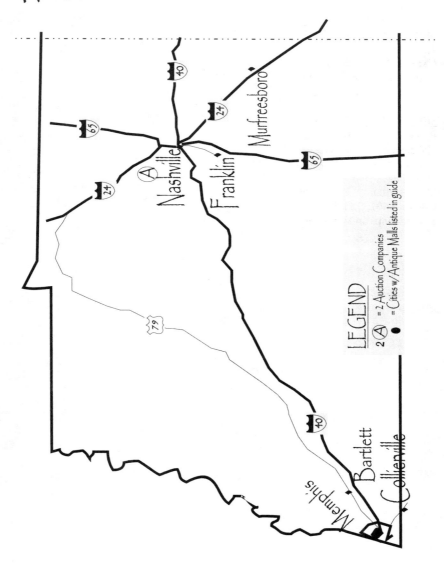

<u>TENNESSEE</u> - West

<u>WEEKEND ANTIQUE EVENTS</u>
Nashville Fairgrounds Antique Flea Market, 1000-2000 dealers,
4th weekend of every month.
Memphis Fairgrounds Mid South Flea Market, 200 dealers,
3rd weekend of every month except Sep.

<u>ANTIQUE DISTRICT/ VILLAGES</u>
Collierville, Franklin, Nashville 8th Ave

<u>AUCTION/ESTATE SALE CO'S</u>
<u>NASHVILLE, TN 37204</u>
Dealers Choice Antiques and Auction
Antique auction
2109 8th Ave
Every 3rd Fri at 5:30 P.M.
615-383-7030.

<u>ANTIQUE MALLS, MARKETS/</u>
<u>SHOWS</u>
<u>COLLIERVILLE, TN 38017</u>
Sheffield Antique Mall
300 dealers, 70,000 sq. ft.
684 W. Poplar Ave
Mon Wed 10-5,Thur, Fri-Sat 10-6 , Sun
12-6
901-853-7822
At intersection of US Hwy 72 and
Poplar Ave, near Kroger, just off I-385

<u>COLLIERVILLE, TN 38017</u>
Abbington Antique Mall
50 dealers
575 W. Poplar
Mon - Sat 10-6, Sun 12-6
901-854-3568
E of jct of US 72 & Poplar Ave.
13 smaller malls and shops in town,
mostly on historic Town Square, where
we enjoyed great food at *Silver Caboose*.
901-853-0010.

<u>MEMPHIS, TN</u>
Memphis Flea Market, The Big One
1000 dealers; 30% antiques & collectibles
Mid South Fairgrounds,Central & E. Pkwy
Open Sat & Sun 8-6; adm free, park $2.00
901-276-3532
In midtown Memphis
3rd weekend each month
except Sep, twice in Dec
Flea Market
955 Early Maxwell Blvd
Memphis, TN 38104

<u>MEMPHIS, TN 38111</u>
Market Central
70 dealers
2215 Central
Open Mon-Sat 10-5; Sun Closed
901-278-0888
I-240 Exit 29, E on Lamar Ave,
L on Central

<u>MEMPHIS, TN 38104</u>
The Antique Shop
10 dealers
14 N McLean
Open daily 10-5; closed Tue
901-274-8563
Corner of Madison & McLean midtown
Memphis

TENNESSEE - West

MEMPHIS, TN 38122
Bo-Jo's Antique Mall
170 dealers and showcases
3400 Summer
Mon-Sat 10-5; Sun 1-5, clsd Wed
901-323-2050
**On US 64, 70 & 79 one block W
of Highland**

MEMPHIS/
BARTLETT, TN 38134
The Antique Gallery
150 dealers
6044 Stage Rd.
Open Mon-Sat 10-6; Sun 1-5
901- 383-2544
**I-40 Exit 12, N on Sycamore
to Stage, R**

MURFREESBORO, TN 37130
Antique Center I & II
100 dealers in 2 bldgs
2213 S. Church St.
Open Mon-Sun 9-5
615-896-5188
I-24 Exit 81, behind Cracker Barrel

MURFREESBORO, TN 37130
Antiques Unlimited
52 dealers
2303 S. Church St.
Open Mon-Sat 9-5; Sun 1-5
615-895-3183
I-24 Exit 81 behind Cracker Barrel

NASHVILLE, TN
TN State Fairgrounds Flea Mkt
1000-2000 vendors
Wedgewood Ave. & Nolensville Rd.
Fri-12-5, Sat 7-6; Sun 7-4; Adm/Park 3.00
615-862-5016
**I-65 Exit 81 (Wedgewood Ave.) E
4th Sat weekend of every month,
all day; indoors & out.**
TN State Fairgrounds Flea Mkt
P. O. Box 40208
Nashville, TN 37204
www.tennesseestatefair.org

NASHVILLE, TN 37203
Tennessee Antique Mall
150 dealers
654 Wedgewood Avenue
Open Mon-Sat 10-5:30; Sun 1-5:30
615-259-4077
At I-65 Exit 81 E 100 yds.

NASHVILLE, TN 37203
Downtown Antique Mall
80 dealers
612 8th Avenue S
Mon-Sat 10-6; Sun 1-6
615-256-6617
**From I-40 or I-24 Exit on Broadway
to 8th avenue S**

NASHVILLE, TN 37215
Green Hills Antique Mall
150 dealers
4108 Hillsboro Rd.
Open Mon-Sat 10-6; Sun clsd
615- 383-9851
**I-440 Exit 3,
S on US 431 (Hillsboro Rd)**

278

NASHVILLE/
FRANKLIN, TN 37064
Antiques at the Factory
50 dealers
230 Franklin Rd, Bldg 3
Mon - Sat 10-5:30, Sun 1-5
615-591-4612
**I-65 Exit Moores Lane S, 1 mi to
Franklin Rd, L 3.2 mi**

NASHVILLE/
FRANKLIN, TN 37064
Battleground Antique Mall
15,000 sq. ft.
232 Franklin Rd
Mon-Sat 10-5, Sun 1-5
615-794-9444
I-65 Exit 65, W 2 mi

NASHVILLE/
FRANKLIN, TN 37064
Franklin Antique Mall
85 dealers
251 Second Ave S
Open Mon-Sat 10-5; Sun 1-5
615-790-8593
**Downtown, I-65 Exit for Franklin, W
about 2 mi to 2nd Ave and S. Margin St.**

**We enjoyed our lunch of gourmet soup
at *Merridee's Bakery & Restaurant,*
110 Fourth Ave.**

NASHVILLE/
FRANKLIN, TN 37064
Harpeth Antique Mall
80 booths, over 100 dealers
529 Alexander Plaza
Mon-Sat 10-6; Sun 1-6
615-790-7965
**Behind McDonald's at I-65 Exit 65
7 antique malls & 12 shops in Franklin**

GREAT GETAWAY TO ANTIQUE NASHVILLE & FRANKLIN

WHEN: 4th Saturday Weekend every month..

WHERE: Tennessee State Fairgrounds. Fri 12-5PM, Sat 7-6PM, Sun 7-4PM. Adm $3.
615-862-5016 I-65 Exit 81 (Wedgewood Ave) East. 1000 to 2000 vendors.

LODGING: For luxury, the Gaylord Opreyland Resort Hotel, Briley Pkwy, would be a possibility, 615-8891000. There is a Courtyard, Fairfield, Hampton Inn and Embassy Suites all near Opryland and Briley Pkwy. I-40 Exit 215 N. on Briley Pkwy.

ANTIQUING:

1.After the market go back on Wedgwood Ave to Exit 81 and visit the *Tennessee Antique Mall* with 150 dealers at 654 Wedgewood, 100 yards E. of Exit 81.

2. Next, take I-65 S to I-440 W to Exit 3, S on Hillsboro Pike to *Green Hills Antique Mall,* 150 dealers at 4108 Hillsboro. *Green Hills Mall* is closed on Sun. Music buffs will enjoy spending an evening in Nashville's *Bluebird Cafe* in a strip mall just off Hillsboro Pike. Here most any night one can find some of Nashville's song writers trying out their pop songs.

3. Go back on Hillsboro Pike to Broadway, then S on 8th ave to *Downtown Antique Mall* at 612 8th Ave. with 80 dealers. Or I-65 or I-40 Exit on Broadway E to 8th Ave S.

Leisure: Grand Ole Opry, the General Jackson showboat, I-Max theatre, restaurants, shops and entertainment facilities all in the Opryland complex near the Gaylord Opryland Resort Hotel. The Hermitage, General & President Stonewall Jackson's home is on US Hwy 70 E of downtown on Hermitage Ave. (US 70) near Jct with Rte 45, adm. $12.00.

Antiquing: The Historic District in the delightful village of Franklin is 18 mi. S of Nashville on I-65 at Exit 65. Franklin has 7 antique malls and 12 antique stores giving out brochure maps to all the locations. *Harpeth Antique Mall* with over 100 dealers is behind McDonalds at I-65, Exit 65. *Battleground Antique Mall* with 15,000 sq.ft. and *Antiques at the Factory* are both in the 200 block of Franklin Rd which is 2 mi. W of I-65 Exit 65. Also, *Franklin Antique Mall* with 85 dealers is at 251 - 2nd Ave So.

Restaurant: We enjoyed lunch at *Merridee's Bakery & Cafe* at 110 - 4th Ave; informal gourmet.

Leisure: A Civil War Battlefield, Confederate Cemetary & Carter House with 1,000 bullet holes and a Museum with video recounting the Battle of Franklin.

Antiquing: Time permitting your Getaway could continue into Murfreesboro, about 30 minutes travel. E of Franklin on Rte 96 to Murfreesboro, then S on I-24 a few miles to I-24, Exit 81, where you will find 300 dealers in 3 Antique malls behind the Cracker Barrel Restaurant.

Lodging: There is a Hampton Inn, Holiday Inn and several other chain motels in Murfreesboro.

TRAVEL NOTES

TEXAS - North

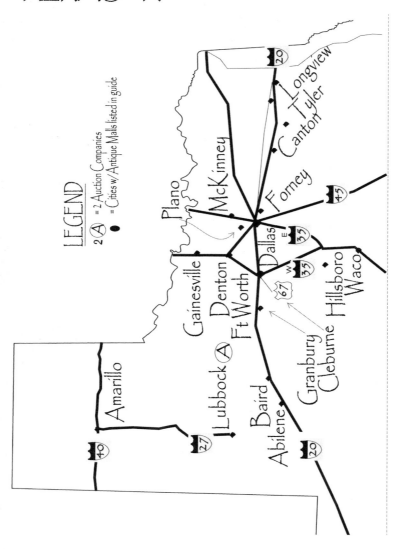

LEGEND

2(A) = 2 Auction Companies

● = Cities w/Antique Malls listed in guide

Amarillo

Lubbock (A)

Baird

Abilene

Gainesville

Denton

Ft Worth

Granbury

Cleburne

Hillsboro

Waco

Plano

McKinney

Dallas

Forney

Longview

Tyler

Canton

TEXAS - NORTH
WEEKEND ANTIQUE EVENTS

Canton, First Monday Trade Days, 1500-3000 dealers,
1st Mon & preceding Fri, Sat & Sun.
Dallas, Buchanan Antique & Collectibles Mkt., 250 dealers,
usually 3rd weekends

ANTIQUE DISTRICT/ VILAGES
Forney

AUCTION/ESTATE SALE CO'S
Ft. Worth, TX 76117
Auction Depot
Antique auctions
2301 Solona
Every Mon at 7 P.M.
817-831-1480

Grand Prairie, TX 75050
Alan Jones Auctions
Antique auctions
2470 NW Dallas St
Fri (and some Sat) at 7:00 P.M.
972-641-7115

ANTIQUE MALLS, MARKETS/ SHOWS
AMARILLO, TX 79106
Village Antique Mall
35 dealers
2821 Civic Circle.
Open Mon-Sat 10-5:30; Sun 1-5
806-372-4472
I-40 Exit 68, S on Georgia St to Woflin, R to Civic Circle, L; 7 antique shops 6th Ave W

ARLINGTON, TX 76013
Antiques & Moore
50,000 sq. ft., 100 plus dealers
3708 W Pioneer Pkwy (Hwy 303)
Open Mon-Sat 10-6; Sun 12-6
817-548-5932
I-20 Exit 453 N to Pioneer (Hwy 303) W or I-30 Exit #30 S to Pioneer, W.

ARLINGTON, TX 76006
Antique Sampler Mall & Tea House
250 dealers
1715 E Lamar Blvd
Open Mon-Sat 10-6; Sun 12-6
817-861-4747
I-30 Exit 30, N on 360 access road, turn L on Lamar Blvd, W 1.5 mi across from Wet & Wild.

ARLINGTON, TX 76013
Antique Marketplace
25,000 sq. ft., 90 dealers
2305 W. Park Row
Open 7 days 10-6
817-274-5533
I-30 Exit 448 , N on Bowen to Park Row R to Mall.

BAIRD, TX 79504
I-20 Exit 307 downtown.
5 antique malls and a dozen antique shops in Baird on or just off Market St.

TEXAS - NORTH

BENBROOK, TX 76126
Benbrook Antique Mall
200 dealers, 65% collectibles
9250 Hwy 377 So.
Open Mon-Sat 10-6, Sun 12-6
817-249-0844
1/2 mile S of I-20

CANTON, TX
First Monday Trade Days
1500-3000 dealers
I-20 Exit 527 S Hwy 19 at Canton
Adm free; park $2.00
903-567-6556
**First Monday of every month
and the preceding Fri, Sat & Sun,
dawn to dusk.**
City of Canton,
P.O. Box 245
Canton, TX 75103

CLEBURNE, TX 76031
Cleburn Antique Mall
75 dealer spaces
215 S Main
Tue-Sat 10-5; Sun 1-5
817-641-5550
**Downtown; I-35 W Exit 26A, the Red
Horse Mall is on Henderson close to
downtown
11 mi W on US Hwy 67**

DALLAS, TX
Buchanan Antique & Collectibles
Market
300 dealers; all antiques & collectibles
Fairgrounds, Garage Sale Feb & Nov
Fri 10-7 $10 early; Sat 9-5 & Sun 11-5, $3
regular Adm. 405-478-4050; call for exact
dates
**Fairpark exit of I-30 E of downtown
Usually 3rd weekends
Shows at Market Hall in Sep-Oct**
Buchanan Productions
P.O. Box 6534
Edmond, OK 73083-6534
www.buchananmarkets.com

DALLAS/ADDISON, TX 75001
Unlimited, Ltd /Antiqueland USA
175 shops/135 showcases
15201 Midway Rd
6 days 10-6, Sun 11-6
972-490-4085
I-635 Exit 23, N 2 mi
www.antiquelandusa.com

DALLAS, TX 75244
Forestwood Antique Mall & Tea Room
200 plus dealers
5333 Forrest Lane
Mon-Sat 10-7; Sun 12-6
972-661-0001
**W of Forest Lane Exit of Dallas N
Tollway**

DALLAS, TX 75235
Love Field Antique Mall
250 dealers
6500 Cedar Springs
Mon-Fri 10-7; Sat 10-7; Sun 12-7
214-357-6500
**At Mockingbird across from entrance
to Love Field Airport**

DALLAS, TX 75209
Lovers Lane Antique Market
30 shops
5001 W Lovers Lane
Open Mon-Sat 10-5, Sun 1-5
214-351-5656
**3 blocks west of Inwood, 2 other antique
shops nearby**

For Italian food in Dallas, we like
Amore **at 6931 Snider Plaza. One
block south of Lovers Lane and one
block west of Hillcrest. We like their
old world neighborhood atmosphere &
half orders of Lasagne.** *Amore* **is open
7 days, dinner only on Sat & Sun. 214-
739-0502. Next door to** *Amore* **is a
small mall specializing in rare and
elegant antiques.**

We have always enjoyed eating at *La
Madelaine's* **in Dallas. It is located in
the strip shopping center just west of
Mockingbird Exit of Central Expressway (US Hwy 75).**

Another location for *La Madelaine's* **is
inside the North Park Shopping Mall,
and 3906 Lemmon Ave.**

DALLAS, TX 75204
McKinney Ave Antique Market
40 dealers, 2 floors, 8000 sq. ft.
2710 McKinney Ave
Mon-Sat 10-5, Sun 1-5
214-871-9803
**Near downtown, 35E exit Pearl, go R on
Pearl, R on McKinney**

DALLAS /
PLANO, TX 75075
Antiqueland /Design Center, Tea Room
250 dealer spaces
1300 Custer
Mon-Wed 10-6; Thur-Sat 10-8; Sun 11-6
972-509-7878
**US Hwy 75 N Exit 15th St, W to Custer,
turn left, Bldg on left
There are a dozen other antique shops
in Plano; ask for map or directions.**

**30 miles South of Dallas is the town of
Waxahachie for antique shops & malls.
See** WAXAHACHIE, TX **listing.**

DENTON, TX 76201
Antiqueland, USA
30,000 sq. ft. 60 % collectibles, 20% new
5800 N. I-35 at Loop 288
Open 7 days
1-877-486-2872-ext 22
At the Denton Factory Stores, Loop 288

TEXAS - NORTH

DENTON, TX 76201
Antique Experience
60 dealers
5800 N I-35, suite 307
Open Mon-Fri 10-6, Sat 9:30-6, Sun
10:30-6
940-565-0688
**In same shopping center w/
Antiqueland,
Factory Outlet Stores Exit at Loop 288.**

FORNEY, TX 75126
Antiques East I, II
200 shops
Hwy 80 & County Road
Mon-Sat 10-5; Sun 12-5
972-564-1303
**20 mi E of Dallas on US 80 Hwy
(Old I-20), exit County Road**

FORNEY, TX 75126
Little Red's Antiques
40,000 sq. ft
US Hwy 80 at County Rd.
Open Mon-Sat 9-5, Sun 1-5, closed Wed
972-564-2200
**Exit US 80 Hwy at County Rd., Hwy 212
Also 4 smaller malls & a half dozen
large antique stores at Forney.**

FT. WORTH, TX 76107
Montgomery Street Antique Mall
240 booths & showcases
2601 Montgomery Street
Open Mon-Sat 10-6; Sun 12-6
817-735-9685
At I-30 Exit 11, northside of I-30

GAINESVILLE, TX 76240
Antique & Design Center of North
Texas
50,000 sq. ft
502 E. California Street
Mon-Sat 10-5:30, Sun clsd (winter hrs
10-5)
940-665-8847
**I-35 Exit California St East to RR
tracks**
www.adcnt.com

GRANBURY, TX 76049
Antique Mall of Granbury
100 dealers
4303 E Hwy 377
Open 7 days 10-6
817-279-1645
**30 mi S of Ft. Worth on Hwy 377
6 single and multi dealer shops
around the court house square.**

HILLSBORO, TX 76645
Hillsboro Antique Mall
55 dealers
114 S. Waco St.
Open Mon-Sat 10-5, Sun 1-5
254-582-8330
**I-35 Exit 3, W to downtown
There are 8 antique malls and
shops in downtown Hillsboro**

LUBBOCK, TX 79407
Antique Mall of Lubbock
50 booths
7907 W 19th St.
Open 7 days, 10-6
806-796-2166
**I-27 Exit 3, 3 mi W of Loop 289
on W 19th St. 20-25 scattered
antique shops in Lubbock**

TEXAS - NORTH

MCKINNEY, TX 75069
The Antique Company Mall
150 dealers
213 E. Virginia
Open 7 days
972-548-2929
Just off Courthouse Square.
8 shops near town square on
LA, KY, & TN Streets

TYLER, TX 75702
Front Street Antiques
50 dealers
202 W. Front Street
Open Mon-Sat 10-5:00; Sun clsd
903-531-0008
Downtown; I-20 Exit 556S or 568 S

TYLER, TX 75702
Antiques on Broadway
55 dealers
320 S Broadway at Front St
Open Mon-Sat 10-5; Sun 1-5
903-531-2399
Downtown

TYLER, TX 75702
Tyler Square Antiques
40 dealers
117 S Broadway
Open Mon-Sat 10-5:30; Sun 12-5
903-593-6888
Downtown
French & English antique furniture-
Vignette settings.

GLADEWATER, TX 75647
From Tyler off US 271
 More collectibles on Main and side
streets w/over 200 dealers.

WAXAHACHIE, TX 75165
Gingerbread Antique Mall
 42 booths
310 S. College St.
Open 10-5 Mon-Fri, Sat 10-5:30, Sun 12-5:30
972-937-0968
Downtown across from historic
Courthouse with 10 other shops and
malls.

In Waxahachie, the *Doves Nest*, 105
Jefferson St., is a unique shop of
goodies, with an atmospheric room for
a great meal. We had a tasty lunch of
apricot chicken salad, homemade soup
and desert of Texas style Buttermilk
pie. 972-938-3683

WAXAHACHIE, TX 75165
Annie Loyd's Design Center & Antiques
308 College St.
Mon-Sat 10-5, Sun 1-5
972-937-7325
Off 35E exit 401B, or off 287 Hwy
exit for downtown.

TEXAS
Dallas/FtWorth

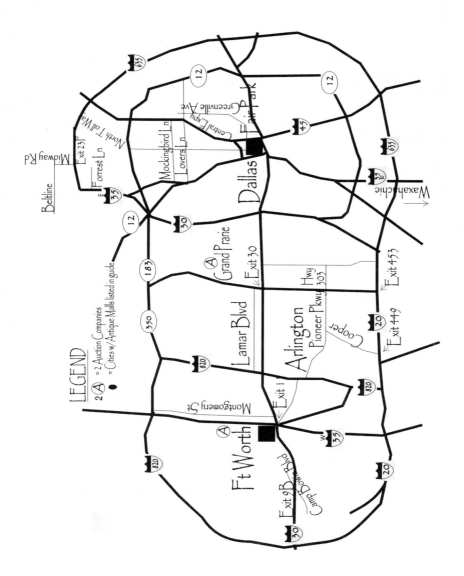

LEGEND

2 Ⓐ = 2 Auction Companies

● = Cities w/Antique Malls listed in guide

GREAT ANTIQUE WEEK-END IN DALLAS/ FT. WORTH

WHEN: Usually 3rd weekends are best because: Dallas Fair Park Antique & Collectible Market is usually on 3rd weekend, but not always, so call 405-478-4050 to be sure. Friday shopping during set-up $10.00 adm, 10-7, Sat 9-5 and Sun 11-5pm $3. adm.400 dealers, indoor market.

WHERE; Fair Park Exit off I-30, E of downtown.

ANTIQUE AUCTIONS: Allen Jones Auctions, 2470 N W Dallas St. in Grand Prairie, auction every Fri at 7 PM, 972-641-7115
Auction Depot, 2301 Solona, Ft. Worth, 817-831-1480 has auction every Mon at 7 PM.

RESTAURANTS: Dallas's most elegant restaurant is probably The Mansion on Turtle Creek at 2821 Turtle Creek Blvd; if a fancy celebration is your desire. Luxury accomodations are available there also.214-559-2100.
Our favorite Dallas lower priced restaurants are *La Madeline French Bakery & Cafe,*with several locations. One at Mockingbird exit off Central Expwy.(US 75) on corner of shopping center. "*Amore*", a neighborhood Italian restaurant with an Old World atmosphere located in Snider Plaza at Lovers Lane & Hillcrest across from SMU. 214-739-0502 Reservations needed for most Dallas restaurants for dinner on weekends.

1ST DAY ANTIQUING:
1. Antique Fair Park Market (see above directions and details.)

2. I-30 W to Exit 30 will take you to Arlington, N on 360 Access Rd to Lamar Blvd, W to *Antique Sampler & Tea House* at 1715 E Lamar, set back in shopping Center, across from Wet & Wild Park.

3. I-30 W to Exit 11 in Ft. Worth, is the *Montgomery St. Antique Mall* on Montgomery St. facing the Hwy on the N side of I-30 with 240 booths, save some time for this one. You might be ready for lunch after this at a *La Madeline* 1 mi West on Camp Bowie Blvd.

4. I-30E to I-820S to Exit 30C, Hwy 303 E to *Antiques & Moore,* 3708 W Pioneer Pkwy.
5. E on Pioneer Pkwy to Bowen N to Park Row W to *Market Place Mall,* 2305 W. Park Row.

2ND DAY ANTIQUING:
1. Take I-635 Exit 23 N on Midway Rd. to #15201, *Unlimited Mall* with 175 booths. Opens 11AM Sun.

2. Go So. on Midway to Forrest Lane, E to #5333 *Forrestwood Antique Mall* & Tea Room.

3. Take Inwood Rd or Tollway S to Lovers Lane, W to #5001 *Lovers Lane Antique Mall.*

4. Take Inwood Rd. So to Mockingbird Lane W to *Love Field Antique Mall a*cross from entrance to Love Field, 6500 Cedar Springs, 250 dealers.

5. Located on 2710 McKinney close to downtown Dallas, is *McKinney Ave Antique Market.* Complicated directions that you should get by phone from where you are coming from, 214-871-9803.It is near Pearl exit off 35E, Cole and McKinney. It is worth finding for high quality antiques.

If you are on an extended trip you may wish to continue with the San Antonio Getaway. To do so, just head South on I-35.

Happy Antiquing!

TEXAS - NORTH

TRAVEL NOTES

TRAVEL NOTES

TEXAS - South

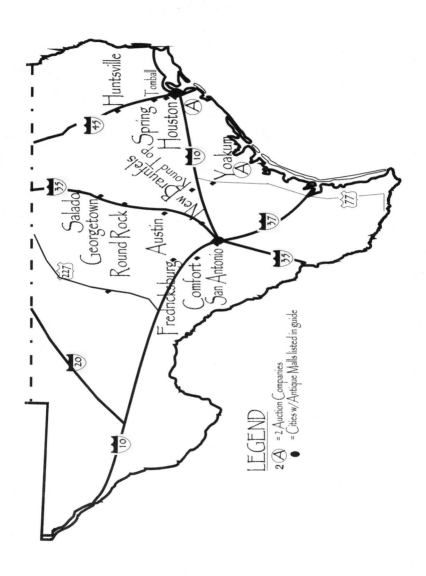

Huntsville
Tomball
Spring
Houston
Round Top
Yoakum
New Braunfels
Salado
Georgetown
Round Rock
Austin
Fredricksburg
Comfort
San Antonio

45
10
35
37
35
77
281
10
20

LEGEND
2 (A) = 2 Auction Companies
● = Cities w/Antique Malls listed in guide

TEXAS - SOUTH

WEEKEND ANTIQUE EVENTS

Houston/Pearland, Coles Antique Village, 100 dealers, **every Sat & Sun.**
Round Top, Marburger Farm Antique Show, 400 tent spaces,
Several days in April & Oct., call for dates

ANTIQUE DISTRICTS / VILLAGES

Comfort, Corpus Christie, El Paso, Fredricksburg, Houston, Salado, San Angelo & downtown San Antonio.

AUCTION/ESTATE SALE CO'S

AUSTIN, TX
Austin Auction Co.
Antique & collectible auction
8414 Anderson Mill Rd
Every Sat Night, every week at 7PM
preview fri-12-3, Sat after 4PM
512-258-5479

YOAKUM, TX 77995
Griffin Auction House
Antique & collectible auction
4850 E Hwy 111
1st Sun of every month at noon
361-293-7479
Hwy 111, 5 mi E of Yoakum, at Sale Barn
I-10 Exit 661, S 28 mi

ANTIQUE MALLS, MARKETS/ SHOWS

AUSTIN, TX 78758
Whit Hanks Antiques & Decorative Arts
40 dealers
1009 W 6th Street
Mon- Sat 10-6; Sun 1-5
512-478-2101
Take 5th St Exit W off I-35 & 1 block

N to 6th St, then to 1009 W 5th St.

Exit Whit Hanks back door and walk one block to *Castle Hill Cafe* at 1101 W. 5th St. - for a very good healthy food meal. 512-476-0728, closed Sun.

AUSTIN, TX 78757
Austin Antique Mall
100 dealers
8822 McCann
Open 7 days; 10-6
512-459-5900
Off US Hwy 183 one block W of Burnet Rd in N Austin behind Maxwell Nissan Auto Agency.
Austin's largest mall,
with the friendliest staff. All kinds of western & Native American, Vintage clothing, jewelry, furniture and interesting artifacts!

AUSTIN, TX 78756
Antique Marketplace
65 dealers
5350 Burnet Road
Mon-Sat 11-7; Sun 12-6
512-452-1000
I-35 Exit 238-B W on Hwy 2222 (Koenig) to Burnet Rd. S 3 blocks

TEXAS - South

AUSTIN/
ELGIN, TX 78621
Elgin Antique Mall
50 dealers
195 N Hwy 290
Open 7 days 10-6
512-281-5655
22 miles E of Austin on US Hwy 290

AUSTIN/
ROUND ROCK, TX 78664
Old Time Treasures
150 dealers
1601 S IH-35
Open Mon-Sat 10-6, Sun 12-6
512-218-4290
**E side of I-35 between Hwy 1325 & 620
in Renaissance Square Shopping Center,
about 8 mi N of Austin.**

COMFORT, TX 78013
Comfort Antique Mall
35 dealers
734 High St.
Open 7 days 10-5, Sat 10-6
830-995-4678
I-10 Exit 523 into Comfort
10 antique shops, 2 B & B's and a cafe.

FREDERICKSBURG TX 78624
**I-10 Exit 523, or Exit 508 N 22 mi
There are 15 antique shops
in downtown Fredericksburg**

HOUSTON, TX 77074
Southwest Antique & Collectibles
60 dealers
6735 Bissonnet
Tue-Sat 10-6; Sun 12-6
713-981-6773
**SW part of city; exits off I-610 & US 59.
6 shops in 2100-2400 blocks Bissonnet.**

HOUSTON, TX 77055
Carolyn Thompson's Antique Center
200 dealers
1001 W. Loop N., or 7200 Old Katy Rd.
7 days 10-6
713-688-4211
**2 miles N of the Galleria on Loop 610,
E on Katy Rd to mall.
From 610 S Exit Memorial**

**In Houston, there is a *La Madelaine*
French Bakery & Cafe at 5015
Westheimer Rd. , Suite 1420,
Westheimer Exit off I-610. There is
another at 10001 Westheimer. One of
our favorite places to eat in Houston.**

HOUSTON, TX 77098
Antique Pavilion
80 dealers, 95% antiques
2311 Westheimer
7 days 10-6
713-520-9755
**2 blocks E of Kirby St., off I-610
Westheimer exit**

HOUSTON/
PEARLAND
Cole's Antique Village and Flea Maarket
Over 200 dealers, antiques & col-
lectibles
1014-1022 N. Main St.
Market Open 8AM-5; Closed Wed
adm free; park $1.00
Village Open 9:30-5:30PM
281-485-2277
**I-45 S to Telephone Rd (Hwy 35)
Every Sat & Sun,
indoors & out**
Cole's Antique Village
1014 N. Main
Pearland, TX 77581

HOUSTON/
PASADENA, TX 77502
Antique Junction Mall
70 dealer spaces
111W Southmore
Open Tue-Sat 10-6, Sun 1-5
713-473-9824
Fwy 225 S on Shaver to Southmore Av W

HOUSTON/
SPRING TX 77388
Antiqueland, USA
Over 200 dealers, 87,000 sq. ft
21127 Spring Town Dr.
Mon-Sat 10-6, Sun 12-6
281-350-4557
I-45 Exit 70A W on FM 2920 1/2 mi
Also shops in Old Spring, on Gentry,
Main, Midway and Spring Cypress.

HOUSTON/
TOMBALL, TX 77375
Granny's Korner
25 dealers
201 Market
Mon-Sat 10-5; Sun 12:30-5:30
281-351-8903
I-45 Exit 70, W 13 mi.
In downtown Tomball, is a village of 18
antique shops

HUNTSVILLE, TX 77340
Sam Houston Antique Mall
30 dealers, 4 floors 80% collectibles
1210 Sam Houston Avenue (US 75 Hwy)
Open 7 days 10-5
936-295-7716
From I-45-Exit 116 E to Town Square,
turn R on Sam Houston Ave
There are 4 other nearby antique shops

HUNTSVILLE, TX 77340
Bluebonnet Square
25 dealers
1110 11th St.
Open 7 days 10-5:30
936-291-2800
At Town Square

There are several other multi-dealer
shops in Huntsville on and just off
the Square. Also a great place for
lunch or dinner is an 1830 log home
at 1215 19th St., *The Homestead.* **We**
certainly enjoyed our meal there. 936-
291-7366

NEW BRAUNFELS, TX 78130
Palace Heights Antique Mall
40 dealers
1175 Business IH 35N
830-620-4934, 830-625-0612
I-35 Exit 189, west 2 blocks on left

NEW BRAUNFELS, TX 78130
Hillcrest Antiques Gallery
35 dealers & 40 showcases
7570 IH-35N
open 7 Days 10-6
830-620-5056
I-35 Exit 195, 5 miles S of San Marcos
Outlet malls.

NEW BRAUNFELS, TX 78130
Gruene Antique Co.
28 dealers
1607 Hunter Rd.
Open daily, hours vary by season
830-629-7781
I-35 Exit 191 W 1.5 mi to 2nd light,
then turn L

TEXAS - South

There are several other antique shops here plus the Historic *Gruene Manson Inn* where we dined overlooking the Gaudelupe River and where you can sleep in a room furnished in antiques. Room reservations 830-629-2641. 1275 Gruene Rd., New Braunfels, TX

ROUND TOP, TX 78954
Marburger Farm Antique Show
350 tent spaces
Hwy 237, PO Box 448
Wed-Sat 9-6; free; early adm Tue 9am, $15
800-947-5799 or 800-999-2148
Located on Hwy 237, south of Hwy 290
Between Round Top & Warrenton
I-10 Exit 674, N on US 77 to Hwy 237
In Mar or April & Oct. or Sept, call for dates. www.roundtop.marburger.com
Simultaneous markets in nearby towns of Warrenton, Shelby and Carmine

SALADO, TX 76517
Remember This Antiques
40 dealers
702 N. Main St.
Open Mon-Sat 10-6; Sun 11-5
254-947-0858
IH-35 Exit 283,284 or 85 downtown,
E side of IH-35, 50 miles N of Austin
10 Antique Shops in Salado
Salado is also known for it's old stagestop, historic buildings and famous old Stagecoach Inn. It is a stop we always enjoy.

SAN ANTONIO, TX 78217
Center for Antiques
35,000 sq. ft. of shops
8505 N Broadway
Mon-Fri 10-5:30, Sat 10-6, Sun 12-5
210-804-6300
At I-410, Broadway Exit
N 1 block on Broadway

SAN ANTONIO, TX 78209
Avalon-Riklin Antiques & Estate Services
30 dealers
3601 Broadway
Open Mon-Sat 10-6, Sun clsd
210-222-0265 or 0263
Downtown 3 miles from the Alamo,
between Hildebrand & Mulberry
Half dozen other antique shops on or just off McCullough

SAN ANTONIO, TX 78205
Alamo Antique Mall
55 dealers
125 Broadway
Open 7 days 10-6
210-224-4354
At Travis downtown,
2 blocks from the Alamo

SAN ANTONIO, TX 78205
Echoes From The Past
3 floors
517 E. Houston St.
Open 7 days 10-6
210-225-3714
On Houston btwn Alamo St & Broadway
We have always enjoyed eating at *La Madelaine's* in New Orleans and Dallas and were pleased to discover a *La Madelaine's* in San Antonio at 4820 Broadway. On the River Walk we found the best food at the major hotels.

ANTIQUE GETAWAY DOWN SAN ANTONIO WAY

WHEN: Anytime

WHERE: Salado to San Antonio ,

LODGING: Salado is an enjoyable place to spend the night at the " Stagecoach Inn" where you can also enjoy a sumptous meal, 254-947-5111.Other choices for food and good lodging are available.

ANTIQUING: First stop, Salado at I-35, Exit 283.

1.This charming old town with about 10 antique shops was once a stage stop and the old stone building is still there. This whole town is historical. *Remember This Antique Mall* with 40 dealers at 702 .Main.

2. Round Rock, I-35 Exit 251 N in Renaissance Square Shopping Center is *Old Time Treasure Antique Mall*, 150 dealers, 8 mi N of Austin.

3. Austin, I-35 Exit 240 N on US 183 one block W of Burnet Rd., *Austin Antique Mall,* with 100 dealers at 8822 McCann behind Nissan Auto Agency.

4. Get back on Burnet Rd., go S 3 blocks past Koenig Ln (Hwy 2222) to 5350 Burnet Rd. to *Antique Market Place*, 55 dealers, opens at 11 AM.

5. Take Koenig Rd back to I-35 S to 5th St Exit W, go 1 block N to 6th St. W to *Whit Hanks Antiques*, 40 dealers at 1009 W. 6th St.

RESTAURANT: Nearby, 1 block S of *Whit Hanks* is "Castle Hill Cafe", 1101 W. 5th St., has good healthy food.

6. New Braunfels, I-35 Exit 195 E. side, *Hillcrest Antique Gallery,* 40 booths & 40 showcases.

7. New Braunfels, I-35 Exit 189 W to 1175 I-35 N, *Palace Heights Antique Mall*. 40 dealers.

8.New Braunfels/ Gruene, I-35 Exit 191 W 1.5 mi to 2nd light, left is *Gruene Antique Co.*, with 28 dealers.

FOOD & LODGING: "Gruene Mansion" provides a view overlooking the river while dining, or sleep in a room furnished with antiques. 830-629-2641.

San Antonio: Our favorite on the River Walk is the Hilton Palacio Del Rio for lodging and food. There is a *La Madeline French Bakery & Cafe* at 4820 Broadway. Best food on River Walk is at the major hotels.

ANTIQUING: 1.Downtown Antique Malls are *Alamo Antique Mall* at 125 Broadway at Travis,and *Avalon-Riklin* at 3601 Broadway.

2.North on Broadway angle to left on McCullough to several shops just off or on McCullough.

3. Return to Broadway, north to 8505 N. Broadway, *Center for Antiques,* 35,000 sq. ft.Mall is at the Broadway Exit of I-410 N 1 block.

LEISURE: The Alamo, downtown, no charge, just donations. Established as a Spanish Mission in 1718. And of course, the last stand for 189 Texans when they refused to surrender to Santa Ana's army of 4000. Jim Bowie and Davy Crockett among the Texans that died that day. Festivals galore on the River Walk, Jan.- Mud Fest, Feb.- Rodeo Fiesta, March-St. Patricks Fiesta, May-Cinco De Mayo, June-Folklife Festival. Greek Festival in Oct. and the Christmas season. At the end of Sept The Great Country River Festival has well known Texas bands with Nashville sounds, in a 3 day Jamboree at 6 staging areas along the river.

UTAH

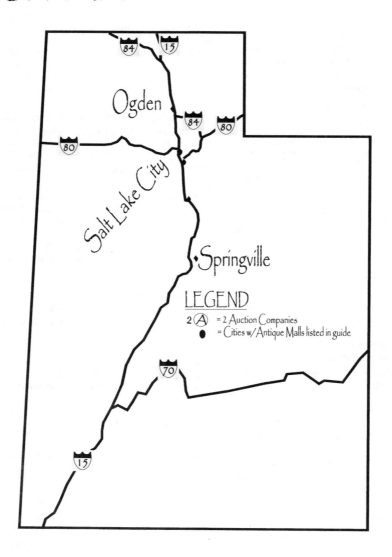

UTAH

ANTIQUE MALLS, MARKETS/ SHOWS

OGDEN, UT 84401
Abby's Antique Mall
55 booths
180 31st Street,
Open Mon-Sat 10-6, closed Sun
801-394-9035
I-15/84 Exit 344 E

SALT LAKE CITY, UT 84101
Kennard Antiques
One of 12 antique shops, 169E 300 S to
407E
65 W 300 South
Most shops open 11-5; closed Sun
801-328-9796
blocks south of the Temple

SALT LAKE CITY, UT 84101
Moriarty's Antiques
50 dealers
959 S. West Temple
Mon-Sat 10-6, Sun 12-5
801-521-7207
5 blocks S of the Temple

SALT LAKE CITY, 84119
Treasures Antique Mall
50 dealers, 8,000 sq. ft.
1940 W 3500 S.
6 days 10-6, closed Sun
801-973-7742
West Valley area between I-15 & 215

SPRINGVILLE, UT
Treasures Antiques & Collectibles
70 dealers
1045 North 2000 West
6 days 10-6, closed Sun
801-491-0749
2 mi S of Provo, off I-15, west frontage road between Exit 263 & 265

TRAVEL NOTES

VERMONT

St. Albans

LEGEND

2 (A) = 2 Auction Companies
● = Cities w/Antique Malls listed in guide

Burlington

Shelbourne

East Barre

Vergennes

East Middlebury

Rutland

Taftville

Quechee

Bridgewater

White River Junction

Manchester Center

Chester

E. Arlington

Bennington

Brattleboro

Wilmington

Pownal

VERMONT

Quechee Vermont Antiques Festival **in Mid Oct.**
Wilmington Outdoor Antique Flea Mkt, **Sat & Sun, Mid May thru Mid Oct.**

ANTIQUE MALLS, MARKETS/ SHOWS

BENNINGTON, VT 05201
Antique Center at Camelot Village
130+ dealers
66 Colgate Heights
363 days 9:30-5:30
802-447-0039
On Rte 9 W of US 7

BURLINGTON/ SHELBOURNE, VT 05482
Burlington Center for Antiques
80 dealers
1966 Shelbourne Rd (US Hwy 7)
Open 7 days 10-5
802-985-4911
On US Hwy 7, 4 mi S of Burlington.
There is another antique mall nearby.

CHESTER, VT 05143
Stone House Antique Center
100 dealers
Rte 103 South
Open daily year round 10-5
802-875-4477
I-91 Exit 6, Rte 103 N 8 miles

EAST ARLINGTON, VT 05252
East Arlington Antique Center
70 dealers in the Movie Theater
E. Arlington Rd
Daily 10-5, year round
802-375-6144
Off Hwy 7A , 4 mi S of Manchester

BARRE, VT 05649
East Barre Antique Mall
250 dealers & consigners
P.O.Box 308, 133 Mill St
Tu-Sun 10-5, Closed Mon
802-479-5190
Jct US 302E & Route 110S,
I-89 Exit 7, to Barre City,
R on Rte 302

EAST MIDDLEBURY, VT 05740
Middlebury Antique Center
60 dealers
P.O. Box 378
Daily 9-6
802-388-6229, FAX 802-388-6224
Rte 7 & Rte 116, on US Hwy 7, 1/2 way
between Rutland & Burlington

MANCHESTER CENTER, VT 05255
US 7 Exit 4, 10 miles N of Bennington
2 similar sized antique centers
and 5 other antique stores here

POWNAL, VT 05261
Century Barn Antique Center
40 dealer spaces
Rte 7
Open 7 days 10-5
802-823-9308
On Rte 7 S of Bennington

VERMONT

Vermont Antiques Festival
400 dealers
Quechee Gorge Village
Open 10-4 Sat & Sun
631-261-4590, Free adm & parking
First half of Oct.
Rte 4 Exit 1
Flamingo Promotions
P.O. Box 57
Northport, NY 11768

QUECHEE, VT 05059
 Quechee Gorge Village
400 dealers
P. O. Box 730 (Rte 4)
7 days 9:30-5:30, 10-5 winter
802-295-1550, 1-800-438-5565
I-89 Exit 1, W on US 4 by
Quechee Gorge

QUECHEE, VT 05059
Antique Collaborative
150 dealers
Route 4, Waterman Place
Open 7 days year round
802-296-5858
At blinker light in Quechee
I-89 Exit 1, W on US 4

SHELBOURNE
See Burlington

TAFTVILLE, VT 05073
Hartland Antique Center, Inc.
20 dealers
US Rte 4, P.O. Box 80
Open 6 days 12-5, closed Tue
802-457-4745
I-89 Exit 1, W 7 mi on Rte 4
W of Quechee Gorge

WILMINGTON, VT
Outdoor Antique Flea Market
120 dealers; all antiques & collectibles
Jct Rte 9 & Rte100
Dawn to dusk; adm free; park free
802-464-3345
Sat-Sun,
Mid-May thru Mid-Oct
Jct Rts 9 & 100 in S Vermont
Outdoor Antique Flea Market
P.O. Box 22
Wilmington, VT 05363

GREAT GETAWAY TO ANTIQUE PICTURESQUE VERMONT

WHEN: 1st Half of October for the spectacular color and the Vermont Antique Festival one weekend in first half of Oct. Call for dates, 631-261-4590.

WHERE: Vermont's "Little Grand Canyon" at Quechee Gorges is the location of the antique Festival. 400 dealers. Adm free, Park free.

If you are not going to the Antique Festival you can start your Getaway at the 120 dealer Outdoor Flea Market, Sat & Sun in Wilmington, then go to Chester, then Quechee for the rest of your getaway.

SATURDAY: For *Vermont Antique Festival* go to I-89 Exit 1 W on US 4 by Quechee Gorge.
1. Antiquing: Taftville, VT 20 dealers on US Hwy 4, 3 mi W of Quechee Gorge.

2. Next, *Quechee Gorge Village Antique Mall*, 400 dealers. on US Hwy 4 at Quechee Gorge.

3. Then *Quechee Collaborative*, 150 dealers at the blinker light in Quechee.

4. Next, take I-89 S across the river to W. Lebanon, NH, I-89 Exit 20 to *Colonial Antiques Mall* with 75 dealers, in Colonial Plaza, Rte 12A to Airport Rd, 1st L. Also Outdoor Flea Market on Sun.

5. Then I-91N to Exit 16, SR 25N to US 302 W to *East Barre Antique Mall*, 250 dealers and consignors at Jct US 302 & SR 110 S. After the mall continue on I-89 to Burlington.

6. Next S on Rte 7, 5 mi to Shelbourne, VT. *Burlington Antique Center*, 1966 US Hwy 7. There is another antique mall just S of this one on US 7.

7. Then, E *Middlebury Antique Center*, 60 dealers, at Jct US 7 & Rte 116.

8. Continue S on US 7 to 4 mi S of Rutland, take Rte 103 S, 34 mi to Chester, VT. *Stone House Antique Mall,* 100 dealers 8 mi N of Chester on Rte 103. Return on Rte 11 to US 7 at Manchester Center.

9. Manchester Center has 2 antique malls and 5 stores on US 7.

10. Next S on US 7 to E. *Arlington Antique Center,* 70 dealers in movie theater off US 7 on E Arlington Rd.

11. Then, S on Rte 7 to Rte 9 W to antique *Camelot Village*, 130 dealers in Bennington at 66 Colgate Heights.

12. The next town Pownal, 6 mi S of Bennington on US 7 is *Century Barn Antiques,* 40 dealers.

13. *Hoosick Antique Center,* with 65 dealers is 7 mi W of Bennington on Rte 7 in Hoosick, New York. It's 30 miles E of Albany by the state line.

LODGING: At Quechee, the Quechee Inn at *Marshland Farms* would be a good choice. 802-295-3133. During fall color time, it might be difficult to find rooms. Killington, VT, is a ski resort town with many motels, with reduced out of ski season rates. Killington is 15 mi E of Rutland and 25 mi W of Quechee. The Cascade Lodge in Killington has 46 rooms, spectacular mountain views and award winning cuisine. 802-422-3351.

See the New Hampshire Getaway.

VIRGINIA

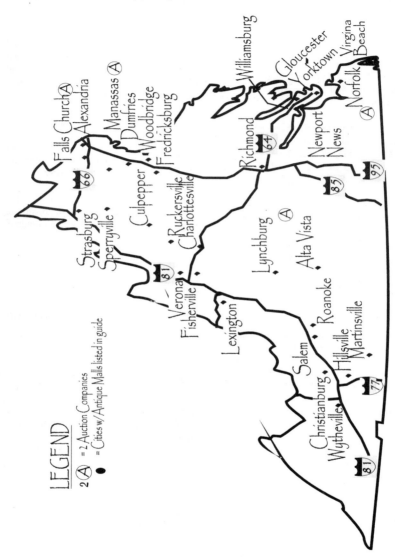

VIRGINIA

WEEKEND ANTIQUE EVENTS

Fisherville, **usually 2nd weekend in May & Oct.**
Hillsville, V.F.W. Flea Market and Gun Show, up to 700 dealers.
 every Labor Day & preceding Fri, Sat & Sun
Norfolk Winter Antiques Show, **4th weekend in Jan**
Richmond, Antiques Extravaganza, 175 dealers,
 last Fri, Sat & Sun in Feb and 1st Fri, Sat & Sun in Oct.

ANTIQUE DISTRICTS / VILLAGES

Alexandria, Fredericksburg, Norfolk, Frederick, Salem, Ruckersville

AUCTION / ESTATE SALE CO'S

FALLS CHURCH, VA 22046
Auction House of Falls Church
Antique & collectible auctions
431 N. Maple Ave.
Wed weekly at 6:30PM, call to confirm
703-532-5632
Easy access I-66 Exit 69

CHESAPEAKE, VA 23323
Cal's Antiques
Antique auctions
928 Canal Dr., call for dates
Last Fri of month at 7:30 P.M.
757-421-99410 or 482-1136

CHESAPEAKE, VA 23323
Strick's Auctioneers
Antique auction
917 Canal Dr.
Every Thurs., 5 PM
757-487-5925call to confirm

MANASSAS, VA 22111
Bull Run auction
Antiques & Collectibles
7209 Centreville Rd.
Auctions about every other week
703-393-0066 for details
www.bullrunauction.com

SMITHFIELD, VA 23431
Smithfield Antique Center
Antique auctions
P.O. Box 157, 131 Main St
1st Wed of every month at 6:30 P.M.
757-365-0223
www.smithfieldantiques.com

RICHMOND, VA 23230
Motley's Auctions
Antique auctions
4402 W. Broad St.
Once a month at 6 P.M., usually
804-355-2100 Call for dates

RICHMOND, VA 23225
Alexander's Antiques and Auctions
Estate, antique & collectible auction
Beaufort Mall, 7114 Midlothian Tpke.
Every Thu at 6:30 P.M.
804-674-4206

VIRGINIA

ANTIQUE MALLS MARKETS/ SHOWS

(SEE WASHINGTON DC)
ALEXANDRIA, VA 22309
Mt Vernon Antique Center
26 individual shops
8101 Richmond Hwy
Open Mon-Fri 10-5; Sat 10-6; Sun 12-5
703-619-5100
I-495 Exit 1-A, S 4 mi on US 1

ALEXANDRIA, VA 22314
French Country Antiques
One of 8 antique shops on King St.
1000 King St.
Mon-Sat 10:30-6; Sun 12-5; closed Tue
703-548-8563
I-95/495 Exit 1 N on US 1 to King St.
Shops both ways on King St.

ALEXANDRIA, VA 22314
Trojan Antiques
One of 16 shops on Lee St. & King St
1100 King St.
Open Mon-Sat 11-6; Sun 12-5
703-549-9766
Antique shops on Washington St.
and in the area which is between US 1
and the Potomac River, N of King St.

CHARLOTTESVILLE, VA 22901
Antiquer's Mall
225 booths
2335 Seminole Trail
Open Mon-Sat 10-5; Sun 12:30-5
434-973-3478
There are 6 antique shops on Main St.
from #201 E to 1211 W Main.
9 others around town.

We had a great lunch at the Old Mill
Room in the Boars Head Inn. It is one
mi W on US 250 from Jct US 29
Bypass in Charlottsville.

CULPEPER, VA 22701
Minuteman Mini Mart
150 booths, antiques & crafts
Rte 3
Open Mon-Sat 9-6; Sun 12-5
540-825-3133
1 block W of US 29 By-Pass on Rte 3

CULPEPER, VA 22701
Country Shops of Culpeper
100 dealers
10046 James Monroe Hwy; US 29
Open Mon-Sat 10-5; Sun 12-5
540-547-4000
US 29

(SEE WASHINGTON DC)
FALLS CHURCH, VA 22046
Falls Church Antique Co.
45 dealers
260 W. Broad St.
Open 7 days
703-241-7074
Rte 7 near Jct with US 29

FISHERVILLE, VA
Shenandoah Antiques Expo
200 dealers inside, 100s outdoors
Augusta County Expoland
Fri, 10 A.M., $10; Sat & Sun $5
434-846-7452 or 434-845-7878
I-64 Exit 91
Generally the 1st weekend in May
& 2nd weekend in Oct. Call for dates
Ray Stokes Heritage Promotions
P.O. Box 3504
Lynchburg, VA 24503

FREDERICKSBURG, VA 22401
Antique Court of Shoppes
140 dealers
1001 Caroline St.
Mon-Fri 10-5; Sat 10-5:30; Sun 12-5
540-371-0685
I-45 Exit 130 E to downtown
14 Shops on Caroline St.

FREDERICKSBURG, VA 22401
Caroline Square
50 dealers
914 Caroline St.
Open Mon-Sat 10-5; Sun 12-5
540-371-4454
I-45 Exit 130 E to downtown

FREDERICKSBURG, VA 22401
Upstairs Downstairs Antiques
35 dealers
922 Caroline St.
Open 6 days, closed Wed
540-373-0370
I-45 Exit 130, E to Caroline St.

In Fredericksburg, 3 smaller malls
and 8 stores in walking distance
in the 600-900 blocks of Caroline
Street, plus 6 shops on
Williams and Sophia Streets.

We enjoyed homemade soup, avocado
chicken salad & bourbon pecan pie at
Merriman's Fresh Natual Foods
Cuisine, **715 Caroline St. 540-371-7723**

GLOUCESTER, VA 23061
Stagecoach Market & Antique Village
45 shops & 75 outdoor table market
Rte. 17
Open Sat & Sun
804-693-3951
40 mi N of Norfolk

HILLSVILLE, VA
36th Annual Antique Show
2000 vendors
1/4 mi along Hwy 58, I-77 exit 14
Open dawn to dusk
Free Adm, Free Parking
4 days ending on Labor Day Monday
919-553-4457
Riley Horne
225 Muirfield Lane
Clayton, NC 27520
Paved walking aisles. Free power.
www.rileyhorne.com

HILLSVILLE, VA
V.F.W. Flea Market and Gun Show
Up to 700 dealers
V.F.W. Complex
8 A.M. to 8 P.M.; adm $1; park free
276-728-2911
I-77 Exit 14 E 1 mi at the
V.F.W. Complex on Rte 221
Fri & Labor Day weekend
VFW Complex
701 Stuart Dr.
Hillsville, VA 24343

LEXINGTON, VA 24450
The Antique Mall
180 dealers
Rte 11 in College Square Shopping
Center
Open Mon-Sat 10-6, Sun 11-6
540-464-5555
I-64 Exit 55, Rte 11 S to 2nd light

VIRGINIA

MANASSAS, VA 22111
Bull Run Antique Mall
20 shops
7217 Centreville Rd.
Open Thur-Mon 11-5, clsd Tue & Wed
703-369-7817
I-66 Exit Centreville, S on Rte 28

LEXINGTON, VA 24450
Duke's Lexington Antique Center
20,000 sq. ft.
1495 N. Lee Hwy
Open 7 days 10-6
540-463-9511
**I-81 Exit 191 & I-64 Exit 55, N on Atell,
3 lights past Walmart, 3/4 mi on L**

NORFOLK, VA 23510
**I-64 Exit 276, US 460 Hwy (Granby St.)
Approx. 50 shops on Granby Street
#819 to 2608.**

NORFOLK, VA
Norfolk Antique Show
100 dealers
At the SCOPE on St. Paul Blvd
Open Sat & Sun 10-5, Adm $5, Park $4
434-846-7452
**I-264 Exit 10, R on St. Paul
4th weekend in Jan every year**
Stokes Show Promotions
P. O. Box 382
Lynchburg, VA

RADFORD/ CHRISTIANSBURG,
VA 24073
Stage Coach Antiques Mall
47 booths
3980 Mudpike Rd. Rte 177
Open Mon-sat 9-5, Sun 1-5
540-639-0397
I-81 Exit 109, South 1/4 mi on R side

RICHMOND, VA
Antiques Extravaganza (Show)
175 dealers; antiques only
3000 Mechanicsville Pike
Fri 10-7; Sat 10-6; Sun 11-5; adm $5.
336-924-4359, call for dates
**I-64 Exit 192, US 360 Hwy, E 1/2 mi
Usually 1st Wk-end Oct, & last in Feb.**
Antique Extravaganza of North Carolina
P.O. Box 11565
Winston-Salem, NC 27116

RICHMOND, VA 23230
West End Antique Mall
200 dealers
2004 Staples Mill Rd.
Open Mon-Sat 10-6; Sun 12-6
804-359-8842 or 359-1600
**I-95 Exit 79 W on I-64 to Staples Mill
Rd. Exit S, 1 mi in Crossroads shopping Center**

RICHMOND/
MIDLOTHIAN, VA 23113
Midlothian Antique Center
125 dealers
13591 Midlothian Tpke
Open Mon-Sat 10-6; Sun 12-5
804-897-4913
**On US Hwy 60 about 5 mi W
of Powhite Pwky Rte 76**

RICHMOND/
MECHANICSVILLE, VA 23116
Antique Village
50 dealers
10203 Chamberlayne Rd.
Open 6 days; closed Wed
804-746-8914
4 mi N of I-295 on US 301

RUCKERSVILLE, VA 22968
Green House Shops
48 dealers
Rte 29 & 33
Open Mon-Sat 10:30-5:30; Sun 12-5
434-985-6053
15 mi N of Charlotteville on US 29
There are 4 other single and multi-
dealer malls on US 29 here

ROANOKE, VA 24012
Roanoke Antique Mall
100 dealers
2302 Orange Avenue
Open 10-6 Mon-Sat, Sun 12-6
540-344-0264
From I-81 take I-581 to US 460 E
4 shops downtown on Campbell Ave.
5 shops Franklin Rd SW Bus. US 220

ROANOKE / SALEM, VA 24153
Wright Place Antique Mall
50 dealers
251 Wildwood Rd.
Open Mon-Sat 10-6; Sun 1-6
540-389-8507
I-81 Exit 137, 500 yds. on R
Furniture, Tools, Railroad items,
Books, Glassware, Advertising, clocks,
Toys, Telephones, Gas Pumps, Rugs,
Art and Brass beds.

ROANOKE/
SALEM, VA 24153
Dixie Caverns Antique Mall
35 dealers
5753 W. Main
7 days 10-6
540-380-5800
5 mi W of town on Rte 11

ROANOKE, VA 24012
Blue Ridge Antique Center
100 dealers
20100 Virgil H. Goode Hwy 220
Mon-Sat 10-5, Sun 12-5
540-483-2362
I-581 S to US220 V.Goode Hwy

SPERRYVILLE, VA 22740
Sperryville Antique Market
150 dealers
P.O. Box 1
Open Thur-Mon 10-5
540-987-8050
US 211/1003, near US 522;
60 mi SW of Washington, DC

STRASBURG, VA 22657
Strasburg Emporium
100 dealers, 60,000 sq ft
160 N. Massanutten Street
Sun-Thur 10-5, Fri-Sat 10-7
540-465-3711
I-81 Exit 298
www.strasburgemporium.com

VIRGINIA

STUARTS DRAFT, VA 24477
Stuarts Draft Antique Mall
50 dealer spaces
Rte 340 South
Open Mon-Sat 10-5; Sun 12-5
540-946-8488
**I-64 Exit 94, S 4 mi on US 340 Hwy
or I-81 Exit 213, N on US 340 4 mi**

VERONA, VA 24482
The Factory Antique Mall
95 dealers, 65,000 sq.ft.
50 Lodge Lane, Ste 106
Mon-Thur 9-5; Fri-Sat 9-6, Sun 1-6
540-248-1110
At I-81 Exit 227

VERONA, VA 24482
Pat's Antique Mall
42 dealers
733 Lee Hwy
Open Thur-Sun 9-5
540-248-7287
Rte 11; I-81 at Exit 227

VIRGINIA BEACH, VA
Barrett St. Antique Center
135 dealers, 28,000 sq. ft.
2645 Dean Dr.
Open Mon-Sat 9-6, Sun 12-5
757-463-8600
**Rte 264 Exit 19B, N 1 block on
Lynnhaver Pkwy. Look for aqua
awnings.**

WILLIAMSBURG, VA 23188
Williamsburg Antique Mall
400 dealers, 45,00 sq. ft
500 L:ightfoot Rd
Open Mon-Sat 10-6; Sun 12-5
757-565-3422
I-64 Exit 234, Lightfoot Rd, Rte 646

WOODBRIDGE, VA 22191
Featherstone Square Antique Mall
200 dealers, plus 80 showcases
14567 Jefferson Davis Hwy
Open Sun-Thur 10-7; Fri & Sat 10-8
703-491-9099
I-95 Exit 161 E to US 1 S
*60,000 sq. ft. with vendors of Civil War
memorabilia, pottery, quilts,
antique clocks , coins, textiles,
antique stained glass & furniture.
Virginia's biggest mall.
Visit our other Featherstone Mall in
Annapolis, MD.(See MD listing)*

WYTHEVILLE, VA 24382
Snoopers Antique Mall
100 booths
P.O. Box 184
Open 7 days 9-6
276-637-6441
**At Ft. Chiswell between
I-77/81 Exits 77 & 80**

310

WYTHEVILLE, VA 24382
Old Fort Antique Mall
80 dealers
Jct of I-81 & I-77
Open 7 days 10-7
276-228-4438
**Exit 77 or Exit 80 off I-81
5 mi E of Wytheville**

YORKTOWN, VA 23692
The Galleria
90 dealers
7628 Geo. Washington Memorial Hwy
Open Mon-Sat 10-6; Sun 12-5
757-890-2950
**US Hwy 17; 15 mi N of Newport News I-
64 Exit 250B.**

TRAVEL NOTES

GREAT GETAWAY TO ANTIQUE FREDERICKSBURG

WHEN: Anytime.
If you prefer trains you could take the train to Fredericksburg instead of driving.

LODGING: If you take the train, there is the Richard Johnson Inn, a Bed & Breakfast Inn in a 1790's home just 2 blocks from the Amtrack Station at 711 Caroline, 540-899-7606. Most major motels are represented here; Fairfield Inn, Hampton Inn, Holiday Inn, Ramada and & Comfort Inn, Quaility Inn and Best Western. Antique stores, antique malls, restaurants and the Richard Johnson Inn, as well as most historical sites are within walking distance of each other.

ANTIQUING: Most of the antiquing is on Caroline St. 600-1000 blocks with some shops on William and Sophia Streets in the same area. This is a great area for Civil War era antiques and militaria.

LEISURE: There are 7 historical homes; including Washington's boyhood home, the James Monroe Museum, which has Louis XVI furniture that he and his wife bought when he was minister to France in 1794. The Fredericksburg Battlefield, Confederate Cemetery, Museums and historical churches, also add interest.

RESTAURANT: We enjoyed our lunch at *Merriman's Fresh Natural Foods*, at 715 Caroline, where homemade soup, avacado chicken salad and bourbon pecan pie really hit the spot. Also recommended to us was *Le Petite Auberge* French restaurant at 311 William St. There are several other very good restaruants in the area.

The great antiquing, charming old town with it's historical architecture, great food, and convenient lodging, combine to make Fredricksburg one of the country's top destinations for a "great antique getaway".

There is more great antiquing in Richmond, Norfolk, Charlottsville and Washington D.C., so use the guide to help you find the antiques on the way home.

TRAVEL NOTES

TRAVEL NOTES

WASHINGTON D.C.

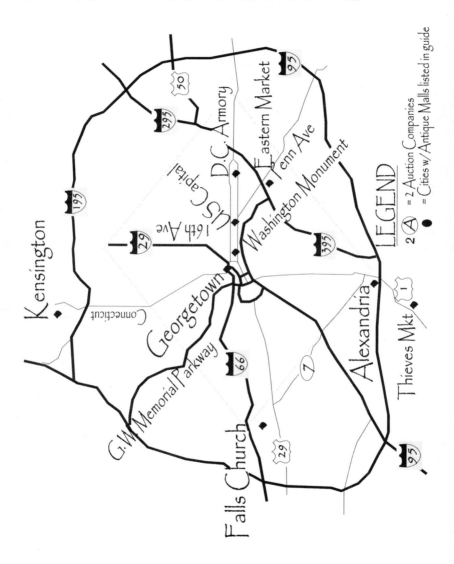

LEGEND

2 (A) = 2 Auction Companies

● = Cities w/ Antique Malls listed in guide

Kensington

Connecticut

29

195

50

295

295

16th Ave

US Capital

D.C. Armory

Eastern Market

Penn Ave

Washington Monument

95

395

Alexandria

Thieves Mkt

1

Georgetown

G.W. Memorial Parkway

Falls Church

66

29

7

95

WASHINGTON D.C.
WEEKEND ANTIQUE EVENTS

See Maryland and Virginia for other D.C. area antiquing and auctions
Washington D.C. Outdoor Flea Market at Eastern Market,
  every Sun, Mar until Sun before Christmas, not 1st Sun in May
Washington, D.C.; Armory Antique Show & Sale,
  1st weekend in Mar, & Dec

ANTIQUE DISTRICTS/VILLAGES
Alexandria, VA-(King & Lee Sts.), Kensington, MD- (Howard St.), DC- Georgetown

ANTIQUE MALLS, MARKETS & SHOWS
WASHINGTON D.C.
The Flea Market at Eastern Market
175 dealers, most outdoor
On 7th St SE between PA Ave & NC Ave
Every Sun 10-5; set-up at 8:30; adm free
703-534-7612
On Capitol Hill, 1/2 blk from
Eastern Market Station, Mar-Dec.
No 1st Sun in May
Tom Rall, Mgr.
1101 N. Kentucky St.
Arlington, VA 22205
www.easternmarket.com

WASHINGTON D.C.
The D.C. Armory Antique Show and
Sale
Over 100 dealers
2001 E. Capitol St., D.C. Armory
Fri-12-8; Sat 11-6; Sun 11-5; adm $7
301-933-9433
I-295 Exit Capitol St W or
1.75 mi E of US Capitol on Capitol St.
First weekend in Mar, & Dec
Pappabello Quality Antique Shows
P.O. Box 12069
Silver Spring, MD 20908

5 antique shops from #1529 to
1665 Wisconsin Ave in Georgetown

WASHINGTON, D.C. 20007
Janis Aldrige, Inc.
Antique shop
2900 M St. NW
Open Tue-Sat 10-6
202-338-7710
One of 4 antique shops in the
2900 block of M St in Georgetown
Ask for directions to nearby shops

KENSINGTON, MD 20895
Kensington Antique Market Center
35 dealers
3760 Howard Ave.
Open Mon-Sat 10-5:30; Sun 12-5:30
301-942-4440
I-495 Exit 33, CT Ave N to Knowles, one
more block to Howard Ave.
There are 29 shops on Howard St.

WASHINGTON D.C.

ALEXANDRIA, VA 22309
Mt. Vernon Antique Center
19 individual shops
8101 Richmond Hwy
Open Mon-Sat 11-5, Sun 12-5
703-619-5100
I-495 Exit 1-A, S 4 mi on US 1

ALEXANDRIA, VA 22314
French Country Antiques
One of 9 antique shops on King St.
1000 King St.
Mon-Sat 10:30-6; Sun 12-5; clsed Tue
703-548-8563
I-95/495 Exit 1, N on US 1 to King St

ALEXANDRIA, VA 22314
Trojan Antiques
Another one of 16 shops on King St
and Lee St.
1100 King St.
Open Mon-Sat 11-6; Sun 12-5
703-549-9766
**Antique shops on Washington St.
and in the area which is between US 1
& the Potomac River N & S of King St.**

FALLS CHURCH, VA 22046
Falls Church Antique Co.
45 dealers
260 W. Broad St.
Open 7 days
703-241-7074
Rte 7 near Jct with US 29
*All consignment antiques:
collectibles, toys dolls, paintings,
prints, furniture, china, jewelry,
glass, porcelain and primitives.*

TRAVEL NOTES

WASHINGTON D.C.

TRAVEL NOTES

WASHINGTON

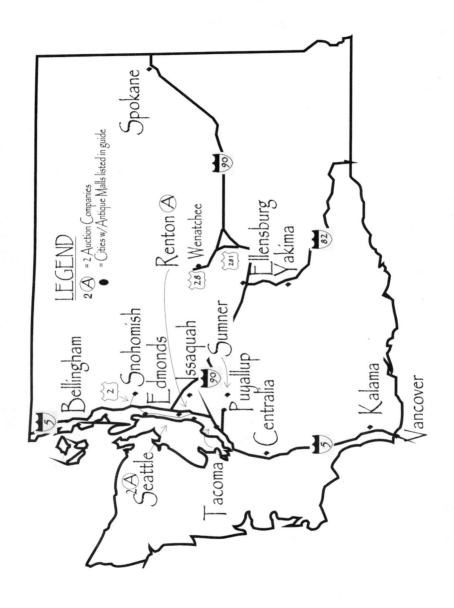

WASHINGTON

WEEKEND ANTIQUE EVENTS
Tacoma Dome Antique and Collectibles Show, 800 booths.;
One weekend in Jan, and Sep; Call to confirm.

ANTIQUE DISTRICTS/VILLAGES
Bellingham, Centralia, Ellensburg, Renton, Snohomish, Seattle 1st Ave, Tacoma -Broadway, Tacoma/Puyallup, Seattle/ Edmonds

AUCTION /ESTATE SALE CO'S
Seattle/
Renton, WA 98055
Mroczek Auctioneers
antique collectible & estate auctions
717 S 3rd St, PO Box 1617
call for date of next antique auction
one about once a week
800-894-6138 or 206-329-6138

Seattle, WA 98103
Pacific Galleries Weekly Auction
Antique collectible & auction
241 S. Lander St.
every Monday at 10AM
206-524-9626
I-90 W Exit 4th Ave. R to Lander R
Call to confirm.

ANTIQUE MALLS, MARKETS/ SHOWS

BELLINGHAM, WA 98226
I-5 Antique Mall
25 dealers
4744 Pacific Hwy
Open Mon-Sat 10-5, Sun 1-4
360-384-5955
At I-5 Exit 260 east side

BELLINGHAM, WA 98225
Old Town Antique Mall
35 dealers
427 W. Holly
Mon-Sat 10-6; Sun 12-5
360-671-3301
I-5 Exit 255, R downtown
Lakely becomes Holly

BELLINGHAM, WA 98225
Aladdin's Antique Mall
30 dealers
427 W. Holly
Mon-Sat 10-6; Sun 12-5
360-647-0066
Downtown.
There are 7 antique stores on
W Holly St from #310 to #705.

CENTRALIA, WA 98531
Centralia Square Antique Mall
135 dealers, plus anex
201 S. Pearl
7 days 10-5
360-736-6406
I-5 Exit 82 E to downtown
200 dealers in 2 other malls plus 10
shops on Tower St.

EDMONDS-SEE / SEATTLE/
EDMONDS

WASHINGTON

ELLENSBURG, WA 98926
Showplace Antique Mall
32 dealers
103 E 3rd Ave.
Open Mon-Sat 10-5:30, Sun 11-4:30
509-962-9331
I-90 Exit 109 to downtown.
8 other nearby shops in downtown
Ellensburg on 3rd, 4th, Main & Pearl.

KALAMA, WA 98625
Memory Lane Antique Mall
32 dealers
413 N 1st St.
Open 7 days 10-5, Clsd Nov - May 1
360-673-3663
I-5 Exit 30 or 32 to downtown Kalama
Walk to 4 other shops on 1st St

RENTON, WA 98055
Downtown Renton Antique Mall
45 dealers
210 Wells Ave S.
Open Mon-Sat 10-5, Sun 11-4
425-271-0511
I-405 Exit 4 into downtown Renton
Walk to 5 other shops and malls

SEATTLE, WA 98103
Pacific Galleries
200 dealers
241 Lander
Mon- Sat 10-6, Sun 11-5, Thur till 8
206-524-9626
I-90 W Exit 4th Ave, R to Lander R
Auction every Mon at 10AM

SEATTLE, WA 98104
Pioneer Square Mall
85 dealers
602 1st Avenue
Open 7 days
206-624-1164
I-5 Exit James St., WI-5 Exit 164 or
165A. About a dozen shops on 1st Ave.
www.pioneersquareantiquemall.com

SEATTLE, WA 98103
Fremont Antique Mall
50 dealers
3419 Fremont Place N.
Open 7 days 11-7PM
206-548-9140
Hwy 99 one block N of Fremont Bridge
on Fremont Pl between 35th & 36th St.s

SEATTLE, WA 98116
Antique Mall of West Seattle
50 dealers
4516 California SW
Mon-Sat 10-6; Sun 11-5
206-935-9774
I-5 Exit 163, W 2 1/4 mi to
California St R

SEATTLE, WA 98101
Antiques at Pike Place
80 dealers
92 Stewart St
Mon-Sat 10-6, Sun 12-5
206-441-9643
One Half block E of Pike Place Market

SEATTLE /
BOTHEL, WA 98021
Town Hall Antique Mall
30 dealers
23716 Bothel/Everett Hwy
Open Mon-Sat 10-6, Sun 11-5
425-487-8979
I-405 Exit 26-B, S 1 mi
There is a 17 dealer Mall next door
& one more shop in the block.

SEATTLE /
EDMONDS, WA 98026
Aurora Antique Pavilion & Expresso
Cafe
250 dealers
24111 Hwy 99
425-744-0566
I-5 Exit 177, W to Hwy 99; N. 100
yards on right.

SEATTLE /
EDMONDS, WA 98020
Old Mill Town Antique Mall
75 dealers
201 5th Ave So.
Mon-Sat 10-6; Sun 12-5
425-771-9466
Downtown Edmonds.
I-5 Exit 177, W on 104; or I-5 Exit 181,
W on 196th St.

SEATTLE /
EDMONDS, WA 98020
Waterfront Antique Mall
150 dealers
190 Sunset Avenue
Open Sat 10-7, Sun- Fri 12-6
425-670-0770
Follow signs to Edmond Ferry,
Across from Edmonds Ferry tickets.

SEATTLE /
EDMONDS, WA 98020
Times Square Antique Mall
100 dealers
10117 Edmonds Way
Sat 10-6, Sun-Fri 12-6
425-673-2858
Follow the signs to the Ferry
across from McDonalds

SEATTLE /
ISSAQUAH, WA 98027
Gilman Antique Gallery
150 dealers
625 NW Gilman Blvd.
Mon-Fri 10-5:30, Sat 10-6, Sun 12-6
425-391-6640
I-90 Exit 15, Gilman Blvd

SEATTLE /
SNOHOMISH, WA 98290
Star Center Antique Mall
225 dealers
829 Second Street
Open 7 days 10-5
360-568-2131
Downtown. I-405 Exit 23 N on
Hwy 522 to Hwy 9 N about 10 mi.
30 mi N of Seattle off Hwy 2

SEATTLE /
SNOHOMISH, WA 98290
Remember When Antique Mall
40 dealers
908 First St.
Open 7 days 11-5
60-568-0757
Downtown. I-5 Exit 194 E on Hwy 2 to
Snohomish Bickford Ave exit to
Historic Shopping District

WASHINGTON

SEATTLE /
SNOHOMISH, WA 98290
Black Cat Antique Mall
80 dealers
1019 First St.
Open 7 days 11-5
360-568-8144
Downtown
You can walk to 24 antique shops in
downtown Snohomish.

SPOKANE, WA 99207
Julie Button's
400 Consignors
2907 N. Monroe
Open Tu-Sat 11-5, Cl Sun & Mon
509-324-2018
I-90 Exit Maple R on Boone L
on Monroe

SPOKANE, WA 99201
Monroe Street Bridge Antique Market
54 dealers
N 604 Monroe
Open 7 days 10-5:30
509-327-6398
From I-90 take theMaple St. Exit and
follow signs

TACOMA, WA
Antique & Collectibles Show
600 booths; antiques & collectibles
Tacoma Dome
Sat 9-6, Sun 10-5, Adm $6, park $6
503-282-0877 Call for dates
at I-5 Exit 133
One weekend in Jan & Sep
Palmer-Wirfs & Assoc.
4001 NE Halsey
Portland, OR 97232

TACOMA, WA, 98444
Pacific Run Antique Mall
125 dealers
10228 Pacific
Mon-Sat 10-6; Sun 11-5
253-539-0117
I-5 Exit 127, E on Hwy 512,
2nd Exit is Pacific Ave, L 6 blocks

TACOMA, WA, 98421
Katy's Antique & Collectibles Mall
60 dealers
602 E 25th St.
Open Mon-Sat 10-6, Sun 12-5
253-305-0203
I-5 Exit 133, 2 blocks from Tacoma
Dome
7 shops in 700 blk of Broadway

TACOMA /
PUYALLUP, WA 98371
Pioneer Antique Mall
35 dealers
113 S Meridian
Daily 10-6
253-770-0981
Take Pioneer Exit Hwy 512 E
downtown. Walk to 3 other shops
on Meridian

TACOMA /
SUMNER, WA 98390
Whistle Stop Antique Mall
45 dealers
1109 Main St.
Open Mon-Sat 10-6, Sun 11-5
253-863-3309
**Sumner Exit off Hwy 410
downtown. 2 shops in the 1000
block of Main, one at 926 Main.**

VANCOUVER, WA 98660
Old Glory Antique Mall
50 dealers
2000 Main St.
Open Mon-Sat 10-5, Sun 12-5
360-906-8823
**I-5 Exit Center City N on Main St.
across the street are 2 antique stores**

WENATCHEE/ CASHMERE, WA 98815
Apple Annie Antique Gallery
85 dealers
603 Cotlets Way
Open 7 days 9-6
509-782-4004 or 866-504-8460
**10 mi W of Wenatchee, just off Hwy 2
at Mile post 112**

WENATCHEE, WA 98801
Antique Mall of Wenatchee
75 dealers
11 N. Wenatchee Ave
Open Mon0
Sat 10-6, Sun 12-4
509-662-3671
In Historic downtown Wenatchee

YAKIMA, WA 98902
Yesterdays Village
75 shops
15 W. Yakima Avenue
Open Mon- Sat 10-6, Sun 12-5
509-457-4981
I-82 Exit 33 W

323

GREAT GETAWAY TO ANTIQUE SEATTLE

WHEN: Anytime, however if you can go when Tacoma Dome Market is in Jan. or Sept., 600 dealers are there to provide lots of shopping Call 503-282-0887 for exact dates.

WHERE: Tacoma Dome is at I-5 Exit 133, Sat 9-6, Sun 10-6. Adm $6, park $6 on specific dates.

Antique Auction: one per week 800-894-6138 and every Mon at 10AM, see below listing for "Next Day".

Casinos: Tulalip Casino, I-5 Exit 142 Hwy 18E to Auburn Way So to Casino. 800-804-4944

ANTIQUING: Anytime or after Tacoma Dome, I-90 E to Exit 15 Gilman Blvd to #1. *Gilman Antique Gallery*, at 625 NW Gilman Blvd, 150 dealers in Issaquah. Opens at 10 AM, Sun noon.

2. Next return on I-90W to 405N to Exit 23N on Hwy 522 to Hwy 9N to Snohomish, an old Victorian town. Go to the Historic District and *Star Center Antique Mall,* 225 dealers at 829 2nd St., Open 7 days 10-5.

3. Then, *Remember When Antique Mall,* 40 dealers at 908 1st St.

4. Next, *Black Cat Antique Mall*, 80 dealers at 1019 First St.

5. There are 20 more single multi-dealer shops on 1st & 2nd Streets in Snohomish.

If you finish in time for more antiquing you could go on to Edmonds, W on Hwy 2 to I-5 So. to Exit 181, W on 196th St. followilng signs to Edmond Ferry to the *Water Front Antique Mall*, 150 dealers at 190 Sunset Ave. across from Ferry tickets. They are open to 6 PM daily, 7 PM Saturday.

6. Next day - Downtown Seattle I-90W Exit 4th Ave R to Lander R to 241 Lander, *Pacific Galleries*, 200 dealers, opens at 11 AM Sundays. Auction every Mon at 10 AM.

7. Now, go N on 4th Ave to James St. W to 1st Ave, *Pioneer Square Antique Mall*, 80 dealers, 602 1st Ave.

8. Then to *Antiques at Pikes Place*, 80 dealers, N on 1st Ave to Pike St., R to 3rd Ave, L to Stewart, L on Stewart to the mall at 92 Stewart. There is a Pike Place Market with cafes, produce sellers and street musicians only 1/2 block away to some good restaurant choices.

9 Continue on Stewart to 1st Ave, L 4 blocks to University, L to I-5 N to Exit 177W to Hwy 99N, 100 yarts to *Aurora Antique Pavillion,* 250 dealers at 24111 Hwy 99 in Edmonds.

10. Across from McDonalds at 10117 Edmonds Way is *Times Square Antique Mall*, 100 dealers, follow the signs to Ferry.

11. If you did not have time to shop the *Waterfront Antique Mall* after Snowhomish, you might be able to now, as it is across from the Ferry Ticket Office at 190 Sunset Ave. The Mall is open until 6 PM daily, 7 PM Sat.

12. Next N. on Hwy 99 a short distance to Hwy 104 W to 201 - 5th Ave. So., for the *Old Mill Antique Mall,* 75 dealers.

RESTAURANT: See all of Seattle at once, have lunch or dinner in the revolving restaurant atop the Seattle Space Needle, downtown. Reservations, 1-800-846-1891. Also consider the Portland Getaway for some great antiquing, if you have time.

TRAVEL NOTES

WEST VIRGINIA

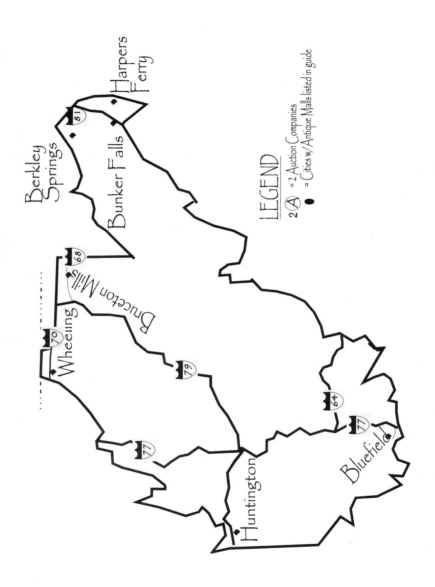

WEST VIRGINIA

WEEKEND ANTIQUE EVENTS

Bluefield City Flea Market.,175 dealers, **every Sat, Mar 15 thru Oct.**.
Harpers Ferry Flea Market,150-200 dealers,
Sat & Sun, Mar 15 thru Oct, also Mon holidays.

ANTIQUE DISTRICT: Huntington

ANTIQUE MALLS, MARKETS/ SHOWS

BERKELEY SPRINGS, WV 25411
Berkeley Springs Antique Mall
32 dealers
#7 Fairfax
Open 10-5; closed Wed
304-258-5676
5 mi S of I-68 Exit 82
Downtown

BERKELEY SPRINGS, WV 25411
Old Factory Antique Mall
55 dealers, 25,000 sq. ft.
282 Williams St.
Open 7 days 10-5
304-258-1788
Downtown.
One block E of US Hwy 522,
watch for signs to mall.

BLUEFIELD, WV
Bluefield City Flea Market
175 dealers; 50% antiques & coll
Princeton Avenue (Route 19)
Adm free; metered street parking
304-327-8031
Downtown; 5 mi E of I-77 Exit 1
Free parking bldg on Princeton Ave
Every Sat, Mar 15-Oct, 5 A.M.
Sharon Lefeel
514 Scott St.
Bluefield, WV 24701

BLUEFIELD, WV 24701
Landmark Antique Mall
20,000 sq ft, 30 dealers
200 Federal St.
Open Mon-Sat 9-5; Sun 1-5
304-327-9686
Downtown, 5 mi E of I-77 Exit 1

BRUCETON MILLS, WV 26525
Bruceton Antique Mall
40 dealers
Rte 26 N.
Open 7 days 10-5
304-379-4040
www.coolsalvage.
At I-68 Exit 23

BUNKER HILL, WV 25413
Bunker Hill Antiques Associates
50 dealers
US Hwy 11
Open daily
304-229-0709
I-81 Exit 5, E at end of ramp, R on US 11
Hwy, 3 mi then R at Runnymeade

327

WEST VIRGINIA

HARPER'S FERRY, WV 25425
Harper's Ferry Flea Market
150-200 dealers; antiques & coll
Outdoors, rain or shine,
dawn to dusk
304-725-0092 or 302-725-4141
20 mi W of Frederick, MD on US 340
Every Sat & Sun and Mon holidays,
Mid-March-Dec 1
Flea Market, Dan Barnett, Mgr
954 Oregon Trail
Harper's Ferry, WV 25425

HUNTINGTON, WV
I-64 Exit 6, N to Washington St, W to
18th St., turn L-15 shops, 10 are on
14th St W

WHEELING, WV 26003
Antiques on the Market
25 shops on 3 floors
2265 Market St.
Open Mon-Sat 10-5; Sun 12-4
304-232-1665
I-70 Exit 1-A,
E 1 block to Market Street.

WEST VIRGINIA

TRAVEL NOTES

WISCONSIN

LEGEND

2 Ⓐ = 2 Auction Companies

● = Cities w/Antique Malls listed in guide

Egg Harbor

Manitowoc

Eau Claire

Wausau

29

Shawano

51

Appleton

41

Tomah

Oshkosh

43

La Crosse

90

Beaver
Dam

Kewaskum

Cedarburg

Wisconsin Dells

90

Columbus

151

45

Milwaukee Ⓐ

Portage

Deerfield

Reedsburg

Elkhorn

Madison

Waterford

Milton

Lake Geneva

Kenoska

Ⓐ Beloit

Clinton

Sturtevant

Walworth

WISCONSIN

WEEKEND ANTIQUE EVENTS
Cedarburg, Maxwell Street Day. 1000 dealers, **last Sun in May & Jul, Labor Day Mon, and 1st Sun in Oct.**
Elkhorn Antique Flea Market, 500 dealers,
One Sun in May, Jun, Jul, Aug & Sep.
Shawano Flea Market, 200 dealers, 80% antiques & collectibles,
Sundays Apr-Mid-Oct.

ANTIQUE DISTRICTS/VILLAGES
Kensoha downtown, Princeton

AUCTION/ESTATE SALE CO'S

Beloit, WI, 53511
Beloit Auction Service
Antique, collectible, household auction
534 W. Grand Ave.
Wed at 4:30 P.M.
608-364-1965

Milwaukee, WI 53215
Betthauser's Auction Service
Antique and collectibles auctions
2918 S.13th St.
Auction held at 5101 W. Oklahoma Ave
414-282-6987
1st, 2nd and 3rd Wed
of every month at 6 P.M.

ANTIQUE MALLS, MARKETS / SHOWS

APPLETON, WI 54913
Memories Antique Mall
100 dealers
400 Randolph Drive
Open 7 days 10-6; Fri 'til 8
920-788-5553
On side of US Hwy 41

Exit 146, Little Chute

BEAVER DAM, WI 53916
Beaver Dam Antique Mall
50 dealers
Jct Hwy 33 & BU 151
Open 7 days 10-5
920-887-1116
35 mi NE of Madison
on US Hwy 151, downtown

BRISTOL, WI
Benson Corners Antique Mall
100 dealer spaces
Jct Hwy 50 & Hwy 45
20000 75th St.
Open 7 days 10-5
262-857-9456
Just W of Hwy 45 on Hwy 50, behind
Shell station. 5 mi N of Illinois line.

BRISTOL, WI 53104
Hawthorn Antiques & Galleries
100 dealer spaces
Hwy 50 & County Rd. MB/North
Open 7 days 10-5
262-857-2226
I-94 Exit Hwy 50 W 2 mi, 5 mi N of IL
line. Two other shops in Bristol.

WISCONSIN

CEDARBURG, WI
Maxwell Street Days
1000 dealers; antiques, collectibles
Fireman's Park, 796 N. Washington
Open 6-4:30; adm free; park $2
262-377-8412 Call for dates
I-43 Exit 89, W to Hwy 143, N 3 mi
Always last Sun in May & Jul,
Labor Day Mon, & 1st Sun in Oct
Cedarburg, Fireman's Park
P.O. Box 344
Cedarburg, WI 53012-0344

CEDARBURG, WI 53012
Creekside Antiques
One of a dozen antique shops
N69 W 6335 Bridge Rd.
Open Mon-Sat 10-5; Sun 11-5
262-377-6131
I-43 Exit 89, W to Washington Ave.,
N to Historic District. Wisconsin's last
covered bridge is here.

CLINTON , WI 53525
Clinton Antiques
multi- dealers
244 Allen Street
Mon-Sat 10-4; Sun 12-4
608-676-5535
I-43 Exit 6; 1 mi S of I-43

COLUMBUS, WI 53925
Columbus Antique Mall & Museum
400 booths; 72,000 sq. ft.
239 Whitney, P. O. Box 151
Open 7 days 8:15-4
920-623-1992
20 mi NE of Madison on US 151,
take Exit 115 and follow signs
to Museum.

Have a tasty lunch at the *Fireman's*
***Tavern* in Columbus at the corner of**
Water & James. Great prime rib &
vegatable soup from the 12 house
varieties and fresh berry pie from 14
homemade deserts. Also 24 sandwiches
on the menu.

COLUMBUS,WI 53925
Antique Shoppes of Columbus Mall
multi-dealer shop
141 W. James
Mon-Sat 10-4:30; Sun 12-5
920-623-2669
Downtown at stop light
There are 4 antique malls in Columbus

DEERFIELD, WI 53531
Old Deerfield Antiques
40 dealers
37 N. Main (Hwy 73)
7 days 10-5
608-764-5743
I-94 Exit 250 S on Hwy 73,
4 mi (10 mi E of Madison)

EGG HARBOR, WI 54209
Olde Orchard Antique Mall
105 dealers
7381 State Hwy 42
May 1-Oct 31; Mon-Sat 9-5; Sun 10-5
920-868-3685
40 mi NW of Green Bay on Hwy 42
3 shops on Hwy 42 in Egg Harbor

ELKHORN
Elkhorn Antique Flea Market
500 dealers; 90% antiques/collectibles
Fairgrounds
Open 7-3; adm $2; indoors & out
414-525-0820; call for dates
I-43 Exit 29, Hwy 11 W 2 mi
One Sun in May, Jun,
Jul, Aug, & Sep
N L. Promotions
P.O. Box 544
Elkhorn, WI 53121

KEWASKUM, WI 53040
General Store Antique Mall
75 dealers
Jct Hwys 45 & 28
Open 7 days 10-5
262-626-2885
40 mi N of Milwaukee

LA CROSSE, WI 54601
Antique Center
75 booths
110 S. 3rd St.
Mon-Sat 9-5:30; Sun 11-5:30
608-782-6533
I-90 Exit 3, downtown

LACROSSE, WI 54603
Caledonia Street Antique Mall
40 dealers
1215 Caledonia St.
Open Mon-Sat 10-5; Sun 11-4:30
608-782-8443
I-90 Exit 3, Hwy 35, L on Clinton St.,
R on Caledonia St.

LAKE GENEVA ,WI 53147
Lake Geneva Antique Mall
60 booths
829 Williams Street
7 days 10-5
262-248-6345
75 mi N of Chicago on US 12
Downtown, R on Broad St. which turns
into Williams.

MADISON, WI 53716
Antiques Mall of Madison
130 dealers
4748 Cottage Grove Road
M-F 10-6; Th 'til 9; Sat 10-5; Sun 11-5
608-222-2049
From US 51 (Stroughton Rd) take
Cottage Grove E 2 blocks, behind Pizza
Hut

MADISON, WI 53716
Broadway Antiques Mall
55 dealers
115 E. Broadway
Mon-Sat 10-5; Thur 'til 9; Sun 11-5
608-222-2241
I-90 S to US 12/18 W
to Monona Drive exit

MADISON/ MIDDLETON , WI 53562
Middletown Antiques Mall
90 dealers
1819 Parmenter St.
Mon-Fri 10-6, Sat 10-5, Sun 11-4
608-831-5515
US Hwy 12 Exit University Ave E 2
blocks to Paramenter St. S.

WISCONSIN

MANITOWOC, WI 54220
Washington St. Antique Mall
45 dealers
910 Washington St.
Open 11-5, 7 days
920-684-2954
I-43 Exit 149, downtown
10 dealer mall at 301 8th St
& 6 more shops around town.

MILTON, WI 53563
Campus Antiques Mall
100 dealers, in old College Gym
609 Campus St.
Mon-Sat 10-5; Sun & holidays 12-5
608-868-3324
I-90 Exits 161 or 171-A into Milton
at Burger King on Hwy 26, go W
2 blocks, then R on campus

In downtown Milwaukee we like
Mader's _German Restaurant_ at 9 N 3rd
St. for lunch or dinner. Nearby at 320
E. Mason St. is another favorite,
Karl Ratch's for dinner, (only) closed
Sunday. Both there for over 100 years.
Mader's 414-271-3377
Ratch's 414-276-2720

MILWAUKEE, WI 53202
Milwaukee Antique Center
75 dealers
341 N. Milwaukee
Open 7 days
414-276-0605
Downtown E of Milwaukee River

MILWAUKEE, WI 53204
Antique Center Walker's Point
48 dealers
1134 S. 1st Street
Closed Tuesdays
414-383-0655
12 blocks S of Grand Avenue Mall

PORTAGE, WI 53901
Antique Mall of Portage
200 dealers & consignors
114 W. Crook Street(Hwy 33)
Open Mon- Sat 9-5, Sun 11-4
608-742-1640
35 mi N of Madison on I-90/94
I-90/94 Exit Hwy 33 E downtown

PRINCETON,WI 54968
River City Antique Mall
7,200 sq. ft.
328 S. Fulton (Hwy 23/73)
Open Mon-Sat 10-4, Sun 12-5
920-295-3475
I-39 Exit 113 E 20 mi
9 other shops nearby
Sat-May-Oct 170 booth Flea Market

REEDSBURG , WI 53959
Big Store Plaza Antique Malls
multi-dealer spaces in 3 malls
195 Main Street (Hwy 23/33)
Open 7 days
608-524-4141
I-90/94 Exit 92; S 3 mi on US 12
to Hwy 33 W 10 mi
antique shop across the street

REEDSBURG , WI 53959
Antique Mall of Reedsburg
60 dealers
121 S. Webb
Mon-Sat 10-5, Sun 10-4
608-524-0000
**I-90/94 Exit 92 S, 3mi to Hwy 33 W, 10 mi.
1/2 block S of Star Cinema**

SHAWANO, WI 54166
Shawano Antique & Flea Market
200 dealers; 80% antiques & collectibles
Shawano County Fairground
6 A.M.-4 P.M.; adm $2; park free
715-526-9769
**32 mi W of Green Bay,
On Hwys 29/47; outdoors
Every Sunday April thru Mid-Oct**
Zurko's Promotions
211 W. Green Bay Street
Shawano, WI 54166

STURTEVANT, WI 53177
School Days Mall
50 dealers
9500 Durand Ave.
Open Tue-Sat 10-5; Sun 12-5
262-886-1069
**Hwy 11, 5 mi W of Racine,
2 mi E of I-94**

STURTEVANT, WI 53177
Antique Castle Mall
40 dealers
1701 S.E. Frontage Rd.
Open 10-5, 7 days
262-886-6001
I-94 Exit 333 S, 5 blocks S of Hwy 20

TOMAH, WI 54660
Antique Mall of Tomah
60 dealers
P.O. Box 848
summer 7 days 9-7, 10-6 in winter.
608-372-7853
At I-94 Exit 143 on Hwy 21 E

TOMAH/
OAKDALE, WI 54649
Oakdale Antiques Mall
40 dealers
RR 3
Open 9-5; 7days
608-374-4700
At I-90-/94 Exit 48, north side

WALWORTH ,WI 53184
On The Square Antique Mall
100 dealers
Jct Hwy 14 & 67
Open 7 days 10-5
262-275-9858
I-43 Exit 15, S 8 mi.

WATERFORD, WI 53185
Freddy Bears Antique Mall
45 dealers
2819 Beck Dr.
Open 7 days 9:30-5
262-534-BEAR
**At Jct Hwy 36 & Hwy 20
17 mi W of Racine**

WISCONSIN

WATERTOWN, WI
Watertown Antiques Market (Mall)
50 dealers
210 S. Water St.
Mon- Thu 10-6, Fri 10-8, Sat 10-5, Sun
11-4
920-206-0097
I-94 Exit 267, N 7 mi, on Rte 26
Downtown

WAUSAU, WI 54660
Rib Mt. Antique Mall
68 dealers
3300 Eagle Avenue
Open 7 days
715-848-5564
On US 51 in Northern WI
At Hwy 51 and 29 Exit 190, I-39.

WISCONSIN DELLS, WI 53965
Antique Mall of Wisconsin Dells II
250 dealers
So. 2276 Hwy 12
Open 10-8, 7 days
608-356-7600
At I-90/94 Exit 92 S 1/2 mi

WICONSIN DELLS, WI 53965
Days Gone By
40 dealers
729 Oak St.
10-9 ,7 days except in winter 10-5
608-254-6788
Downtown, Oak crosses Broadway (the
main Street).

TRAVEL NOTES

WYOMING

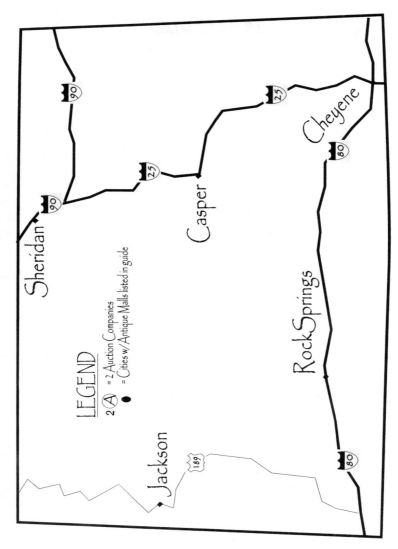

LEGEND

2 (A) = 2 Auction Companies
● = Cities w/ Antique Malls listed in guide

Sheridan

Casper

Cheyene

Jackson

Rock Springs

WYOMING

WEEKEND ANTIQUE EVENTS
Casper Antique Show, 40 dealers, **1st full weekend in Jun & Oct**
Jackson Hole, Mangy Moose Antique Show, **1st weekend after July 4th**

ANTIQUE MALLS, MARKETS/ SHOWS

TRAVEL NOTES

CASPER, WY
Antique Show
40 dealers
Central Wyoming Fairgrounds
Sat 10-5; Sun 10-4; Adm $2.00
307-266-5613
On Rte 220 in SW part of Casper
1st fukll weekend in Jun & Oct
Mary Hobson Hemmingan
2033 W. 42nd St.
Casper, Wy 82604

JACKSON HOLE, WY
Mangy Moose Antique Show & Sale
65 dealers; quality antiques
In Teton Village
Fri, Sat & Sun 9-5
208-345-0755 or 314-962-7016 call for
exact dates
1st weekend after 4th of July
Adm & park free
Outdoors
Jeffery Perkins Productions
P.O. Box 56541
St. Louis, MO 63156

SHERIDAN, WY 82801
Best Outwest Antique Collectibles Mall
100 booths
109 N. Main
Open Mon-Sat 9-6; closed Sun
307-674-5003
Downtown